GLOSSARY

MICHIGAN PROFICIENCY

SKILLS BUILDER

DIANE FLANEL PINIARIS

REVISED EDITION 2007

Australia • Brazil • Japan • Korea • Mexico • Singapore • Spain • United Kingdom • United States

**Michigan Proficiency Skills Builder Glossary
(Revised Edition 2007)**
Diane Flanel Piniaris

Acknowledgements

I would like to extend my heartfelt thanks to Eleni Papaioannou for her invaluable help in refining the Greek equivalents that appear in the Glossary.

© 2008, Cengage Learning EMEA

ALL RIGHTS RESERVED. No part of this work covered by the copyright herein may be reproduced, transmitted, stored or used in any form or by any means graphic, electronic, or mechanical, including but not limited to photocopying, recording, scanning, digitizing, taping, Web distribution, information networks, or information storage and retrieval systems, except as permitted under Section 107 or 108 of the 1976 United States Copyright Act, or applicable copyright law of another jurisdiction, without the prior written permission of the publisher.

While the publisher has taken all reasonable care in the preparation of this book, the publisher makes no representation, express or implied, with regard to the accuracy of the information contained in this book and cannot accept any legal responsibility or liability for any errors or omissions from the book or the consequences thereof.

Products and services that are referred to in this book may be either trademarks and/or registered trademarks of their respective owners. The publishers and author/s make no claim to these trademarks. The publisher does not endorse, and accepts no responsibility or liability for, incorrect or defamatory content contained in hyperlinked material.

> For product information and technology assistance,
> contact **emea.info@cengage.com**.
> For permission to use material from this text or product, and for
> permission queries, email **emea.permissions@cengage.com**.

British Library Cataloguing-in-Publication Data
A catalogue record for this book is available from the British Library.

ISBN: 978-960-403-599-1

Cengage Learning EMEA
Cheriton House, North Way, Andover, Hampshire, SP10 5BE
United Kingdom

Cengage Learning products are represented in Canada by Nelson Education Ltd.

For your lifelong learning solutions, visit **www.cengage.co.uk**

Purchase your next print book, e-book or e-chapter at
www.cengagebrain.com

Printed in the United Kingdom by Lightning Source
Print Number 06 Print Year 2019

Contents

Abbreviations and symbols 4

1. Perspectives on personality 5

2. Flora and fauna 17

3. Health and medicine 30

4. Environmentalism 101 43

5. Technological transitions 56

Alphabetical word list 67

Abbreviations and symbols

English

abbr	abbreviation (e.g., *FBI, MRI*)
adj	adjective
adv	adverb
Brit	British spelling
C	countable noun
C/U	countable and uncountable noun
e.g.	for example
fig	figurative meaning
idm	idiom
i.e.	that is
irreg v	irregular verb
lit	literal meaning
n phr	noun phrase: adjective + noun combination (e.g., *military conflict*)
n/adj	noun used as adjective (e.g., *baseball* in the phrase *baseball game*)
n	noun
phr v	phrasal verb
pl n	plural noun
pp	past participle
sb	somebody
sing n	singular noun
sth	something
U	uncountable noun
v phr	verb phrase: verb + noun combination (e.g., *take pity on*)
v	verb
c.	*circa*, Latin for "around, about" (e.g., c. 100 years, c. 1995)
e.g.	*exempli gratia*, Latin for "for example"
esp.	especially
ger	gerund
i.e.	*id est*, Latin for "that is"
prep	preposition
prep phr	prepositional phrase

Greek

evs. 1-2	έννοιες 1 και 2, κλπ
κυρ	κυριολεκτική έννοια
μετ	μεταφορική έννοια
πληθ	πληθυντικός
π.χ.	παραδείγματος χάριν
κτ	κάτι
κπ	κάποιος, κάποιον

Symbols

•	example sentence
~	the target word (used in example sentence)
➤	derivatives
❖	Greek equivalent
📖	see dictionary for other meanings
★	technical/scientific term accompanied by shortened entry because word is explained in Student's Book or unlikely to be tested directly

Perspectives on personality

1.1 perspective (n) – (C/U) way of looking at sth, point of view, attitude, outlook • *Westerners who experience the difficulties of life in a developing country often return home with a different ~.* ❖ άποψη

Introduction — Vices versus virtues (and vice versa) (page 8)

1.2 vice (n) – 1. (C) bad or negative moral quality • *Greed and laziness are ~s.* 2. (U) evilness/badness of character • *Demons are traditionally associated with ~.* ❖ 1. ηθικό ελάττωμα, κακή συνήθεια 2. ανηθικότητα, κακία

1.3 versus (prep) – (same as **vs.**) against, as compared to • *The judge called the next case: Smith ~ Jones. / What are the advantages of renting a flat ~ buying a home?* ❖ εναντίον, κατά

1.4 virtue (n) – 1. (C) a good moral quality • *Honesty and modesty are his most attractive ~s.* 2. (U) goodness of character, moral goodness • *Tom is a man of unquestionable ~ ; he's the most ethical person I know.* ➤ virtuous (adj), virtuously (adv) ❖ 1. προτέρημα, προσόν 2. αρετή

1.5 vice versa (adv) – (Latin) the reverse or opposite (is also true) • *If John loves Mary and ~, then why don't they get married?* ❖ αντίστροφα

Warm-up (page 8)

1.6 trait (n) – personal characteristic or quality, attribute • *Among his many admirable ~s are honesty, patience, and loyalty.* ❖ χαρακτηριστικό γνώρισμα

A A moral primer (page 8)

1.7 primer (n) – (C) (slightly dated) book that contains basic, introductory facts about a subject • *The children laughed when they leafed through the old-fashioned ~s their grandmother had used in elementary school.* ➤ prime (adj), primary (adj), primarily (adv) ❖ βιβλίο στοιχειωδών γνώσεων

1.8 dawn (of) (n) – (C) (fig) beginning, first signs of sth • *Do you ever wonder what it would have been like to have lived at the ~ of civilization?* ➤ dawn (on) (v) ❖ (μετ) η αυγή

1.9 struggle (to do sth) (v) – (fig) try hard to do sth • *Many foreigners ~ to learn Greek, but don't make very much progress.* ➤ struggle (n), struggling (adj) ❖ αγωνίζομαι

1.10 make sense of (v phr) – understand the logic behind sth • *She tried hard to ~ why her teenage son had become so moody lately, but she could find no explanation.* ❖ βγάζω νόημα

1.11 human nature (n phr) – (U) the general character of men and women • *Optimists believe that ~ is essentially good, not evil.* ❖ ανθρώπινη φύση

1.12 conduct (n) – (U) behavior • *The child's ~ has improved since his parents decided not to get a divorce.* ➤ conduct (v) ❖ διαγωγή, συμπεριφορά

1.13 branch (of sth) (n) – (C) part of a subject or large area of study • *Botany and zoology are ~es of biology.* ❖ κλάδος. See also **2.93**.

1.14 ethics (n) – 1. (U) moral philosophy • *The philosophy professor's specialty is ~.* 2. (pl n) principles or standards of behavior, set of ideas about what is right and wrong • *Her ~ prevent her from cheating on tests.* ❖ 1. ηθική 2. ηθικές αρχές, ήθη

1.15 ethical/moral (adj) – having high principles or standards of behavior • *She's a(n) ~ person who would never knowingly break the law.* ➤ ethicality (n), ethically (adv); moral (n), moralize (v), morally (adv). Opp: unethical (adj), immoral (adj) ❖ ηθικός

1.16 unethical/immoral (adj) – bad, wrong, unethical • *Most people believe that stealing is ~.* ➤ immorality (n), immorally (adv). Opp: ethical (adj), immoral (adj) ❖ ανήθικος

1.17 wickedness (n) – (U) the state of being **wicked** (i.e., bad, evil) • *Everyone was shocked by the intentional ~ of his actions.* ➤ wicked (adj) ❖ κακία, κακοήθεια

1.18 personality (n) – (C) wide range of characteristics and qualities of a person, seen as a whole • *Psychologists now believe that early upbringing plays a strong role in determining a child's ~.* ❖ προσωπικότητα

1.19 attribute (n) – (C) characteristic, quality, trait (see **1.6**) • *His sense of humor is his greatest ~.* ➤ attribute (v), attributive (adj) ❖ χαρακτηριστικό γνώρισμα, ιδιότητα

1.20 fault/flaw (n) – (C) weak point or imperfection in sb/sth • *No one is perfect; we all have ~s.* ➤ fault (v), faulty (adj); flaw (v), flawed (adj) ❖ ελάττωμα, σφάλμα, ατέλεια

1.21 shortcoming (n) – (C) drawback, fault, defect • *From what I can see, the only ~ our new employee has is that she works too hard!* ❖ ελάττωμα, αδυναμία

1.22 temperament (n) – (C) one's basic nature, the general way in which one is inclined to think and behave • *The baby has a bright, cheerful ~ ; she almost never cries.* ➤ temperamental (adj), temperamentally (adv) ❖ ψυχοσύνθεση, ταμπεραμέντο

1.23 paradigm (n) – (C) representative model, example • *Mike is a ~ of good behavior; I wish his brother were more like him.* ❖ παράδειγμα

1.24 epitome (n) → **the ~ of (sth)** (n) – (U) the perfect example of sth • *Mary is the ~ of everything that is good about human nature. She's the finest person I know.* ➤ epitomize (v) ❖ επιτομή

1.25 paragon of virtue (n phr) – (C) perfect example of a person who lives by the highest moral standards • *She's a good person at heart, but I wouldn't call her a ~ ; like the rest of us, she's got a few faults.* ❖ υπόδειγμα αρετής

B Vices and virtues: A sketchy sampler (page 9)

1.26 sketchy (adj) – incomplete, not very detailed • *The witness's description was ~, so police are having a hard time finding the burglar.* ➤ sketch (n, v), sketchily (adv) ❖ πρόχειρος, σε γενικές γραμμές

1.27 sampler (n) – (C) a collection of sth • *As always, her unimaginative husband gave her a chocolate ~ for Valentine's Day.* ➤ sample (n, v), sampling (n) ❖ δειγματολόγιο

1. VICES (page 9)

1.28 pride (n) – (U – negative meaning) the quality of having too high an opinion of yourself and your achievements • *Ever since his promotion he's been puffed up with ~. / P~ was the tragic flaw of Oedipus Rex.* ➤ pride (v), proud (adj), proudly (adv) ❖ υπεροψία. **Note: pride** also has a positive meaning: feeling of satisfaction or pleasure (e.g., that sb gets from doing sth well or watching sb succeed) • *The amateur photographer took great ~ in the prize she won.* ❖ υπερηφάνεια

1 Perspectives on personality

1.29 proud (adj) – (negative meaning) having too high an opinion of yourself and your achievements • *Ever since she got into Harvard, she's been too ~ to go out with her old classmates.* ➢ pride (n, v) proudly (adv) ❖ φαντασμένος. **Note: proud** also has a positive meaning: pleased with oneself or others (e.g., for having done a good job) • *Tim's parents are ~ of his achievements.* ❖ υπερήφανος

1.30 arrogance (n) – (U) the quality of treating others as worthless inferiors • *The director's ~ made it impossible for him to win the respect of the employees.* ➢ arrogant (adj), arrogantly (adv) ❖ αλαζονεία

1.31 arrogant (adj) – treating others as worthless inferiors; overly proud, self-important, conceited • *He was an ~, self-important person who did little to hide the fact that he thought he was better than everyone else around him.* ➢ arrogance (n), arrogantly (adv) ❖ αλαζόνας

1.32 greed (n) – (U) strong, unhealthy desire for money, power or possessions; same as **avarice** • *G~ and ambition motivated the businessman's every move.* ➢ greedy (adj), greedily (adv) ❖ απληστία, λαιμαργία

1.33 greedy (adj) – having an extreme desire for wealth or gain; same as **avaricious** • *The ~ businessman will do anything to make more money.* ➢ greed (n), greedily (adv) ❖ άπληστος, λαίμαργος

1.34 envy (n) – (U) quality of being jealous of other people • *She was filled with ~ when her colleague was promoted.* ➢ envy (v), envious (adj), enviable (adj), enviously (adv) ❖ ζήλια, φθόνος

1.35 envious (adj) – jealous, wanting what others have • *He was ~ of his brother's success, and the emotion poisoned their relationship.* ➢ envy (n, v), enviable (adj), enviably (adv) ❖ ζηλόφθονος

1.36 gluttony (n) – (U) the quality of eating and drinking to excess • *The Roman emperor Nero was known for ~.* ➢ glutton (n), gluttonous (adj), gluttonously (adv) ❖ λαιμαργία

1.37 gluttonous (adj) – tending to eat and drink to excess; greedy for food/drink • *Teenage boys are known for their ~ appetites.* ➢ glutton (n), gluttony (n), gluttonously (adv) ❖ λαίμαργος, αχόρταγος

1.38 indolence (n) – (U) laziness, inactivity • *You work hard all year, so it's OK to give into a feeling of ~ for a few weeks in the summer.* ➢ indolent (adj), indolently (adv) ❖ νωθρότητα

1.39 indolent (adj) – lazy, idle • *The August heat makes many people feel ~.* ➢ indolence (n), indolently (adv) ❖ νωθρός, ράθυμος

2. VIRTUES (page 9)

1.40 integrity (n) – (U) the quality of having high moral standards • *The politician proved he had ~ when he refused to accept the bribe.* ➢ integruous (adj – rare) ❖ (ηθική) ακεραιότητα

1.41 honesty (n) – (U) the quality of being truthful and forthright; same as **candor** • *If I were you I'd tell the boss the truth. H~ is always the best policy.* ➢ honest (adj), honestly (adv). Opp: dishonesty (n) ❖ τιμιότητα, εντιμότητα, ειλικρίνεια

1.42 honest (adj) – truthful, forthright, candid • *He's usually ~, but this time I think he's lying.* ➢ honesty (n), honestly (adv). Opp: dishonest (adj) ❖ τίμιος, έντιμος, ειλικρινής

1.43 moderation (n) – (U) the quality of being self-controlled and avoiding extremes; same as **temperance** • *Sean is a paragon of ~ ; he never does anything to excess.* ➢ moderate (v, adj), moderately (adv). Opp: immoderation (n) ❖ μετριοφροσύνη, μετριοπάθεια

1.44 moderate (adj) – (of people) self-controlled; (of things) neither large nor small in amount or degree, within logical limits • *If you want to get fit, start with a program of ~ exercise (e.g., walking or swimming twice a week).* ➢ moderation (n), moderate (v), moderately (adv). Opp: immoderate (adj) ❖ (άνθρωπος) μετριόφρων, σεμνός, μετριοπαθής · (πράγμα) μέτριος

1.45 prudence (n) – (U) the quality of being careful and exercising good judgment; same as **cautious** • *It's wise to exercise ~ if you live in a big city with a high crime rate.* ➢ prudent (adj), prudently (adv). Opp: imprudence (n) ❖ σύνεση, φρονιμάδα, προνοητικότητα

1.46 prudent (adj) – careful, cautious, not taking unnecessary risks • *P~ parents always leave their children with a babysitter in case an emergency arises.* ➢ prudence (n), prudently (adj). Opp: imprudent (adj) ❖ συνετός, φρόνιμος, προνοητικός

1.47 valor (n) – (U) the quality of being brave or courageous, especially in war • *The soldier was given a medal for ~ in combat.* ➢ valiant (adj), valiantly (adv) ❖ γενναιότητα, ανδρεία

1.48 valiant (adj) – brave, courageous • *The soldier received a medal for his ~ actions during the battle.* ➢ valor (n), valiantly (adv) ❖ γενναίος

1.49 tolerance (n) – (U) the quality of being open-minded and patient • *Teachers are trained to display ~ towards students of all skill levels.* ➢ tolerate (v), tolerant (adj), tolerantly (adv) ❖ ανοχή, ανεκτικότητα. 📖 : e.g., ~ to heat

1.50 tolerant (adj) – open-minded, patient; willing to accept people, ideas, or ways that are different from your own • *Society is becoming more and more ~ of unmarried couples with children. / T~ people respect other people's beliefs.* ➢ tolerance (n), tolerantly (adv). Opp: intolerant (adj) ❖ ανεκτικός

1.51 loyalty (n) – (U) the quality of staying firm in friendship or support; similar to **faithfulness, trustworthiness** • *We've been friends for almost 20 years, so I'm not questioning your ~.* ➢ loyal (adj), loyally (adv). Opp: disloyalty (n) ❖ πίστη

1.52 loyal (adj) – faithful, trustworthy • *Anthony has been a ~ supporter of the Democratic party for many years.* ➢ loyalty (n), loyally (adv). Opp: disloyal (adj) ❖ πιστός

1.53 diligence (n) – (U) the quality of working hard and conscientiously • *The employee's ~ earned her a substantial raise.* ➢ diligent (adj), diligently (adv) ❖ επιμέλεια, εργατικότητα

1.54 diligent (adj) – 1. (people) hard-working, conscientious • *He's a ~ student who always gets high grades.* 2. (things) careful and thorough, painstaking • *The biography is the result of years of ~ research.* ➢ diligence (n), diligently (adv) ❖ 1. (άνθρωποι) επιμελής, εργατικός 2. (πράγματα) προσεκτικός, σχολαστικός

1.55 resolve (n) – (U) the quality of making firm, lasting decisions; same as **determination** • *It takes a good deal of ~ to lose weight; it takes even more not to gain it back!* ➢ resolution (n), resolute (adj), resolved (adj), resolutely (adv) ❖ αποφασιστικότητα

Perspectives on personality

1.56 resolute (adj) – determined, intent on achieving a goal, fixed on succeeding • *The ~ young man did everything he could to succeed in his new job.* ➤ resolve (n, v), resolution (n), resolutely (adv). Opp: irresolute (adj) ❖ αποφασισμένος

Writing (1) Paragraph Development (page 10)

Model paragraph

1.57 epitomize (v) – be a perfect example of sth • *His rude remarks last night ~ everything that is wrong with his attitude.* ➤ epitome (n) ❖ αποτελώ μικρογραφία, εκπροσωπώ

1.58 needless to say (idm) – (informal) as you would expect, it goes without saying • *The company is in deep financial trouble so, ~, the employees are worried about losing their jobs.* ❖ είναι περιττό να πω, δεν χρειάζεται να πούμε

1.59 unmotivated (adj) – without motivation (i.e., the inner force or energy that pushes sb to act) • *He's a couch potato who is ~ to do anything but watch TV all day.* ➤ motive (n), motivation (n), motivate (v), motivated (adj) ❖ χωρίς κίνητρο

1.60 count on (phr v) – depend on sth/sb, put your trust in sth/sb • *Children ~ their parents to provide them with food, clothing, and love.* ❖ βασίζομαι σε κτ/κπ

1.61 barely (adv) – only just, scarcely • *She whispered so softly that we could ~ hear her.* ➤ bare (adj) ❖ σχεδόν καθόλου, ελάχιστα, μόλις (και μετά βίας)

1.62 lend (sb) a hand (idm) – help (out) • *I offered to ~ when I heard they were moving, but they said they didn't need help.* ❖ δίνω χέρι βοήθειας, βοηθώ

Vocabulary (1) It takes all kinds (Part I) (pages 11-13)

1. Amiable Amy (page 11)

1.63 amiable (adj) – friendly, good-natured • *The ~ young woman has many friends.* ➤ amiability (n), amiably (adv) ❖ αξιαγάπητος, φιλόφρων

1.64 animated (adj) – energetic, active, full of life • *Everyone at the party became more ~ as soon as we put on some dance music.* ➤ animation (n), animate (v), animatedly (adv) ❖ ζωντανός, ζωηρός

1.65 articulate (adj) – able to speak/write clearly • *She's an ~ writer, but she doesn't present her ideas as clearly when she gives a speech.* ➤ articulation (n), articulate (v), articulately (adv) ❖ σαφής, ευκρινής

1.66 ardent (adj) – enthusiastic, passionate • *He's an ~ football fan who hardly ever misses a game.* ➤ ardor (n), ardently (adv) ❖ φλογερός, ένθερμος

1.67 agitated (adj) – upset, disturbed • *She knew something terrible had happened the moment she saw how ~ he was.* ➤ agitation (n), agitate (v), agitating (adj) ❖ ταραγμένος, αναστατωμένος

1.68 aggressive (adj) – unfriendly, argumentative • *A ~ people are always looking to start an argument.* ➤ aggression (n), aggressor (n), aggress (v), aggressively (adv) ❖ επιθετικός

2. Antagonistic Algernon (page 12)

1.69 antagonistic (adj) – hostile, attacking • *A ~ people often try to push others to fight with them.* ➤ antagonism (n), antagonize (v), antagonistically (adv) ❖ ανταγωνιστικός, εχθρικός

1.70 arrogant (adj) – see **1.31**

1.71 appalling (adj) – horrible, awful • *We found the film's violence so ~ that we left after half an hour.* ➤ appall (v), appallingly (adv) ❖ φοβερός, φρικιαστικός

1.72 aloof (adj) – distant, uncommunicative • *He's an ~ person who keeps to himself, so it's hard to know what's bothering him.* ➤ aloofness (n), aloofly (adv) ❖ επιφυλακτικός, ακατάδεχτος, ψυχρός

1.73 absentminded (adj) – preoccupied, forgetful • *He's so ~ that he never remembers where he puts anything.* ➤ absentmindedness (n), absentmindedly (adv) ❖ αφηρημένος, απορροφημένος σε σκέψεις

1.74 austere (adj) – serious, self-controlled • *She's a rather ~, closed person who rarely laughs or shows any emotion.* ➤ austerity (n), austerely (adv) ❖ σοβαρός, αυστηρός (στο ήθος)

1.75 avaricious (adj) – greedy, wanting more and more • *She's an aggressive competitor with an ~ desire for profit and personal gain.* ➤ avarice (n), avariciously (adv) ❖ φιλάργυρος

1.76 aggravating (adj) – annoying, irritating • *He's got an ~ habit of always being 15 minutes late for a meeting.* ➤ aggravation (n), aggravate (v), aggravated (adj), aggravatingly (adv) ❖ εξοργιστικός

3. Baffling Bernice (page 12)

1.77 baffling (adj) – mysterious, puzzling • *I find it ~ that the couple is always arguing as they've been together for fifty years!* ➤ bafflement (n), baffle (v), baffled (adj) ❖ που φέρνει σε αμηχανία

1.78 biased (adj) – prejudiced, intolerant • *Thanks to equal opportunity laws, ~ employers are no longer common.* ➤ bias (n). Opp: unbiased (adj) ❖ προκατειλημμένος

1.79 belittling (adj) – insulting, humiliating • *The boss's ~ remarks made her want to crawl under the table.* ➤ belittle (v), belittled (adj) ❖ υποτιμητικός

1.80 benevolent (adj) – kind, humane • *Donating 20% of your salary to the children's orphanage was a ~ gesture which the institution greatly appreciated.* ➤ benevolence (n), benevolently (adv) ❖ καλοκάγαθος, φιλάνθρωπος

1.81 broad-minded (adj) – open to new ideas • *The ~ company has never discriminated against women or people of racial and religious minorities.* ➤ broad-mindedness (n), broad-mindedly (adv). Opp: narrow-minded (adj) ❖ ανεκτικός, προοδευτικός

1.82 boisterous (adj) – noisy, cheerful, rough • *Inexperienced teachers find it difficult to discipline a class of ~ students.* ➤ boisterously (adv) ❖ θορυβώδης

4. Commendable Carl (page 12)

1.83 commendable (adj) – praiseworthy, admirable • *The boss congratulated her on doing a ~ job.* ➤ commend (v), commendably (adv) ❖ αξιέπαινος

1.84 congenial (adj) – pleasant, agreeable • *She found her new boss an easy-going ~ person who was easy to get along with.* ➤ congeniality (n), congenially (adv) ❖ ευχάριστος

1.85 cooperative (adj) – helpful, willing • *She found her new colleagues ~ and always willing to help.* ➤ cooperation (n), cooperate (v), cooperatively (adv) ❖ συνεργάσιμος

1 Perspectives on personality

1.86 coercive (adj) – using force or threats • *It is against the law for the police to use ~ tactics to get people to confess.* ➢ coercion (n), coerce (v), coercively (adv) ❖ πιεστικός

1.87 conscientious (adj) – thorough, devoted to doing a job well • *He's a ~ employee who approaches every task with great thoroughness and care.* ➢ conscience (n), conscientiousness (n), conscientiously (adv) ❖ ευσυνείδητος

1.88 composed (adj) – calm, in control • *The bright young candidate was confident and ~ during the interview, unlike the others who were extremely nervous.* ➢ composure (n), compose (v) ❖ ήρεμος, ατάραχος

5. Dejected Debby (page 13)

1.89 dejected (adj) – sad, depressed • *He was ~ for weeks after learning that he had failed the exam.* ➢ dejection (n), deject (v), dejectedly (adv) ❖ κατηφής, αποθαρρημένος

1.90 detached (adj) – separate, cut off • *Since his divorce, he's been very ~ and difficult to talk to.* ➢ detachment (n), detach (v) ❖ ξεκομμένος, απομονωμένος

1.91 determined (adj) – strong-minded, resolute • *The ~ young lawyer will do anything to succeed.* ➢ determination (n), determine (v) ❖ αποφασισμένος

1.92 desperate (adj) – wild with pain or anger • *The woman was so ~ that she attempted to rob a bank to get money for her son's operation.* ➢ desperation (n), despair (n), desperately (adv) ❖ απελπισμένος

1.93 distracted (adj) – unable to concentrate • *What's wrong? You're so ~ that you haven't done any work today.* ➢ distraction (n), distract (v), distracting (adj), distractingly (adv), distractedly (adv). Opp: undistracted (adj) ❖ αναστατωμένος

1.94 disillusioned (adj) – disappointed, stripped of false hope • *D~ by the increasing difficulty of the Proficiency Exam, she decided to stop her English lessons.* ➢ disillusionment (n), disillusion (v) ❖ απογοητευμένος, χωρίς ψευδαισθήσεις

6. Exuberant Eddy (page 13)

1.95 exuberant (adj) – excited, full of joy • *The children woke up feeling ~ about their trip to Disneyland.* ➢ exuberance (n), exuberantly (adv) ❖ διαχυτικός, ενθουσιώδης

1.96 enchanting (adj) – charming, fascinating • *We found her to be an ~ companion whose stories we couldn't get enough of.* ➢ enchantment (n), enchant (v), enchanted (adj), enchantingly (adv) ❖ γοητευτικός, μαγευτικός

1.97 eloquent (adj) – well-spoken, articulate (*see* **1.65**) • *The former politician is now an ~ spokesperson for the environment.* ➢ eloquence (n), eloquently (adv) ❖ εύγλωττος

1.98 enterprising (adj) – hard-working, ambitious • *The ~ young employee worked long hours in hopes of getting a promotion.* ➢ enterprise (n) ❖ τολμηρός

1.99 erratic (adj) – unpredictable, inconsistent • *His teacher is concerned about his ~ test scores; apparently, he's in danger of failing the course.* ➢ erratically (adv) ❖ αλλοπρόσαλλος

1.100 efficient (adj) – fast, effective, and competent • *The ~ secretary is not only fast but accurate as well.* ➢ efficiency (n), efficiently (adv). Opp: inefficient (adj) ❖ αποτελεσματικός, αποδοτικός

7. Frugal Fran (page 13)

1.101 frugal (adj) – careful with money • *She's always been ~, which is why she never has trouble paying her bills.* ➢ frugality (n), frugally (adv). Opp: spendthrift (adj) ❖ (για ανθρώπους) λιτοδίαιτος, οικονόμος· (για πράγματα) λιτός

1.102 frank (adj) – open, honest • *I appreciate a person who is ~ in giving opinions, even if the truth hurts from time to time.* ➢ frankness (n), frankly (adv) ❖ ειλικρινής

1.103 foolhardy (adj) – overly risky, foolish • *It was ~ of him to drive you home after he'd been drinking; you're lucky he didn't have an accident.* ➢ foolhardiness (n) ❖ απερίσκεπτος, παράτολμος

1.104 farsighted (adj) – able to plan ahead • *If you're ~, you will be able to save enough money to live comfortably after you retire.* ➢ farsightedness (n) ❖ προνοητικός, διορατικός

1.105 fickle (adj) – changing, unstable • *Fate can be ~ ; one day luck seems like it's on your side, the next day your life might be turned upside down.* ➢ fickleness (n) ❖ ευμετάβλητος, άστατος

1.106 frustrated (adj) – angry, disappointed • *No wonder she feels ~. She lost her job six months ago and still hasn't found a new one.* ➢ frustration (n), frustrate (v), frustrating (adj), frustratingly (adv) ❖ απογοητευμένος και θυμωμένος

Grammar (1) Adjectives (pages 15-16)

Try it! (page 15)

1.107 scrambled (adj) – mixed up, not in the correct order • *The teacher asked us to put the ~ list of words in alphabetical order.* ➢ scramble (n, v). Opp: unscrambled (adj) ❖ ανακατωμένος, μπερδεμένος

1.108 slender (adj) – attractively long and thin • *a ~ ballerina, ~ palm trees swaying in the wind* ➢ slenderness (n) ❖ λεπτός, λυγερός

1.109 chubby (adj) – softly rounded, pleasantly fat • *It's hard to believe that in a few short years the ~ baby had grown into a slim five-year-old ready for her first day of school.* ➢ chubbiness (n) ❖ παχουλός

Vocabulary (2) It takes all kinds (Part II) (pages 17-19)

1. Gregarious Gerty (page 17)

1.110 gregarious (adj) – sociable, loving company • *The twins are as different as night and day: John is ~ and loves parties, but Jim prefers the company of a good book.* ➢ gregariousness (n) ❖ αγελαίος, κοινωνικός

1.111 gracious (adj) – charming and polite • *It was ~ of you to invite my parents to visit you at your summer home.* ➢ grace (n, v), graciously (adv). Opp: ungracious (adj) ❖ ευγενικός, πρόσχαρος

1.112 generous (adj) – giving freely and unselfishly • *Sara is a ~ child who always shares her toys with other children.* ➢ generosity (n), generously (adv) ❖ γενναιόδωρος

1.113 gloomy (adj) – sad, melancholy, dejected • *He's been in a ~ mood since his girlfriend told him she wouldn't marry him.* ➢ gloom (n), gloominess (n), gloomily (adv) ❖ μελαγχολικός, απαισιόδοξος

Perspectives on personality 1

1.114 genial (adj) – cheerful, good-tempered • *She's such an optimistic, ~ person that it's a joy to spend time with her.* ➤ geniality (n), genially (adv) ❖ καλοδιάθετος, πρόσχαρος

1.115 gullible (adj) – too trusting, easily tricked • *The ~ old woman really believed that she had won a million dollars in a contest that she never entered.* ➤ gullibility (n), gull (v), gullibly (adv) ❖ ευκολόπιστος

2. Hopeless Harriet (page 17)

1.116 hopeless (adj) – without hope for improvement • *Ann is a ~ math student who never gets above a D in her math classes.* ➤ hopelessness (n), hopelessly (adv). Opp: hopeful (adj) ❖ απελπισμένος

1.117 heedless (of) (adj) – careless, not attentive • *Drivers cannot afford to be ~; they must pay attention to every detail on the road.* ➤ heedlessness (n), heed (n, v), heedlessly (adv) ❖ απρόσεκτος

1.118 hesitant (adj) – uncertain, hesitating • *Policemen are trained to act quickly; they must not be ~.* ➤ hesitation (n), hesitate (v), hesitantly (adv) ❖ διστακτικός

1.119 helpless (adj) – unable to look after oneself • *Far from being upset and ~, the lost child told the police exactly how they could help him get back home.* ➤ helplessness (n), helplessly (adv) ❖ ανίκανος, ανήμπορος

1.120 humble (adj) – modest, unpretentious • *She prefers riding around town on a ~ bicycle rather than spending a lot of money on maintaining a car.* ➤ humble (v), humbly (adv) ❖ ταπεινός

1.121 humiliated (adj) – totally embarrassed • *Failing the exam left him feeling totally ~.* ➤ humiliation (n), humiliated (adj), humiliatingly (adv) ❖ ταπεινωμένος, εξευτελισμένος

3. Ignorant Izzy (page 17)

1.122 ignorant (adj) – unaware, uninformed • *With so much information in the media and on the Internet, there's no excuse for being ~ today.* ➤ ignorance (n), ignore (v), ignorantly (adv) ❖ ανίδεος, αδαής, απληροφόρητος

1.123 intolerant (adj) – narrow-minded, biased • *Racists and sexists are by nature ~.* ➤ intolerance (n), intolerantly (adv). Opp: tolerant (adj) ❖ μη ανεκτικός

1.124 impertinent (adj) – rude, offensive, bold • *The child was punished for being ~ to his parents.* ➤ impertinence (n), impertinently (adv) ❖ αναιδής, αυθάδης. **Note: pertinent** (adj) means unrelated, irrelevant ❖ άσχετος; it is *not* the opposite of **impertinent**.

1.125 indignant (adj) – morally offended, angry • *The customer became ~ when the manager refused to refund her money.* ➤ indignation (n), indignantly (adv) ❖ αγανακτισμένος

1.126 impetuous (adj) – acting hastily, unpredictably • *It would be ~ of you to quit your job before you found another.* ➤ impetuousness (n), impetuously (adv) ❖ απερίσκεπτος, ορμητικός

1.127 irksome (adj) – annoying, irritating • *After a full day of teaching, she found the noisy students in her last class especially ~.* ➤ irk (v) ❖ δυσάρεστος, ενοχλητικός

4. Jovial Judy (page 18)

1.128 jovial (adj) – cheerful, pleasant • *The sun's out and I'm on vacation with good friends. Of course, I'm feeling ~!* ➤ joviality (n), jovially (adv) ❖ χαρούμενος, κεφάτος

1.129 juvenile (adj) – childish, childlike • *"I would expect such ~ behavior from your younger brother,"* scolded his mother, *"but you, young man, should know better."* ❖ ανώριμος, νεανικός. 📖 : e.g., ~ court

1.130 jubilant (adj) – joyful, exuberant • *The fans were ~ when their team won the national championship.* ➤ jubilation (n), jubilantly (adv) ❖ περιχαρής, ενθουσιώδης

1.131 jealous (adj) – envious • *Of course, I was ~ when I saw my fiancé walking down the street with a beautiful woman!* ➤ jealousy (n), jealously (adv) ❖ ζηλιάρης

1.132 just (adj) – morally right, fair • *King Solomon had a reputation for being a ~ judge.* ➤ justice (n), justness (n), justly (adv). Opp: unjust (adj) ❖ δίκαιος

1.133 judicious (adj) – showing good judgment • *No matter how ~ you are, investing money in the stock market is always a risky business.* ➤ judiciousness (n), judiciously (adv) ❖ νουνεχής, συνετός

5. Kindhearted Kenneth (page 18)

1.134 kindhearted (adj) – caring, considerate • *Our ~ neighbor always brings us a plate of cookies whenever she bakes for her own family.* ❖ καλόκαρδος

1.135 knowledgeable (adj) – well-informed • *The science writer is said to be one of the most ~ experts in his field.* ➤ knowledge (n), knowledgeably (adv) ❖ γνώστης, ενήμερος

1.136 keen (adj) – 1. strong, sharp; deeply felt • *The lawyer has a ~ sense of justice.* 2. enthusiastic • *The businessman is a ~ supporter of the local environmental group; he made several large donations last year.* ➤ keenness (n), keenly (adv) ❖ 1. οξύς, κοφτερός 2. ενθουσιώδης, φανατικός

1.137 keyed-up (adj) – anxiously excited, nervous • *She always gets ~ before she has to speak in public.* ❖ σε αγωνία

1.138 knowing (adj) – having secret knowledge • *"Of course, we didn't have ice cream,"* said Grandpa, giving us a wink and a *~ smile.* ➤ knowingly (adv) ❖ με σημασία

6. Liberal Linda (page 18)

1.139 liberal (adj) – progressive, tolerant • *Don't you wish your parents had more ~ ideas about child-rearing?* ➤ liberalness (n), liberalize (v), liberally (adv) ❖ φιλελεύθερος, προοδευτικός

1.140 loyal (adj) – see **1.52**

1.141 lucid (adj) – clear, easily understood • *After surgery, patients usually take an hour or so to wake up and become ~ again.* ➤ lucidity (n), lucidly (adv) ❖ σαφής, διαυγής

1.142 literate (adj) – 1. well-educated • *The boss was quick to hire the refined and ~ young woman.* 2. able to read and write (though not necessarily at a high level) • *His great grandfather only attended school for two years, so he was barely ~.* ➤ literacy (n), literately (adv). Opp: illiterate (adj) ❖ 1. μορφωμένος 2. εγγράμματος. 📖 : e.g., barely ~

1.143 lenient (adj) – gentle, not strict • *He's a ~ judge who does not believe in imprisoning first-time offenders.* ➤ leniency (n), leniently (adv) ❖ επιεικής

1.144 laudable (adj) – deserving praise or approval • *All of the critics agreed that the actor's brilliant performance was the most ~ they had seen all year.* ➤ laud (v), laudably (adv) ❖ επαινετός

Perspectives on personality

7. Modest Maxine (page 18)

1.145 modest (adj) – humble, not arrogant • *Given his money and position, you'd expect him to be snobbish, but in fact he's a very ~ man.* ➢ modesty (n), modestly (adv) ❖ μετριόφρων, σεμνός, μετριοπαθής

1.146 mediocre (adj) – ordinary, commonplace • *He's a ~ language student who will probably not pass the ECPE on his first try.* ➢ mediocrity (n) ❖ μέτριος, παρακατιανός

1.147 malicious (adj) – with bad intentions, spiteful • *She is a ~, jealous person who does not have a nice bone in her body.* ➢ malice (n), maliciousness (n), maliciously (adv) ❖ κακόβουλος, μοχθηρός

1.148 materialistic (adj) – desiring money and things • *We live in a consumer-oriented, ~ society, where spiritual values are not as important as in the past.* ➢ materialism (n), materialistically (adv) ❖ υλιστικός

1.149 magnanimous (adj) – generous, big-hearted • *Philanthropists are known for their ~ gestures to charitable organizations.* ➢ magnanimity (n), magnanimously (adv) ❖ μεγάθυμος, μεγαλόψυχος

1.150 maternal (adj) – motherly • *Watching her friend holding her newborn child brought out her ~ instinct.* ➢ maternity (n), maternally (adv) ❖ μητρικός

8. Notorious Ned (page 19)

1.151 notorious (adj) – infamous, known for sth bad • *He is ~ for cheating on tests, so all the teachers keep a close eye on him.* ➢ notoriety (n), notoriously (adv) ❖ διαβόητος, περιβόητος

1.152 nosy (adj) – snoopy, curious • *My ~ next-door neighbor is always asking questions about my friends.* ➢ nosiness (n), nose (v), nosily (adv) ❖ αδιάκριτος, περίεργος

1.153 nasty (adj) – unpleasant, not nice • *She refused to babysit for the ~, ill-mannered child.* ➢ nastiness (n), nastily (adv) ❖ κακός, πρόστυχος

1.154 narrow-minded (adj) – intolerant, prejudiced • *His ~, racist remarks have made him very unpopular with his colleagues.* ➢ narrow-mindedness (n). Opp: broad-minded (adj) ❖ στενόμυαλος

1.155 negligent (adj) – neglectful, inattentive • *It is illegal for parents to be ~ of their children's health and other basic needs.* ➢ negligence (n), neglect (v), negligently (adv) ❖ αμελής, απρόσεκτος

1.156 noble (adj) – worthy, excellent • *The doctor's ~ effort to save the dying patient was unfortunately in vain.* ➢ noble (n), nobility (n), nobly (adv). Opp: ignoble (adj) ❖ ευγενής, μεγαλοπρεπής

9. Obnoxious Olivia (page 19)

1.157 obnoxious (adj) – annoying, aggravating • *I'm not sure why I find him so annoying, but I do. He's one of the most ~ people I know.* ➢ obnoxiously (adv) ❖ απεχθής, αποκρουστικός. See also **2.351**.

1.158 outspoken (adj) – blunt, frank, honest • *Theresa is an ~ person who always says exactly what she's thinking* ➢ outspokenness (n), speak out (v), outspokenly (adv) ❖ ειλικρινής, ντόμπρος

1.159 offensive (adj) – rude, insulting • *He was thrown out of class for using ~ language.* ➢ offense (n), offence (n – Brit), offend (v), offensively (adv). Opp: inoffensive (adj) ❖ προσβλητικός. 📖 : e.g., an ~ military operation

1.160 outrageous (adj) – shocking, scandalous • *Everyone was insulted by his ~, drunken remarks* ➢ outrage (n, v), outrageously (adv) ❖ σκανδαλώδης, εξωφρενικός

1.161 obstinate (adj) – stubborn, insistent • *O~ people rarely change their mind, even if they're wrong!* ➢ obstinacy (n), obstinately (adv) ❖ ισχυρογνώμων, πεισματάρης

1.162 ostentatious (adj) – showy, pretentious • *O~ people are always bragging about their fancy cars, jewelry, and other possessions.* ➢ ostentation (n), ostentatiously (adv) ❖ φανταχτερός, φιγουρατζής

1.163 oblivious (adj) – unconscious, unaware • *She's so self-centered that she's ~ to everyone's problems except her own.* ➢ oblivion (n), obliviously (adv) ❖ που δεν επικοινωνεί με το περιβάλλον, που δεν ξέρει τι γίνεται γύρω του

1.164 objectionable (adj) – worthy of disapproval • *I found his insulting behavior totally ~.* ➢ objection (n), object (v), objectionably (adv). Opp: unobjectionable (adj) ❖ απαράδεκτος, δυσάρεστος

10. Prudent Paul (page 19)

1.165 prudent (adj) – *see* **1.46**

1.166 pensive (adj) – deep in thought, thoughtful, reflective • *Is something troubling you? You're usually not this ~.* ➢ pensiveness (n), pensively (adv) ❖ συλλογισμένος, σκεπτικός

1.167 persistent (adj) – insistent, set on continuing • *She finally gave in to her son's ~ requests and bought him a puppy.* ➢ persistence (n), persist (v), persistently (adv) ❖ επίμονος

1.168 poised (adj) – dignified, self-controlled • *She's a ~ and confident young woman who rarely loses her temper.* ➢ poise (n, v) ❖ αξιοπρεπής

1.169 personable (adj) – admirable, likable • *I'm sure you'll like her; she's very ~.* ❖ ευπαρουσίαστος

1.170 pretentious (adj) – arrogant (*see* **1.31**), conceited • *She's highly intelligent, but the refreshing thing is that she's not at all ~.* ➢ pretension (n), pretentiousness (n), pretentiously (adv) ❖ ξιπασμένος

Cloze: A closer look (pages 21-23)

Cloze practice – Amelia Earhart (pages 22-23)

Passage (page 23)

Paragraph 1

1.171 invasion (n) – (C) (used figuratively in text) the action or an act of enemy armed forces entering a country • *Hitler's ~ of Poland in 1939* ➢ invade (v), invasive (adj), invasively (adv) ❖ εισβολή

1.172 daring (n) – (U) courage combined with a willingness to take risks • *Many lives were saved as a result of the firemen's ~.* ➢ dare (n, v) ❖ τόλμη

1.173 aviator (n) – (C) sb who flies or is a crewmember on an aircraft • *Charles Lindbergh is one of the most famous ~s of all time.* ➢ aviation (n), aviate (v) ❖ αεροπόρος

Perspectives on personality

1.174 barrier (n) – (C) sth that prevents or controls progress, a limit or boundary • *Language was never a ~ between them because her Greek was quite good by the time she met him.* ➢ bar (v) ❖ φράγμα, εμπόδιο

1.175 embody (v) – be a living symbol or expression of an abstract idea or quality • *In his eyes, she ~ied every quality that he thought a woman should have: intelligence, virtue, and beauty.* ➢ embodiment (n) ❖ ενσωματώνω, εκφράζω

1.176 breezy (adj) – cheerful, relaxed • *How can you be so ~ at 6 a.m.? I'm still half asleep!* ➢ breeziness (n), breeze (v), breezily (adv) ❖ (άνθρωποι) χαρωπός, κεφάτος

1.177 mobility (n) – (U) the ability to move easily from one place to another (e.g., within a country or a work environment) • *Cars have given people great ~.* ➢ mobilize (v), mobile (adj). Opp: immobility (n) ❖ κινητικότητα, ευκινησία

1.178 dashing (adj) – (appearance) impressive and attractive in a stylish, sophisticated way • *The army officer looked ~ in his dress uniform.* ❖ (εμφάνιση) εντυπωσιακός, κομψός

1.179 evolving (adj) – gradually developing into a higher, more complex form • *Anthropologists are fascinated by the ~ culture of mankind.* ➢ evolution (n), evolve (v) ❖ που εξελίσσεται

1.180 sought (pp) → **seek – sought – sought** (irreg v) – search for and try to find or obtain sth/sb • *~ a job, ~ happiness* ❖ αναζητώ, ψάχνω

1.181 fulfillment (n) – (U) satisfaction that comes from achieving one's goals • *Having a wonderful family and a successful career gave her a great sense of ~.* ➢ fulfill (v), fulfilled (adj), fulfilling (adj) ❖ ικανοποίηση, εκπλήρωση

Paragraph 2

1.182 mettle (n) → **prove (sb's) ~** (idm) – show what one's capabilities are • *The U.S. space program proved its ~ by landing astronauts on the moon in the summer of 1969.* ❖ δείχνω τι αξίζω

1.183 fatal (adj) – ending in death or disaster • *a ~ traffic accident, a ~ mistake* ➢ fatality (n), fatally (adv) ❖ θανατηφόρος, μοιραίος

1.184 hazard (n) – (C) danger • *Smoking is a known ~ to your health.* ➢ hazard (v), hazardous (adj), hazardously (adv) ❖ κίνδυνος

1.185 trouble-plagued (adj) – full of problems • *The politician was forced to resign after a ~ year of scandal and accusations.* ❖ γεμάτος από προβλήματα

1.186 constant (adj) – continuous, occurring again and again without stopping • *Having grown up in a village, he found it hard to cope with the ~ noise of city traffic.* ➢ constant (n), constancy (n), constantly (adv) ❖ συνεχής, αδιάκοπος

Paragraph 3

1.187 aspiration (n) – (C) strong desire or ambition to achieve sth • *The young senator has ~s of becoming president someday.* ➢ aspire (v), aspiring (adj) ❖ φιλοδοξία

1.188 enlightened (adj) – free of ignorance or prejudice, having great knowledge and understanding • *The founders of the new American nation had ~ ideas about liberty and freedom.* ➢ enlightenment (n), enlighten (v), enlightening (adj). Opp: unenlightened (adj) ❖ διαφωτισμένος

1.189 indulge (in) (v) – engage in sth you find pleasurable • *After winning the lottery, he ~d in luxuries like expensive trips and designer clothing.* ➢ indulgence (n), indulgent (adj) ❖ παραδίδομαι σε

1.190 shallow (adj) – (of people and their actions) superficial, overly simple • *The art critic's ~ review made it clear that he had not understood the artist's intent.* ➢ shallowness (n), shallowly (adv) ❖ ρηχός, επιπόλαιος

1.191 transform (v) – change/be changed into a totally different form • *Time had ~ed the skinny child into a beautiful young woman.* ➢ transformation (n), transformed (adj), transforming (adj) ❖ μετατρέπω, μεταβάλλω, αλλάζω

Choices: Item 1a

1.192 erect (v) – (used figuratively in text) build, put up • *~ a building, ~ a statue in sb's honor, ~ a tent at a campsite* ➢ erection (n), erect (adj) ❖ κτίζω, στήνω, ανεγείρω

Grammar (2) Predicate adjectives (pages 24-25)

Point 1 (page 24)

1.193 ablaze (adj) – burning, on fire • *The children's eyes were ~ with excitement.* ➢ blaze (n, v) ❖ φλεγόμενος

1.194 afloat (adj) – floating, on the surface (e.g., of a body of water) • *The crew fought to keep the fishing boat ~ in the storm.* ➢ float (n, v), floating (adj) ❖ επιπλέων, στην επιφάνεια

1.195 aghast (adj) – shocked, horrified • *The jury was ~ when they heard how the murder had been committed.* ➢ ghastly (adj) ❖ κατάπληκτος, εμβρόντητος

1.196 aglow (adj) – glowing, shining • *When the child saw his birthday cake, his eyes were all ~.* ➢ glow (n, v), glowing (adj), glowingly (adv) ❖ λάμπων, φλογερός

1.197 averse (adj) → **be ~ to sth/doing sth** – be opposed to sth/doing sth, have a strong dislike of sth/doing sth • *lazy people are ~ to hard work, strict parents are ~ to their children staying out late at night* ➢ aversion (n) ❖ αντιτίθεμαι, απεχθάνομαι

Vocabulary (3) It takes all kinds (Part III) (pages 26-28)

1. Quirky Quentin (page 26)

1.198 quirky (adj) – peculiar, idiosyncratic • *Tom is a ~ eater; he eats chicken for lunch and dinner seven days a week.* ➢ quirk (n), quirkiness (n), quirkily (adv) ❖ εκκεντρικός, παράξενος

1.199 querulous (adj) – complaining, finding fault • *Q~ people make difficult friends as they're always complaining and finding fault with everyone.* ➢ querulously (adv) ❖ μεμψίμοιρος, γκρινιάρης

1.200 quarrelsome (adj) – argumentative, fond of starting quarrels • *Q~ people always seem to start arguments wherever they go.* ➢ quarrel (n, v) ❖ φιλόνικος, καβγατζής

1.201 quibbling (adj) – critical about small details • *His mother-in-law is a ~ creature who rarely has anything nice to say.* ➢ quibble (n, v) ❖ λεπτολόγος, που φέρνει μικρο-αντιρρήσεις

1.202 quixotic (adj) – unrealistic, impractical, overly idealistic (e.g., like Don Quixote) • *It's rather ~ of the elderly woman to think she's going to find the perfect husband after all these years.* ❖ δονκιχωτικός (δηλ., που επιδεικνύει ψεύτικη παλικαριά)

Perspectives on personality

1.203 quackish (adj) – pretending to know medicine (like a **quack/charlatan**) • *I expected the acupuncturist to be a bit ~, but in fact he seems quite knowledgeable.* ➢ quack (n) ❖ τσαρλατάνος, αγύρτης

2. Reputable Rita and Ruthless Ruth (page 26)

1.204 reputable (adj) – respected, having a good reputation • *Harrods of London is one of the most ~ department stores in the world.* ➢ reputation (n), repute (n), reputed (adj), reputedly (adv) ❖ τίμιος, ονομαστός

1.205 reliable (adj) – dependable, trustworthy • *After 15 years, they decided that the car was no longer ~ and would have to be replaced.* ➢ reliability (n), rely (v), reliably (adv). Opp: unreliable (adj) ❖ αξιόπιστος, σίγουρος

1.206 refined (adj) – cultured, courteous • *As one would expect, the aristocrat was a ~ person with a taste for the finer things in life.* ➢ refinement (n), refine (v) ❖ ραφινάτος, καλλιεργημένος, εκλεπτυσμένος

1.207 righteous (adj) – morally good, virtuous • *It's rare to find such a fine and ~ politician who is truly interested in helping the poor.* ➢ righteousness (n), righteously (adv) ❖ δίκαιος, ενάρετος

1.208 ruthless (adj) – cruel, without mercy • *The ~ dictator thought nothing of making his enemies "disappear."* ➢ ruthlessness (n), ruthlessly (adv) ❖ αδίστακτος, ανελέητος, άσπλαχνος

1.209 rash (adj) – hasty, impulsive • *It was ~ of you to quit your job before finding another.* ➢ rashness (n), rashly (adv) ❖ (άνθρωποι) παράτολμος, απερίσκεπτος, ορμητικός · (πράξεις) απερίσκεπτος

1.210 remote (adj) – (people) distant, unfriendly, aloof • *He was a ~ person who kept his distance from his co-workers.* ➢ remoteness (n), remotely (adv) ❖ (άνθρωποι) ψυχρός, επιφυλακτικός. 📖 : e.g., a ~ village, ~ control

1.211 rigid (adj) – (people) stiff, unbending, inflexible • *He's a ~ person who never bends the rules he has made for himself.* ➢ rigidity (n), rigidly (adv) ❖ αυστηρός, αδιάλλακτος. *See also* **2.66**.

3. Sarcastic Seymour (page 26)

1.212 sarcastic (adj) – ironic, cutting • *Your ~ comments really hurt her. You really should apologize.* ➢ sarcasm (n), sarcastically (adv) ❖ σαρκαστικός

1.213 sophisticated (adj) – cultivated, cosmopolitan • *She grew up in a village, but she's much more ~ now that she's been living in a big city.* ➢ sophistication (n) ❖ ραφινάτος, εκλεπτυσμένος. *See also* **3.314**.

1.214 shrewd (adj) – clever, cunning • *S~ businessman make lots of money by making ~ decisions.* ➢ shrewdness (n), shrewdly (adv) ❖ έξυπνος, καπάτσος

1.215 superficial (adj) – shallow, not deep • *She's such a ~ person that it's impossible to have a serious conversation with her.* ➢ superficiality (n), superficially (adv) ❖ επιφανειακός, επιπόλαιος

1.216 stubborn (adj) – strong-willed, obstinate (*see* **1.161**) • *That child is as ~ as a mule; she insists on getting her own way.* ➢ stubbornness (n), stubbornly (adv) ❖ πεισματάρης, ισχυρογνώμων

1.217 sensitive (adj) – (people) aware, caring how others feel • *All she ever wanted was to find a husband who was kind and ~.* ➢ sensitivity (n), sense (v), sensitively (adv). Opp: insensitive (adj) ❖ ευαίσθητος, αισθαντικός. 📖 : e.g., ~ to light, a ~ performance

4. Temperate Ted (page 27)

1.218 temperate (adj) – (people) self-controlled, moderate • *Her new boyfriend is more ~ than the race-car driver she used to date.* ➢ temperance (n), temper (v), temperately (adv) ❖ εγκρατής, μετρημένος, συγκρατημένος. *See also* **2.326**.

1.219 tenacious (adj) – firm, unwilling to give up • *The old man is a ~ fighter who isn't ready to give up living.* ➢ tenacity (n), tenaciously (adv) ❖ επίμονος, ανυποχώρητος

1.220 tolerant (adj) – *see* **1.50**

1.221 thrifty (adj) – careful with money • *Thanks to her ~ ways, she was able to buy her own home before she was 30.* ➢ thrift (n), thriftily (adv) ❖ οικονόμος, φειδωλός

1.222 trusting (adj) – having faith in others • *His parents are ~ because he has always shown himself to be responsible and reliable.* ➢ trust (n, v), trustingly (adv) ❖ γεμάτος εμπιστοσύνη

1.223 trustworthy (adj) – reliable, dependable • *My best friend has proven herself to be ~ again and again; I know I can rely on her.* ➢ trustworthiness (n) ❖ αξιόπιστος

5. Uproarious Ursula (page 27)

1.224 uproarious (adj) – extremely funny, hilarious • *His ~ jokes had us laughing until we had tears in our eyes.* ➢ uproar (n), uproariously (adv) ❖ πολύ αστείος, εύθυμος, θορυβώδης

1.225 unique (adj) – one of a kind, exceptional • *Critics agree that the artist's work is ~ ; they have never seen anything like it.* ➢ uniqueness (n), uniquely (adv) ❖ μοναδικός

1.226 unbearable (adj) – intolerable, not endurable • *Ted is an ~ bore whom I find difficult to be in the same room with!* ➢ unbearably (adv) ❖ ανυπόφορος

1.227 uncanny (adj) – unusual, mysterious, strange • *Her ~ ability to remember names and dates was a big help to her in history class.* ➢ uncannily (adv) ❖ παράξενος, αφύσικος, αλλόκοτος

1.228 urbane (adj) – refined, courteous • *We found the actor charming and ~ ; you'd never guess he grew up on a farm in the Midwest.* ➢ urbanity (n), urbanely (adv) ❖ αβρός, ευγενικός, πολιτισμένος

1.229 uncouth (adj) – rude, unrefined • *I'll be embarrassed if you tell any ~ jokes in front of my parents.* ➢ uncouthness (n), uncouthly (adv) ❖ άξεστος

6. Villainous Victor (page 27)

1.230 villainous (adj) – bad, evil • *In the end, the ~ dictator was overthrown and executed.* ➢ villain (n), villainy (n) ❖ αχρείος, παλιάνθρωπος

1.231 vicious (adj) – cruel, fierce • *The ~ criminal was sentenced to life in prison for his ~ crimes.* ➢ viciousness (n), viciously (adv) ❖ φαύλος, αισχρός

1.232 vague (adj) – unclear, indefinite • *Your explanation is rather ~. Could you give us a few more details?* ➢ vagueness (n), vaguely (adv) ❖ ασαφής, ακαθόριστος

Perspectives on personality

1.233 vindictive (adj) – spiteful, wanting revenge • *I can understand you're feeling ~, but is it worth going to jail to get your revenge?* ➣ vindictiveness (n), vindictively (adv) ❖ εκδικητικός

1.234 versatile (adj) – (people) good at many things • *The ~ actor is comfortable playing both dramatic and comic roles.* ➣ versatility (n) ❖ (άνθρωπος) πολύπλευρος, πολυμήχανος. 📖 : e.g., a ~ material

1.235 vigorous (adj) – active, energetic • *Ed and Sue are ~ supporters of the local environmental group.* ➣ vigor (n), vigorously (adv) ❖ ρωμαλέος, δυνατός. 📖 : e.g., a ~ plant

1.236 voracious (adj) – greedy, wildly hungry • *Teenage boys are notorious for having ~ appetites. / She's a ~ reader who can devour a 600-page book in a few days.* ➣ voraciously (adv) ❖ αχόρταγος, ακόρεστος, άπληστος

1.237 vain (adj) – conceited, arrogant, proud • *Yes, she's beautiful and intelligent, but does she have to be so ~ about it?* ➣ vanity (n), vainly (adv) ❖ ματαιόδοξος, καμαρωτός

7. Whimsical William (page 28)

1.238 whimsical (adj) – strange yet amusing • *Everyone enjoys his ~ sense of humor, though not everyone understands it!* ➣ whim (n), whimsy (n), whimsicality (n), whimsically (adv) ❖ ιδιότροπος, άστατος

1.239 wishy-washy (adj) – indecisive, vague • *W~ people have trouble making up their minds.* ➣ wishy-washiness (n) ❖ ανούσιος, αναποφάσιστος

1.240 wary (adj) – cautious, suspicious • *He's understandably ~ about driving on icy roads.* ➣ wariness (n), warily (adv) ❖ προσεχτικός, επιφυλακτικός

1.241 whiny (adj) – complaining, irritating • *I hate babysitting for children who are ~ and spoiled; nothing seems to satisfy them.* ➣ whine (n, v) ❖ παραπονιάρης, κλαψιάρης

1.242 witty (adj) – amusing in a clever way • *Educated audiences tend to prefer ~ comedians to silly ones.* ➣ wit (n), wittily (adv) ❖ σπιρτόζος, πνευματώδης, έξυπνος

1.243 wily (adj) – sly, deceptive, sneaky ➣ wiliness (n) ❖ πανούργος, πονηρός

8. Exasperating Xenophon (page 28)

1.244 exasperating (adj) – highly annoying, irksome • *It's ~ to be highy qualified and not be able to find a job.* ➣ exasperation (n), exasperate (v), exasperated (adj) ❖ εκνευριστικός, που φέρνει σε απόγνωση

1.245 take exception (to sth) (v phr) – object strongly to sth, be insulted or offended by sth • *What I'm about to tell you is for your own good. I hope you won't ~ to it.* ❖ θίγομαι, φέρνω αντίρρηση, προσβάλλομαι

1.246 excessive (adj) – much more than is reasonable or necessary • *The police were criticized for using ~ force in their attempt to quiet the protest.* ➣ excess (n), exceed (v), excessively (adv) ❖ υπέρμετρος, υπερβολικός

1.247 figure out (phr v) – think about sth until you understand it • *I can't ~ why they broke up. They seemed so happy together.* ❖ θεολογίζω, καταλαβαίνω

1.248 xenophobic (adj) – fearing/hating foreigners • *The politician's extreme patriotism is beginning to have ~ overtones, which many voters find unattractive.* ➣ xenophobia (n) ❖ ξενόφοβος

1.249 exceptional (adj) – unusually good, outstanding • *She has an exceptional memory, so she has no problem learning new vocabulary.* ➣ exception (n), except (v, prep), exceptionally (adv). Opp: unexceptional (adj) ❖ εξαιρετικός

9. Yellow Yolanda (page 28)

1.250 yellow (adj) – (fig) cowardly, not brave • *The other soldiers knew he was ~ and refused to go into battle with him.* ❖ δειλός

1.251 yielding (adj) – surrendering, giving in • *Tom is aggressive and argumentative, while his twin brother Tim is a much more ~ character.* ➣ yield (n, v) ❖ υποχωρητικός, διαλλακτικός

1.252 young (adj) – immature, childish • *College graduates tend to be ~ and a bit wet behind the ears.* ❖ νέος, άπειρος. 📖 : e.g., ~ at heart

1.253 youthful (adj) – fresh, full of youth • *For an 80-year-old man, her grandfather is very energetic and has a very ~ outlook on life.* ➣ youth (n) ❖ νεανικός

10. Zany Zelda (page 28)

1.254 zany (adj) – absurdly funny, crazy • *The ~ comedian made the audience laugh till their sides ached.* ➣ zaniness (n) ❖ παλαβός, τρελός

1.255 zestful (adj) – refreshing, enthusiastic, full of life • *For an elderly man, he's very active and ~.* ➣ zest (n), zestfully (adv) ❖ γεμάτος από κέφι και ενθουσιασμό

1.256 zippy (adj) – lively, energetic • *I woke up feeling ~ and went for a five-mile hike in the woods.* ➣ zippiness (n), zip (v) ❖ ζωηρός, γεμάτος από ζωή

1.257 zealous (adj) – committed, ardent • *The senator is a ~ supporter of human rights.* ➣ zeal (n), zealot (n), zealously (adv) ❖ γεμάτος από ενθουσιασμό/φλόγα

Reading — Skimming and scanning (pages 30–31)

STEP 2: Scanning for detail
Questions 1-4 (choices)

1.258 extent (n) – (U) size, area, or degree to which sth spreads or extends • *They examined the wrecked car carefully to determine the ~ of the damage.* ➣ extension (n), extend (v), extensive (adj), extensively (adv) ❖ βαθμός, σημείο

1.259 intolerant (adj) – see **1.123**

1.260 prudent (adj) – see **1.46**

1.261 compassionate (adj) – sympathetic, caring • *I have never met such a ~ person; she's always there to listen to your problems and help you find a way to make things better.* ➣ compassion (n), compassionately (adj) ❖ συμπονετικός

1.262 concerned (adj) – showing an active personal interest in sb/sth • *The teacher was a concerned person who cared about all of her students.* ➣ concern (n, v), concerning (prep). Opp: unconcerned ❖ που νοιάζεται, που δείχνει ενδιαφέρον για τους άλλους

1.263 vindictive (adj) – see **1.233**

1.264 arrogant (adj) – see **1.31**

1.265 quirky (adj) – see **1.198**

1.266 impetuous (adj) – see **1.126**

1 Perspectives on personality

1.267 minor (adj) – not very great, serious or important, of secondary importance • *Luckily, the driver's injury was ~ and he did not need to go to the hospital.* ➤ Opp: major (adj) ❖ μικρός, ασήμαντος, δευτερεύων

1.268 determined (adj) – see **1.91**

Presidents at gunpoint (page 31)
Paragraph 1

1.269 campaign (v) – take part in or lead a **campaign** (i.e., a series of planned activities with a specific aim) • *politicians ~ for re-election, feminists ~ for women's rights* ❖ εκστρατεύω, αγωνίζομαι, κάνω καμπάνια

1.270 auditorium (n) – (C) large room or hall in which an audience sits • *The students had a meeting in the school ~.* ❖ αίθουσα (συναυλιών, διαλέξεων, συνεδριάσεων κλπ)

1.271 strode (v – past tense) → **stride – strode – strode** (irreg v) – walk with long, confident steps • *Everyone turned to watch the handsome actor as he ~ confidently down the street.* ❖ βαδίζω με μεγάλα βήματα, δρασκελίζω

1.272 burst (v – past tense) → **burst – burst – burst** (irreg v) – explode noisily • *We all jumped when the balloon ~ without warning!* ❖ σπάζω, σκάω

1.273 smash (v) – hit with great force • *The car ~ed into the tree, but luckily no one was hurt.* ➤ smash (n), smashing (adj) ❖ συντρίβω, κάνω κομμάτια

1.274 spatter (v) – splash (with a liquid) • *Be careful or you'll ~ yourself with tomato sauce!* ➤ spatter (n), spattering (adj), spattered (adj) ❖ πιτσιλίζω

1.275 seep (v) – leak or flow out/through in small quantities • *blood ~s out of a wound and through a bandage, oil ~s out of the ground* ➤ seepage (n), seeping (adj) ❖ διαρρέω, διαποτίζω

1.276 mere (adj) – simple, only (i.e., nothing more than or better than what sth/sb actually is) • *Her parents objected to the idea of her marrying a ~ car mechanic.* ➤ merely (adv) ❖ απλός, μόνος, τίποτα άλλο από

1.277 bystander (n) – sb who stands by/near sth that takes place but who does not participate; onlooker, witness • *After the accident, police interviewed several ~s to find out what had happened.* ➤ stand by (phr v) ❖ παριστάμενος, παρατυχών, θεατής

1.278 subdue (v) – control using force • *Prison guards quickly ~d the angry prisoners and returned them to their cells.* ➤ subdued (adj) ❖ υποτάσσω

1.279 wrestle (v) – fight, struggle with • *~ an attacker to the ground, ~ with a difficult problem* ❖ παλεύω, βασανίζομαι (π.χ., με προβλήματα)

1.280 would-be (adj) – trying or hoping to be sth (but perhaps not having the right qualities) • *The ~ writer refuses to give up even though he has received countless rejection letters.* ❖ επίδοξος

1.281 assassin (n) – (C) person who murders an important or well-known person (usually for money or political reasons) • *President John F. Kennedy and his brother Robert were both murdered by ~s.* ➤ assassinate (v), assassinated (adj) ❖ δολοφόνος

1.282 adamantly (adv) – firmly, resolutely, stubbornly • *Not realizing how seriously he was injured, he ~ refused to be taken to the hospital.* ➤ adamant (adj) ❖ ανένδοτα, ανυποχώρητα

1.283 thunder (v) – shout loudly/angrily • *"Freeze!" ~ed the policeman.* ➤ thunder (n), thundering (adj) ❖ βροντώ. See also **2.259**.

1.284 compose (oneself) (v) – calm oneself, bring one's feelings under control • *It's important to try to ~ yourself before a job interview.* ➤ composure (n), composed (adj) ❖ ηρεμώ

Paragraph 2

1.285 lodge (v) – become stuck • *The bullet grazed his shoulder and ~d in the wall in back of him.* ❖ σφηνώνω/-ομαι, χώνω/-ομαι

1.286 rousing (adj) – exciting, inspiring, enthusiastic • *The crowd gave a ~ cheer when the teams came onto the field.* ❖ ενθουσιώδης

1.287 charismatic (adj) – having charisma (i.e., strong personal appeal or charm) • *What the country needs now is a ~ leader who can take charge and inspire the citizens.* ➤ charisma (n), charismatically (adv) ❖ χαρισματικός

1.288 orator (n) – public speaker • *Great ~s like Winston Churchill are articulate, eloquent, and capable of inspiring their audiences.* ➤ oratory (n), orate (v), oratorical (adj) ❖ ρήτορας

1.289 circumstances (pl n/singular meaning) – situation, all of the conditions that characterize an event or period of time • *If my ~ were different, I'd be happy to lend you the money; unfortunately, I've just lost my job.* ➤ circumstantial (adj) ❖ συνθήκες

1.290 tend (v) – take care of • *After the birth of her third child, she decided to give up her career and ~ her family.* ❖ φροντίζω, περιποιούμαι

Paragraph 3

1.291 mortally (adv) – ending in death • *Luckily, he's not ~ wounded; the doctors expect him to make a full, if slow, recovery.* ➤ mortal (n, adj) ❖ θανάσιμα

1.292 gasp (v) struggle to breathe • *By the time we reached the top of the steep hill, we were ~ing for air.* ➤ gasp (n), gasping (adj) ❖ ασθμαίνω, αγκομαχώ

Paragraph 4

1.293 temperament (n/adj) – see **1.22**

1.294 extraordinary (adj) – very special, outstanding • *He has an ~ memory for dates, which is why he is such a good history student.* ➤ extraordinarily (adv) ❖ εξαιρετικός

1.295 vigorous (adj) – see **1.235**

1.296 fierce (adj) – intense, strong • *Competition is ~ in today's job market.* ➤ ferocity (n), fiercely (adv). ❖ σφοδρός. See also **2.249**.

1.297 persistent (adj) – see **1.167**

1.298 determined (adj) – see **1.91**

1.299 considerate (adj) – thoughtful, careful not to hurt or bother others • *a kind and ~ person, a ~ offer, a person who is ~ of others' feelings* ➤ consideration (n), consider (v), considerately (adv). Opp: inconsiderate (adj) ❖ διακριτικός, αβρός, ευγενικός.

1.300 compassion (n) – sympathy and understanding for sb's suffering • *His cruel remarks showed a distinct lack of ~ for the suffering of the poor.* ➤ compassionate (adj), compassionately (adv) ❖ οίκτος, συμπόνια

Perspectives on personality

1.301 impetuous (adj) – see **1.126**

1.302 consistent (with) (adj) – in agreement (with), showing the same pattern or behavior (as) • *The second doctor's opinion was ~ with the first: both said the patient needed immediate surgery.* ➢ consistency (n), consistently (adv). Opp: inconsistent ❖ σύμφωνος (με)

1.303 spontaneous (adj) – natural, unplanned, done or happening as a result of a sudden strong feeling • *A look of ~ joy appeared on the child's face when her grandparents appeared at their door.* ➢ spontaneity (n), spontaneously (adv) ❖ αυθόρμητος

1.304 ardent (adj) – see **1.66**

Exam Practice (pages 34–37)
Cloze (page 35)
Text

1.305 ethics (n) – see **1.14**

1.306 welfare (n) – (U) the general well-being of a person or group (e.g., their health, comfort, economic status, etc.) • *Her main concern is the ~ of her children.* ❖ ευημερία

1.307 ultimately (adv) – in the end, after everything has been taken into consideration • *The decision to perform the risky surgery was ~ in the hands of the boy's parents.* ➢ ultimate (adj) ➢ ultimatum (n), ultimate (v) ❖ τελικά, σε τελευταία ανάλυση

1.308 obligation (n) – duty, moral responsibility • *When his sister's husband died, he felt he had an ~ to help.* ➢ oblige (v), obligatory (adj), obliged (adj) ❖ υποχρέωση

1.309 prudent (adj) – see **1.46**

1.310 tendency (n) – (C) natural leaning or inclination to be or behave in a certain way • *He has a ~ to put things off and do them at the last minute.* ➢ tend (v) ❖ τάση

1.311 hint (at sth) (v) – be a possible indication or sign (of sth); also, express an idea or information in an indirect way • *His elegant clothing and flashy car ~ at how successful he is. / What are you ~ing at: that he may not be as honest as he seems?* ➢ hint (n) ❖ υπονοώ, κάνω νύξη (για κτ)

1.312 integrity (n) – see **1.40**

1.313 consciously (adv) – deliberately, knowingly • *He ~ tries to impress her whenever he sees her.* ➢ consciousness (n), conscious (adj). Opp: unconsciously (adv) ❖ συνειδητά, επίτηδες

Vocabulary (page 36)

All of the answer choices in questions 21-30 appear in previous entries in this unit. Consult the Alphabetical Word List at the back of the book to locate any words you wish to review.

Reading (page 37)

Paragraph 1

1.314 range wide (v phr) – cover a wide variety of things (e.g., subject areas, interests) • *The journalist's interests ~ : from sports and local politics to technology and the environment.* ❖ καλύπτω μεγάλη/ευρύ ποικιλία θεμάτων

1.315 conceive (v) – (of ideas, theories, etc.) imagine, form sth in the mind, especially for the first time • *The writer claims that he ~d the idea for his new novel while taking a shower.* ➢ conception (n), concept (n), conceptual (adj), conceivable (adj) ❖ συλλαμβάνω (π.χ., ιδέα, θεωρία). See also **3.336**.

1.316 theory of relativity (n phr) – (U) (physics) Einstein's famous theory, which explains the relationship between time, space, and motion • *Afraid of not being able to understand difficult concepts like Einstein's ~, she avoided taking physics courses in college.* ❖ θεωρία της σχετικότητας

1.317 indispensable (adj) – absolutely necessary, vital • *A good bilingual dictionary is ~ if you want to enjoy reading literature in a foreign language.* ➢ Opp: dispensable (adj) ❖ απόλυτα απαραίτητος

Paragraph 2

1.318 drop out (of sth) (phr v) – stop attending or participating in sth before it is finished (e.g., school, a race) • *When his father died, he had no choice but to ~ of college and get a job to help support his family.* ➢ drop-out (n) ❖ εγκαταλείπω (π.χ., σπουδές, αγώνα)

1.319 mere (adj) – See **1. 276**

1.320 postdoctoral (adj) – related to academic work done after a doctorate has been completed • *Sue has a bachelor's degree, a master's, and a Ph.D. Now she's working on a ~ degree!* ❖ μεταδιδακτορικός

1.321 appointment (n) – (C) job, position; (U) the act or process of assigning or giving sb a position • *It was his lifelong dream to receive an ~ as a professor at Harvard University.* ➢ appoint (v), appointed (adj) ❖ διορισμός

1.322 reject (v) – (used passively in text) refuse to accept or consider sb/sth • *The company ~ed her application because she did not have enough experience.* ➢ rejection (n), rejected (adj) ❖ απορρίπτω

Paragraph 3

1.323 eccentric (adj) – strange, peculiar, odd • *Some people dislike him for being ~, but I find his strangeness quite refreshing.* ➢ eccentricity (n), eccentrically (adv) ❖ εκκεντρικός

1.324 introverted (adj) – quiet, shy, concerned with your own inner world rather than things outside you • *She prefers people who are lively and outgoing rather than serious and ~.* ➢ introvert (n), introversion (n), introvert (n). Opp: extroverted (adj) ❖ εσωστρεφής

1.325 remote (adj) – see **1.210**

1.326 icon (n) – (C) symbol • *Adolf Hitler will go down in history as a twentieth-century ~ of evil.* ➢ iconography (n), iconic (adj) ➢ iconic (adj) ❖ εικόνα, σύμβολο. 📖 : e.g., a religious ~

1.327 absentminded (adj) – see **1.73**

1.328 frizzy (adj) – (of hair) curly and hard to manage (as opposed to smooth or straight) • *She hates rainy days, because her hair gets all ~ and out of control.* ❖ κατσαρός, σγουρός

1.329 legion (adj) → **be ~** (v phr) – (formal, literary) exist in large numbers • *Her admirers are ~; half the boys in the school would love to date her.* ❖ αφθονώ, υπάρχω σε μεγάλους αριθμούς

1.330 succinct (adj) – briefly and clearly expressed, concise • *Mother's answer, as always, was ~ : "No!"* ➢ succinctness (n), succinctly (adv) ❖ περιληπτικός, σύντομος

Perspectives on personality

Paragraph 4

1.331 vague (adj) – see **1.232**

1.332 abstracted (adj) – in a world of one's own, distracted (see **1.93**), absentminded (see **1.73**) • *I knew from the ~ look on his face that he was daydreaming and hadn't heard a word I said.* ➤ abstraction (n), abstract (adj), abstractedly (adv), abstractly (adv) ❖ αφηρημένος, απορροφημένος

1.333 oblivious (adj) – see **1.163**

1.334 inattentive (adj) – not paying attention to what one is doing, unable or unwilling to concentrate • *Sorry if I seem so ~ ; I've got a lot on my mind and it's hard for me to concentrate.* ➤ inattentiveness (n), inattentively (adv). Opp: attentive (adj) ❖ αφηρημένος, απρόσεκτος

1.335 resent (v) – feel bitter and angry about sth • *The child ~ed the attention his newborn sister was getting.* ❖ θίγομαι (από κτ), αγανακτώ με κτ/κπ, δυσανασχετώ (με κτ/κπ)

1.336 resist (v) – oppose, fight against • *The rebellious teenager ~ed his parents' strict rules and always did exactly what he wanted. / A healthy diet helps the body ~ disease.* ➤ resistance (n), resistant (adj) ❖ ανθίσταμαι, αντιστέκομαι

1.337 authority (n) – (U/C) sb/sth with official power to give orders, make decisions, and enforce rules; also, the power or right to do these things • *The President is the highest authority in the country.* ➤ authorization (n), authorize (v), authorized (adj), authoritarian (adj) ❖ εξουσία. 📖 : e.g., an ~ on theater

1.338 defy (v) – resist, stand up to sb/sth by refusing to obey or show respect • *She was an obedient girl who found it difficult to ~ her parents' wishes.* ➤ defiance (n), defiant (adj), defiantly (adv). Opp: obedient (adj), compliant (adj) ❖ αντιστέκομαι, αψηφώ

1.339 decorum (n) – (U) correct and dignified behavior • *Don't expect to find ~ at a championship football match, where everyone goes wild as soon as the game starts.* ➤ decorous (adj) ❖ ευπρέπεια, κοσμιότητα

1.340 function (n) – (C) formal social event, reception, affair • *She hates getting dressed up so she avoids weddings, cocktail parties, and other social ~s.* ❖ επίσημη τελετή, δεξίωση. See also **5.123**.

1.341 oversight (n) – (C) failure to notice or do sth (e.g., because of forgetfulness or carelessness) • *Not inviting him to the party was an ~, not a personal insult. I simply forgot to put his name on the list.* ❖ αβλεψία, παράλειψη

1.342 needle (v) – (informal) intentionally irritate, annoy or tease sb • *The rebellious teenager stayed out late, knowing it would ~ his parents.* ❖ (καθομ.) προκαλώ, ερεθίζω κάποιον

1.343 pretension (n) – (C) (often plural) snobbish air or attitude; feeling of superiority that is often unjustified • *I'm tired of all his arrogant ~s. He thinks he's the only intelligent being on the plant. / Despite the musician's many achievements, he was a modest man without ~s.* ➤ pretentious (adj), pretentiously (adv) ❖ αξίωση, εκζήτηση

1.344 convention (n) – (C) generally accepted rule concerning the way things are done • *He grew up in China and is unfamiliar with Western ~s regarding birthdays and other celebrations.* ➤ conventional (adj), conventionally (adj). ❖ έθιμο, τύπος. 📖 : e.g., a medical/teachers' ~, the Geneva C~

1.345 subjectivity (n) – (U) interpretation based on feelings or opinion rather than on facts or evidence • *Good journalists report the facts and let readers draw their own conclusions; there is no place for ~ in their articles.* ➤ subjective (adj), subjectively (adv). Opp: objectivity (n) ❖ υποκειμενικότητα

Flora and fauna

Introduction Biodiversity (pages 38-39)

A What on earth is "biodiversity"? (page 38)

2.1 **vast** (adj) – huge, enormous • *The Sahara is a ~ desert. / The government spends ~ sums of money on national defense.* ➣ vastness (n), vastly (adv) ❖ απέραντος

2.2 **teeming** (adj) – overflowing, crowded • *The mountain stream was ~ing with fish. / The ~ rain came down for hours.* ➣ teem (v) ❖ που ξεχειλίζει (από)

2.3 **species** (n/pl n) – (C) kind of plant, animal, or other living thing • (singular) *Scientists think they have discovered a new ~ of fish.* / (plural) *The region is home to robins, sparrows, and other common bird ~s.* ❖ είδος.

2.4 **flora** (pl n) – (u) plant life • *The botanist specializes in orchids and other tropical ~.* ➣ florist (n), floral (adj). Opp: fauna (n) ❖ χλωρίδα

2.5 **fauna** (pl n) – (U) animal life • *The national park was established to protect tigers and other endangered ~.* ➣ Opp: flora (n) ❖ πανίδα

2.6 **primitive** (adj) – simple, at an early stage of development • *Creatures such as sponges and jelly fish are ~ life forms.* ➣ primitiveness (n), primitively (adv). Opp: sophisticated (adj), highly developed (adj) ❖ πρωτόγονος, αρχέγονος

2.7 **bacteria** (pl n) → **bacterium** (n) – small, often disease-carrying organism • *Meat and eggs should be thoroughly cooked to prevent food poisoning from ~.* ➣ bacterial (adj) ❖ βακτηρίδιο, μικρόβιο

2.8 **algae** (pl n) → **alga** (n) – (C) simple form of plant life that grows in water • *The water of the pool is treated to prevent the growth of slimy, green ~ on the sides of the pool.* ❖ άλγη

2.9 **scratch the surface** (idm) – explore a subject superficially (i.e., without going into too much detail) • *Investigators have only begun to ~ ; you will be shocked when all the details of the scandal come out.* ❖ (μετ.) θίγω επιφανειακά

2.10 **bewildering** (adj) – amazing yet puzzling/confusing • *She looked at the ~ mass of files on her desk and didn't know where to begin.* ➣ bewilderment (n), bewildered (adj) ❖ που φέρνει σύγχυση, ζάλη ή αμηχανία

2.11 **concept** (n) – (C) general idea, principle, or notion • *The advertising director has come up with a brilliant ~ for the spring ad campaign.* ➣ conceptualize (n), conceptual (adj), conceptually (adv) ❖ έννοια, γενική ιδέα

2.12 **biodiversity** (n) – (U) rich variety of life on earth • *Global warming is posing a great threat to ~.* ❖ βιοποικιλότητα (η ποικιλομορφία των ζωντανών οργανισμών)

2.13 **range (of)** (n) – (C) selection, variety, number of things of the same general type • *The music shop carries a wide ~ of music, including classical, folk, jazz, and rock.* ➣ range (v) ❖ ποικιλία, κλίμακα

2.14 **ecosystem** (n) – (C) system in which plants, animals, and simpler life forms exist and interact with each other within a certain environment • *The logging industry is responsible for damaging the ~ in the Amazon basin.* ❖ οικοσύστημα

2.15 **interact** (v) – relate to, have an effect on, or work together with (sth/sb) • *School helps children learn how to ~ with each other.* / *Plants and animals ~ in an ecosystem.* ➣ interaction (n), interactive (adj) ❖ αλληλεπιδρώ

2.16 **habitat** (n) – (C) natural environment or home of an animal or plant • *deserts, seas, forests, and other ~s* ➣ inhabitant (n), inhabit (v), habituate (v) ❖ φυσικό περιβάλλον

B Home sweet home (page 38)

2.17 **wasteland** (n) – (C) area of land that is not or cannot be used; similar to **wilderness** (see **2.19**) • *The middle of the country is a vast desert ~ with very little plant and animal life.* ❖ χερσότοπος

2.18 **reef** (n phr) – (C) wall of coral, sand, or rock near the surface of the sea • *The tiny fishing boat sank after crashing into a coral ~.* ❖ ύφαλος

2.19 **wilderness** (n) – (C) area of wild, uncultivated land • *The explorers Lewis and Clark spent several years exploring the American ~ west of the Mississippi River.* ➣ wild(s) (n/pl n), wild (adj), wildly (adv) ❖ αγριότοπος

C Biodiversity under attack (page 39)

2.20 **beleaguered** (adj) – under attack • *The ~ city has been surrounded by the invading army for more than a month.* ➣ beleaguer (v) ❖ πολιορκημένος

2.21 **on the verge of** (prep phr) – at or close to the point where sth is about to begin or happen; similar to **on the brink** (see **2.32**) • *Each year more and more species are reported to be ~ extinction.* ❖ στο χείλος, στα πρόθυρα

2.22 **extinction** (n) – (U) the state of no longer existing; (C) the death of all remaining members of an animal or plant species • *(U) an animal on the verge of ~, (C) Ice Age ~s* ➣ extinct (adj) ❖ εξαφάνιση, αφανισμός

2.23 **endangered** (adj) – (plants, animals) in danger of being harmed or destroyed, facing extinction • *Many governments now have agencies that fight to protect ~ species.* ➣ endangerment (n), endanger (v) ❖ απειλούμενος με αφανισμό

2.24 **evolution** (n) – (U) (biology) the slow development of plants and animals over many generations • *human ~, Darwin's theory of ~* ➣ evolve (v), evolving (adj), evolved (adj) ❖ εξέλιξη

2.25 **wipe out** (phr v) – destroy completely • *If illegal hunting is not controlled, it will ~ the elephant population here.* ❖ εξαφανίζω, εξολοθρεύω

2.26 **climate** (n) – (C/U) weather and atmospheric conditions of an area (e.g., temperature, rainfall, etc.) • *Much of central Europe has a temperate ~.* ➣ climatic (adj) ❖ κλίμα

2.27 **natural disaster** (n phr) – (C) event in nature that causes great damage or harm • *Floods and hurricanes are examples of ~s.* ❖ φυσική καταστροφή

2.28 **volcanic eruption** (n phr) – (C) sudden forceful explosion of smoke, fire, rock, ash, and lava • *The ~ continued for several hours, with ash and rock shooting into the air and lava pouring down the slopes of the once-quiet mountain.* ❖ έκρηξη ηφαιστείου

2.29 **collision** (n) – (C) crash, an instance of one thing hitting violently into another • *The driver drove off the road to avoid a head-on ~ with an oncoming car.* ➣ collide (v) ❖ σύγκρουση

17

2 Flora and fauna

2.30 **adapt** (v) – adjust or change to suit new circumstances • *It took her a few months to ~ to living on her own, but now she enjoys it.* ➣ adaptation (n), adaptable (adj) ❖ προσαρμόζω/-ομαι

2.31 **accelerate** (v) – cause sth to go faster or happen sooner; also, speed up, go faster • *Industrialization has ~d the destruction of the environment. / Cars ~ when more gas is pumped into the engine.* ➣ acceleration (n), accelerated (adj). Opp: decelerate (v) ❖ επιταχύνω, επισπεύδω

D On the brink (page 39)

2.32 **on the brink (of sth)** (prep phr) – about to experience (sth disastrous or unwelcome); similar to **on the verge of** (see **2.21**) • *The two nations are ~ of war; if diplomatic efforts fail, there will be bloodshed.* ❖ στο χείλος

2.33 **deforestation** (n) – (U) the act of cutting down huge areas of trees to make room for industrial development • *D~ in the Amazon basin has endangered hundreds of species in the area.* ❖ καταστροφή δασών, αποψίλωση

2.34 **habitat loss** (n phr) – (U) general destruction or shrinking of a species' environment • *The building of dams, mines, and suburban shopping centers have greatly contributed to ~ across the United States.* ❖ καταστροφή του φυσικού περιβάλλοντος

2.35 **overhunting** (n) – (U) the excessive killing of animals for sport, food, and/or commercial exploitation • *Commercial whaling is an example of ~ that has resulted in the endangerment of several whale species.* ➣ overhunt (v), overhunted (adj) ❖ κυνήγι σε υπερβολικό βαθμό

2.36 **overpopulation** (n) – (U) the state of having too many people in an area (and the resulting strain that this puts on the environment) • *O~ and poverty usually go hand in hand.* ➣ overpopulate (v), overpopulated (adj). Opp: underpopulation (n) ❖ υπερπληθυσμός

2.37 **pollution** (n) – (U) the process of making air, water, or land unclean and dangerous • *It's the responsibility of the government to pass laws to control ~.* ➣ pollutant (n), pollute (v), polluted (adj) ❖ μόλυνση (του περιβάλλοντος, της ατμόσφαιρας κλπ)

2.38 **urbanization** (n) – (U) the process of creating towns and cities in areas that were once countryside • *U~ has resulted in a mass exodus from rural areas.* ➣ urbanize (v), urban (adj), urbanized (adj) ❖ αστικοποίηση

Definitions 1-6

2.39 **exploit** (v) – use to gain a fair or unfair advantage • *If we want to win the game, we must ~ the opposition's weaknesses. / The workers went on strike, charging that the company was ~ing them.* ➣ exploitation (n), exploited (adj), exploitative (adj), exploitable (adj) ❖ εκμεταλλεύομαι

2.40 **commercial exploitation** (n phr) – (U) the (often harmful) use of sth for a company's or industry's profit • *The fur industry is an example of how seals and other animals can be endangered as a result of ~.* ❖ εμπορική εκμετάλλευση

2.41 **poaching** (n) – (U) the act of hunting illegally (especially when trespassing on sb's property or defying an official order of protection) • *Elephant ~ has declined since the government has assigned more park rangers to patrol the national park.* ➣ poacher (n), poach (v) ❖ λαθροθηρία

Writing (1) Paragraph development (page 40)

A

2.42 **jumbled** (adj) – mixed up, not in the correct order, scrambled • *Can you put this ~ list of words into alphabetical order?* ➣ jumble (n, v) ❖ ανακατωμένος, μπερδεμένος

2.43 **vicious cycle** (n phr) – (C) (also **vicious circle**) ongoing situation in which one problem leads to another, making everything worse • *Fighting terrorism leads to more and more people becoming terrorists; it's a ~.* ❖ φαύλος κύκλος

2.44 **outskirts** (pl n) → **on the ~ (of)** (prep phr) – on the outer edge (of an area, e.g., a town or city) • *They enjoy living on the ~ of town, far from the noise of the busy city center.* ❖ στα περίχωρα

Vocabulary (1) The plant kingdom (flora) (pages 41-44)

A Our debt to plants (page 41)

Word bank

2.45 **carbon dioxide** (n phr) – (U) the chemical compound CO_2 (a gas) • *When we exhale, we breathe out ~.* ❖ διοξείδιο του άνθρακα

2.46 **erosion** (n) – (U) slow wearing away of soil or rock by natural forces (e.g., water, wind) ❖ διάβρωση. ➣ erode (v), erosive (adj). See also **2.125**.

2.47 **evolution** (n) – see **2.24**.

2.48 **fossil fuel** (n phr) – (C) fuel produced by the very slow decaying of animals or plants over millions of years • *Examples of ~s include coal, petroleum, and natural gas.* ❖ ορυκτό καύσιμο

2.49 **organic matter** (n phr) – (U) material containing compounds of hydrogen and carbon • *When a plant dies, it decays and sends rich ~ back into the soil.* ❖ οργανική ύλη

2.50 **oxygen** (n) – (U) the chemical element O_2 (a gas) • *Water (H_2O) is composed of two parts hydrogen and one part oxygen.* ➣ oxide (n), oxidize (v), oxygenate (v) ❖ οξυγόνο

2.51 **barren** (adj) – empty, lifeless • *A desert is a ~ place, with seemingly little sign of plant or animal life.* ➣ barrenness (n) ❖ άγονος, στείρος, άκαρπος

2.52 **diverse** (adj) – varied, showing variety • *Big cities are often populated by people of ~ ethnic backgrounds. / People with ~ interests are rarely bored.* ➣ diversity (n), diversify (v), diversified (adj) ❖ ποικίλος, διαφορετικός

2.53 **fossilized** (adj) – decayed and hardened, like a fossil (i.e., the ancient remains of an animal or plant which have hardened or been pressed into rock) • *The young boy dreamed that he found the ~ remains of a dinosaur in his yard.* ➣ fossil (n), fossilization (n), fossilize (v) ❖ απολιθωμένος

2.54 **uninhabitable** (adj) – not fit to live in • *The house was ~ as it had a leaking roof and was full of rats.* Opp: inhabitable (adj) ❖ ακατοίκητος

2.55 **decompose** (v) – rot, decay, break down chemically • *After several weeks, the dead body had clearly begun to ~.* ➣ decomposition (n), decomposed (adj) ❖ αποσυνθέτω, σαπίζω

2.56 **modify** (v) – change slightly • *Most scientists now believe that global warming has ~ied worldwide weather patterns.* ➣ modification (n), modified (adj) ❖ τροποποιώ

Flora and fauna 2

2.57 **shelter** (v) – protect • *The walls and roof of a house ~ its inhabitants from rain, wind, and cold.* ➢ shelter (n), sheltered (adj) ❖ προστατεύω, προφυλάσσω

B Plant points to ponder (page 41)
Word bank

2.58 **bog** (n) – (C) wet, muddy area (e.g., marsh, swamp) • *I'd rather not spend my vacation walking through muddy ~s in a tropical rain forest.* ❖ έλος, βάλτος, βούρκος

2.59 **cellulose** (n) – (U) substance in the cell walls of plants • *C~ is responsible for the hardness of a plant's cell walls.* ❖ κυτταρίνη

2.60 **chlorophyll** (n) – (U) green substance in plants that helps convert light into chemical energy that a plant uses for food. • *When tree leaves stop manufacturing ~ in the fall, they turn color and fall to the ground.* ❖ χλωροφύλλη

2.61 **component** (n) – (C) part of sth (e.g., of a chemical compound, a system) • *Hydrogen and oxygen are the main ~s of water. / Speakers and amplifiers are ~s of a music system* ➢ composition (n), compose (v), component (adj) ❖ συστατικό μέρος

2.62 **parasite** (n) – (C) plant or animal that lives off of (or in) another plant or animal • *The tapeworm is a ~ that can live in the intestines of humans.* ➢ parasitic (adj) ❖ παράσιτο

2.63 **saprophyte** (n) – (C) plant or animal that lives off of dead or decomposing matter ➢ saprophytic (adj) ❖ σαπρόφυτο

2.64 **insectivorous** (adj) – (plants/animals) able to capture and live off of insects • *The Venus fly trap is an example of an ~ plant.* ➢ insectivore (n) ❖ εντομοφάγος

2.65 **multicellular** (adj) – having or consisting of more than one cell • *Amoebas are made up of only one cell; they are not ~.* ❖ πολυκύτταρος

2.66 **rigid** (adj) – (things) hard, firm, stiff • *As a dead body begins to decompose, it becomes ~ due to a condition called rigor mortis.* ➢ rigidity (n), rigidly (adv) ❖ άκαμπτος, αλύγιστος. See also **1.211** (people).

2.67 **convert** (v) – change from one form into another • *During photosynthesis, plants ~ light energy into chemical energy, which they use for food.* ➢ convert (n), conversion (n), converted (adj), convertible (adj) ❖ μετατρέπω. 📖: e.g., ~ sb to a cause/religion

2.68 **photosynthesize** (v) – carry out **photosynthesis** (i.e., the process by which plants convert light energy into food) • *Without chlorophyll, a plant loses its ability to ~.* ➢ photosynthesis (n), photosynthetic (adj) ❖ φωτοσυνθέτω · φωτοσύνθεση

2.69 **supplement** (v) – add to (usually in order to complete or improve sth) • *The doctor told her to ~ her diet with a multivitamin pill.* ➢ supplement (n), supplementary (adj), supplemental (adj) ❖ συμπληρώνω

C Plants in action: Who says vegetation just vegetates? (page 42)

2.70 **vegetation** (n) – (U) plant life • *She was amazed at how dense the ~ was in the tropical rain forest shown in the film.* ➢ vegetable (n, adj), vegetate (v), vegetative (adj) ❖ βλάστηση

2.71 **vegetate** (v) – live with a minimum of action, thought, or feeling (e.g., like a vegetable) • *Couch potatoes spend their free time ~ing in front of a TV.* ➢ vegetable (n), vegetation (n), vegetative (adj) ❖ φυτοζωώ

1. Things that plants do by themselves (page 42)
Word bank

2.72 **absorb** (v) – take/draw in, soak up (e.g., what roots do to water) • *The soil was dry and quickly ~ed the falling rain.* ➢ absorption (n), absorbent (adj), absorbed (adj), absorbing (adj) ❖ απορροφώ

2.73 **adapt** (v) – see **2.30**

2.74 **blossom** (v) – produce flowers; same as **bloom**, **bud**, and **flower** • *My favorite time of year is late March, when the cherry trees ~ with pretty pink flowers.* ➢ blossom (n), blossoming (adj) ❖ ανθίζω

2.75 **decay** (v) – rot, decompose • *She always throws her leftover vegetables onto the compost heap in her garden, where they will ~ and later be used to enrich the soil.* ➢ decay (n), decaying (adj), decayed (adj) ❖ σαπίζω

2.76 **germinate** (v) – (seeds) begin to grow and sprout small green shoots; same as **sprout** • *The seeds have just begun to ~. Can you see those tiny white shoots coming out of them?* ➢ germination (n), germinating (adj) ❖ βλαστάνω, φυτρώνω

2.77 **reproduce** (v) – produce fruit/seeds that will grow into new plants; same as **propagate** ➢ reproduction (n), reproductive (adj) ❖ αναπαράγομαι

2.78 **wilt** (v) – (plants, flowers) bend or droop over weakly (e.g., from lack of water) ➢ wilting (adj), wilted (adj) ❖ μαραίνω

2. Things that we do to plants, crops, or the soil (page 42)
Word bank

2.79 **breed – bred – bred** (irreg v) – control the reproduction of plants/animals so as to produce young plants/animals with particular characteristics; similar to propagate • *In the 1860s Gregor Mendel's attempts to ~ peas with certain characteristics opened the way to further experiments in plant genetics.* ➢ breeding (n) ❖ αναπαράγω. See also **2.123** and **2.380**.

2.80 **cultivate** (v) – grow crops; prepare and use land for growing crops; same as **till** • *He owns a small piece of property in southern California where he ~s grapes.* ➢ cultivation (n), cultivated (adj) ❖ καλλιεργώ. See also **2.124**.

2.81 **fertilize** (v) – (of soil) add natural or artificial substances to make crops grow better • *She ~s the soil in her garden with a product called Miracle-Gro.* ➢ fertilizer (n), fertilization (n), fertile (adj), fertilized (adj) ❖ λιπαίνω, εμπλουτίζω. See also **2.388**.

2.82 **harvest** (v) – cut and gather grain or other crops in large quantity; same as **reap** • *It will be wine-making time as soon as the farm workers ~ the grapes.* ➢ harvest (n) ❖ θερίζω, μαζεύω

2.83 **irrigate** (v) – supply water to farmland via special channels or pipes • *Crop yields in the area have greatly increased since farmers began to ~ their fields.* ➢ irrigation (n), irrigated (adj) ❖ αρδεύω

2.84 **pick** (v) – gather flowers, fruits, or vegetables from a field, tree, garden, etc. • *It's a joy to walk into your own garden and ~ vegetables grown with your own hands.* ❖ μαζεύω, συλλέγω

19

2 Flora and fauna

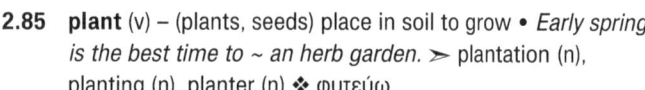

2.85 **plant** (v) – (plants, seeds) place in soil to grow • *Early spring is the best time to ~ an herb garden.* ➢ plantation (n), planting (n), planter (n) ❖ φυτεύω

2.86 **plow** (v) – (Brit: **plough**) dig up and turn over the surface of the soil with a tool of the same name • *In the old days farmers ~ed the soil with the aid of a horse; today tractors are used.* ➢ plow (n), plowed (adj) ❖ οργώνω

2.87 **sow – sowed – sown** (irreg v) – (seeds) place in or scatter on the land • *It's hard work to ~ an entire field with seeds.* ❖ σπέρνω

2.88 **trim** (v) – cut back branches of a tree, bush, etc., to encourage new growth; similar to **prune** ❖ κλαδεύω

D Get the picture? (page 42)

2.89 **canopy** (n) – (C) (trees) protective covering of leaves (e.g., of one tree or many) • *Aerial photography of a rain forest doesn't reveal much detail as the ~ of leaves is too dense to see what's underneath it.* ❖ σκιάδα

2.90 **limb** (n) – (C) main branch of a tree; similar to **bough** • *That ~ looks strong enough, so it's OK for you to climb onto it.* ❖ χονδρό κλαδί. See also **2.116** and **2.158**.

2.91 **trunk** (n) – (C) (tree) thick main stem from which limbs and branches grow • *Olive trees are known for their twisted and gnarled ~s.* ❖ κορμός

2.92 **root** (n) – (C – often plural) underground part of plant that helps hold it firmly in the ground • *The ~s of a plant absorb water and nutrients from the soil.* ➢ root (v), uproot (v), rooted (adj) ❖ ρίζα

2.93 **branch** (n) – (C) arm-like part of a tree growing out of a larger limb (*see* **2.90**); similar to **bough** • *If you want the tree to grow stronger, you'll need to trim the ~es at least once a year.* ➢ branch out (phr v) ❖ κλαδί

2.94 **bush** (n) – (C) woody plant that is smaller than a tree and has multiple woody stems; same as **shrub** • *She spends her weekends caring for the rose ~es in her garden.* ➢ bushy (adj), bush out (phr v) ❖ θάμνος, χαμόδεντρο

2.95 **log** (n) – (C) trunk, limb, or large branch of a tree that has been cut down • *L~s need to dry out before they can be burnt in a fireplace.* ➢ logging (n, adj) ❖ κομμένος κορμός (δέντρου)

2.96 **stump** (n) – (C) part of the tree that is left in the ground after the rest has fallen down or been cut off • *Before they could build their cabin in the forest, they had to cut down a number of trees and remove the ~s from the ground.* ➢ stumpy (adj) ❖ κούτσουρο

2.97 **twig** (n) – (C) small thin branch • *When they go camping, they always collect dry ~s which they then use to help get the campfire burning.* ❖ κλαδάκι

E Itchy eyes, sneezing, and the sex lives of flowers (page 43)

Warm-up

2.98 **pollen** (n) – (U) sticky yellow powder produced by flowers • *In spring, my car is always covered with a layer of ~ that comes from the flowering trees in the area.* ➢ pollinator (n), pollination (n), pollinate (v), pollinated (adj) ❖ γύρη

Text

The starred (★) entries below are technical terms that are explained at length in the course book. For the sake of brevity, the entries for these words include only Greek equivalents. For explanations in English, please consult the relevant texts in the course book.

2.99 ★ **angiosperm** (n) – (C) ❖ αγγειόσπερμα (δηλ., ανθόφυτο)

2.100 **widespread** (adj) – found or distributed over a large area or number of people • *Many people are against the ~ use of chemicals in agriculture.* ❖ πλατιά διαδεδομένος

2.101 **herb** (n) – (C) soft-stemmed plant whose seeds or leaves are used in cooking, perfumes, medicines, etc. • *Oregano and thyme are common ~s.* ➢ herbicide (n), herbal (adj) ❖ βότανο

2.102 **stem** (n) – (C) long, thin, main body of a plant • *The ~ of that sunflower is over two meters tall!* ➢ stem (from) (v), long-stemmed (adj) ❖ βλαστός, μίσχος

2.103 **thorn** (n) – (C) sharp, pointed growth on the stem of certain plants • *Wouldn't it be great if someone invented a breed of roses that didn't have ~s?* ➢ thorny (adj) ❖ αγκάθι

2.104 ★ **sepal** (n) – (C) ❖ σέπαλο

2.105 **bud** (n) – (C) flower or leaf that is not yet fully open • *Look! The ~s on the magnolia tree are just beginning to open. By next week they'll be in full bloom.* ➢ bud (v), budding (adj) ❖ μπουμπούκι

2.106 **petal** (n) – (C) one of several often brightly colored, leaf-shaped parts that make up the head of a flower • *The bouquet of flowers you gave me was beautiful until the ~s started to fall off.* ❖ πέταλο

2.107 ★ **stamen** (n) – (C) ❖ στήμονας

2.108 ★ **anther** (n) – (C) ❖ ανθήρας

2.109 ★ **pistil** (n) – (C) ❖ ύπερος

2.110 ★ **ovary** (n) – (C) (flower) ❖ ωοφόρος κώνος, ωοθήκη

2.111 ★ **ovule** (n) – (C) ❖ ωάριο

2.112 ★ **style** (n) – (C) ❖ στύλος

2.113 ★ **stigma** (n) – (C) ❖ στίγμα. 📖 : e.g., *the ~ of mental illness*

2.114 **pollination** (n) – (U) the action of transferring pollen (*see* **2.98**) from the male reproductive parts of a flower to the female reproductive parts of the same or another flower • *The ~ of plants can occur naturally with the help of pollinators like insects, animals, or the wind.* • pollen (n), pollinator (n), pollinate (v) ❖ επικονίαση, γονιμοποίηση (με γύρη)

Time out for review — Beyond botany (page 44)

Speaking figuratively with plant language

A Nouns (page 44)

2.115 **forest** (n) → **can't see the ~ for the trees** (idm) – fail to understand the main issue because of paying too much attention to detail • *Perfectionists are so worried about detail that they often can't see the ~ for the trees.* ❖ βλέπω το δέντρο και χάνω το δάσος

2.116 **limb** (n) → **go out on a ~ for sb** (idm) – put (oneself) in a difficult position for sb • *John's a true friend. He'll also go out on a ~ for you if he thinks you need help.* ❖ βάζω τον εαυτό μου σε δύσκολη θέση (για κπ). See also **2.90** and **2.158**.

Flora and fauna 2

2.117 **log** (n) → **sit around like a ~ on a log** (idm) – sit around doing nothing and not having fun • *I'd rather not invite her, as she's become a real ~ on a log since she broke up with her boyfriend.* ❖ κάθομαι σαν κούτσουρο

2.118 **root** (n) → **put down new ~s** (idm) – settle down in a new place • *He's been really lonely since he moved to Los Angeles. I guess it's not easy to put down new ~s.* ❖ ρίχνω καινούργιες ρίζες

2.119 **seed** (n) → **go to ~** (idm) – neglect one's looks, fall into bad shape because of neglect • *He's really gone to ~ since he stopped exercising. Look how much weight he's gained.* ❖ παραμελώ την εμφάνισή μου, εγκαταλείπω τον εαυτό μου, μαραίνομαι

2.120 **tree** (n) → **bark up the wrong ~** (idm) – be mistaken about sth • *You're barking up the wrong ~ if you think she'll go out with you!* ❖ χτυπώ λάθος πόρτα

2.121 **thorn** (n) → **be a ~ in (sb's) side** (idm) – be an ongoing problem or source of irritation for sb; same as **be a ~ in sb's flesh** • *Most parents agree that adult children who still live at home are a ~ in their sides.* ❖ είμαι μόνιμος μπελάς, είμαι μόνιμη πηγή στενοχώριας

B Verbs (page 44)

2.122 **branch** (v) → **~ out (into sth)** (phr v) – (fig) diversify; get involved in different activities or areas in addition to a main area of interest • *At first the school only offered English, but now it has ~ed out into French and Spanish as well.* ➢ branch (n) ❖ (μετ) επεκτείνομαι επιχειρηματικά

2.123 **breed – bred – bred** (irreg v) – (fig) bring about, generate (e.g., a feeling, circumstances), cause to develop • *If you don't cheer up, you'll lose all your friends. Misery ~s loneliness, you know.* ➢ breeding (n) ❖ προκαλώ, φέρνω. *See also* **2.79**.

2.124 **cultivate** (v) – (fig) develop sth (e.g., an attitude, relationship, friendship) • *She sees the conference as a chance to ~ new business contacts.* ➢ cultivation (n), cultivated (adj) ❖ καλλιεργώ. *See also* **2.80**.

2.125 **erode** (v) – (fig) (used passively in text) gradually wear away or destroy • *Three unsuccessful attempts to pass the ECPE is enough to ~ anyone's confidence.* ➢ erosion (n), eroded (adj), erosive (adj) ❖ (μετ) διαβρώνω, κατατρώγω. *See also* **2.46**.

2.126 **grow** (v) → **~ on sb** (idm) – (fig) become more appealing or attractive to sb • *At first, I didn't like the group's music, but after playing the CD a few times, it's starting to ~ on me.* ❖ αρέσω διαρκώς περισσότερο

2.127 **reap** (v) → **~ the rewards** (idm) – (fig) derive advantages from sth, usually as a result of hard work • *Study hard and you will ~ the rewards by getting into a good university.* ❖ δρέπω τα οφέλη, ανταμείβομαι

C Adjectives (page 44)

2.128 **budding** (adj) – (fig) just beginning to develop • *The ~ author is trying to find a publisher for his new novel.* ➢ bud (n, v) ❖ πρωτοεμφανιζόμενος, που κάνει τα πρώτα του βήματα

2.129 **bogged down** (adj) → **get ~ (in sth)** (idm) – get/be stuck (in sth difficult) • *People who can't see the forest for the trees (see **2.115**) are also guilty of getting ~ in too much detail.* ➢ bog (n) ❖ (κυρ/μετ) κολλάω σε κτ

2.130 **cultivated** (adj) – (fig – people) well-educated with refined manners • *The opera critic is one of the most ~ and sophisticated people I've ever met.* ❖ καλλιεργημένος

2.131 **fertile** (adj) – (fig) (of a person's imagination, mind) readily able to produce new ideas • *Young children have ~ imaginations, which is why they often imagine things that never happened.* ➢ fertility (n), fertilize (v). Opp: infertile (adj) ❖ γόνιμος. *See also* **4.32**.

2.132 **root** (n/adj) → **~ cause (of sth)** (n phr) – (fig) basic or fundamental cause (of sth) • *Jealousy was the ~ cause of his negative attitude towards his sister.* ❖ αρχική αιτία

2.133 **thorny** (adj) – (fig) complicated and difficult to figure out • *He lost his job yesterday, which leaves him with a ~ problem: how is he going to pay his bills?* ❖ ακανθώδης

Vocabulary (2) The animal kingdom (fauna) (pages 48-51)

A What's what and who's who? (page 48)
Paragraph 1

2.134 **ingest** (v) – take into the body (e.g., by swallowing) • *If someone in your family ~s poison, call the local poison center immediately.* ❖ τρώγω, καταπίνω

2.135 **digest** (v) – (of food) break down into chemicals so it can be used by the body • *Some people find it hard to ~ cabbage and beans.* ➢ digestion (n), digestive (adj), digestible (adj) ❖ χωνεύω. *See also* **2.226** for figurative meaning.

2.136 **tissue** (n) – (C/U) (anatomy) group of cells that perform the same function • *If the cancer cells spread, they will affect healthy ~ elsewhere in the body.* ❖ ιστός. 📖: e.g. ~ paper, a box of ~s

2.137 **contract** (v) – (muscles) tighten or shorten (e.g., in order to produce a desired movement or process) • *The heart muscle ~s about 70 times per minute when the body is at rest.* ➢ contraction (n), contracted (adj). ❖ συστέλλομαι. *See also* **3.172** (disease) *and* 📖: e.g., ~ to do sth

2.138 **nervous system** (n phr) – (C) system that transports nerve signals from one part of the body to the other • *The brain is a key part of the body's ~.* ❖ νευρικό σύστημα

2.139 **sense organ** (n phr) – (C) organ that allows the body to feel, hear, see, smell, etc. • *The tongue is a complex ~ that allows us to experience different tastes.* ❖ αισθητήριο όργανο

2.140 **stimuli** (pl n) → **stimulus** (n) – (C) sth in the environment that causes a physical reaction or response • *Heat is a ~ that can be sensed through nerves in the skin.* ➢ stimulation (n), stimulate (v), stimulating (adj), stimulated (adj) ❖ διέγερση, ερέθισμα

Paragraph 2

2.141 **array** (n) – (C) variety, assortment, collection • *The natural museum has an impressive ~ of butterfly and moth specimens.* ❖ διάταξη

2.142 **primitive** (adj) – *see* **2.6**

2.143 **complex** (adj) – complicated, sophisticated, composed of many parts • *The human nervous system is an incredibly ~ network.* ➢ complexity (n), complexly (adj) ❖ πολύπλοκος, πολυσύνθετος

2.144 **invertebrate** (n) – (C) creature that lacks a backbone (*see* **2.145**) • *Insects and jellyfish are ~s.* ➢ Opp: vertebrate (n) ❖ ασπόνδυλο

2 Flora and fauna

2.145 backbone (n) – (C) line of bones that run down the middle of the back connecting the head and hips; same as **spine** or **spinal column** • *The ~ is composed of bones known as vertebrae.* ❖ σπονδυλική στήλη

2.146 vertebrate (n) – (C) creature that has a backbone and central nervous system • *Man is a ~.* ➢ vertebra (n), vertebrae (pl n). Opp: invertebrate (n) ❖ σπονδυλωτό

2.147 aquatic (adj) – of or related to water • *A~ animals live in water: some live in the sea in a saltwater habitat; others live in freshwater habitats like lakes and rivers.* ❖ υδρόβιος

2.148 marine (adj) – of or related to the sea • *Sharks and dolphins are ~ animals; they cannot survive in lakes or rivers.* ❖ θαλάσσιος

2.149 freshwater (n/adj) – of or found in bodies of water such as rivers, lakes, and streams • *Bass and trout are ~ fish; they do not live in the sea.* ❖ του γλυκού νερού

2.150 terrestrial (adj) – of or related to land • *Deserts and rain forests are ~ habitats.* ❖ χερσαίος, στεριανός

2.151 amphibious (adj) – related to, living in, or suitable for both land and water • *Frogs are ~ animals.* ➢ amphibian (n) ❖ αμφίβιος

C The phylum Chordata (chordates) (page 39)
Word bank

2.152 amphibian (n) – (C) animals that live both in water and on land • *Frogs are ~s.* ❖ αμφίβιο

2.153 mammal (n) – (C) warm-blooded animal whose body is covered with hair and whose females are able to produce milk • *Did you know that dolphins and whales are marine ~s (rather than fish)?* ➢ mammalian (adj) ❖ θηλαστικό

2.154 reptile (n) – (C) cold-blooded animal whose skin is covered by plates or fish-like scales • *The dinosaurs were giant ~s.* ➢ reptilian (adj) ❖ ερπετό

Definitions 1-5

2.155 aquatic (adj) – see **2.147**

2.156 cold-blooded (adj) – (animals) having a body temperature that varies with the environment • *Frogs and fish are ~ animals.* ❖ ποικιλόθερμος, ψυχρόαιμος See also **2.224**.

2.157 gill (n) – (C) one of two small openings on the side of a fish which aids in breathing ❖ βράγχιο

2.158 limb (n) – (animals) arm or leg of a person or four-legged animal • *We have four ~s: two arms and two legs.* ❖ άκρο. See also **2.90** and **2.116**.

2.159 fin (n) – (C) modified limb which a fish uses to propel itself through the water • *Fish use their ~s to move themselves through water, while birds use their wings to move through the air.* ❖ πτερύγιο

2.160 warm-blooded (adj) – (animals) having a constant body temperature that is usually above the temperature of the environment • *Mammals and birds are ~ creatures.* ❖ ομοιόθερμος, θερμόαιμος. 📖: e.g., a ~ young man

2.161 tadpole (n) – (C) new-born frog in the first stages of development • *A newly hatched ~ lives in water and has fish-like gills and a tail, which gradually disappear as the creature develops into an adult frog.* ❖ γυρίνος

2.162 metamorphosis (n) – (U) (insects, amphibians) process of development from an immature form into an adult • *Butterflies undergo several stages of ~ : from a worm-like larva (or grub) to a chrysalis in a cocoon to full-grown adult.* ➢ metamorphose (v) ❖ μεταμόρφωση

2.163 creep – crept – crept (irreg v) – (animals) move quietly and slowly, usually with the body close to the ground • *I watched the kitten ~ slowly toward the fly and ready herself for the kill.* ➢ creeping (adj) ❖ έρπω, γλιστρώ, προχωρώ σιγά-σιγά. 📖: e.g., a plant ~s, traffic ~s

2.164 crawl (v) – (reptiles, insects) move slowly along a surface • *Turtles ~ incredibly slowly, while lizards are reptiles that move much more quickly.* ➢ crawling (adj) ❖ έρπω, σέρνομαι. 📖: e.g., ~ like a baby

2.165 horny (adj) – (skin) hard and rough • *The body of a gila monster is covered with ~ plates, making it look like it wears protective armor.* ❖ (δέρμα) σκληρός και τραχύς

2.166 scale (n) – (C) one of many small, thin overlapping plates that cover the body of many fish • *I love to eat fish, but cleaning the ~s off of them is hard work.* ❖ λέπι. 📖: e.g., the Richter ~

2.167 nourish (v) – keep sb/sth alive by providing food • *Dead organic matter enriches the soil and helps to ~ plants.* ➢ nourishment (n), nourishing (adj) ❖ τρέφω. See also **4.351** for figurative meaning.

2.168 carnivore (n) – (C) meat-eating animal • *Lions and tigers are ~s.* ➢ carnivorous (adj) ❖ σαρκοφάγο

2.169 rodent (n) – (C) small, furry animals with sharp front teeth • *Mice and squirrels are ~s.* ❖ τρωκτικό

2.170 marsupial (n) – (C) animal that carries its young in a pouch • *Most people think of kangaroos when they hear the word "~."* ❖ μαρσιποφόρο

2.171 primate (n) – (C) upright, two-legged mammal with well-developed hands and brains • *With the exception of humans, most ~s are typically tree-dwelling animals like chimps and lemurs.* ❖ πρωτεύον θηλαστικό

D Be fruitful and multiply (page 50)

2.172 fruitful (adj) – (fig) productive • *The all-day meeting was ~ as we found solutions to a number of problems.* ➢ fruitfully (adj) ❖ (μετ) γόνιμος, καρποφόρος

2.173 multiply (v) – increase greatly in number or amount • *The recent closure of several factories has seriously ~ied the number of the city's unemployed.* ➢ multiplication (n) ❖ πολλαπλασιάζομαι

Word bank

2.174 fertilization (n) – (U) (animals) the action or process of a male sperm cell combining with the nucleus of a female egg cell • *After ~, a new life begins to develop.* ➢ fertilize (v), fertilized (adj), fertile (adj) ❖ γονιμοποίηση. See also 📖: e.g., ~ of soil

2.175 embryo (n) – (C) (animal) unborn young, from earliest stages of development • *In birds, the ~ develops within a hard-shelled egg; in humans and other mammals, it develops in an organ known as the uterus.* ➢ embryonic (adj) ❖ έμβρυο

2.176 ovum (n) – (C) female egg cell • *After fertilization by a sperm cell, the ~ soon develops into an embryo.* ➢ ova (pl n) ❖ ωάριο

Flora and fauna

2.177 spawning (n) → **spawn** (v) – (fish, frogs, etc.) produce and release large quantities of unfertilized eggs in water • *After the female fish ~, the males come along and release their sperm into the water so fertilization can take place.* ➢ spawn (n) ❖ (για ψάρια, βάτραχους κλπ) γεννώ. See **2.229** for figurative meaning.

2.178 sperm (n/pl n) – male reproductive cell(s) • *See* **2.177** *for example.* ❖ σπέρμα, σπερματόζωο. **Note: sperm** is both the singular and plural form.

2.179 uterus (n) – (C) female organ in which the embryo develops • *See* **2.175** *for example.* ➢ uterine (adj) ❖ μήτρα

E A guide to -vores and other voracious denizens ... (page 50)

2.180 voracious (adj) – greedy, wildly hungry • *Teenage boys are notorious for having ~ appetites.* ➢ voraciously (adv) ❖ αχόρταγος, ακόρεστος, άπληστος. See **2.230** for figurative meaning.

2.181 denizen (n) – (C) (formal, literary) a person, animal, or plant that is found in a particular place • *Whales and sharks are sometimes referred to as "~s of the deep."* ❖ κάτοικος

Word bank 1

2.182 carnivore (n) – *see* **2.168**

2.183 decomposer (n) – (C) creature that feeds on rotting leaves, dead animals, and/or other decaying matter • *Bacteria and worms are typical examples of ~s.* ➢ decompose (v), decomposed (adj) ❖ αποικοδομητής

2.184 herbivore (n) – (C) plant-eating animal • *Humans are meant to be omnivorous, but Helen has decided to challenge nature and become a ~ ; she's a strict vegetarian now.* ➢ herbivorous (adj) ❖ χορτοφάγος

2.185 omnivore (n) – (C) animal that eats both plants and animals • *By nature, humans are ~s, having a diet of both meat and vegetables.* ➢ omnivorous (adj) ❖ παμφάγο

Text

2.186 fuel (v) – (used passively in text) supply or provide with energy or power • *The digestive process ~s all of our body's vital processes.* ➢ fuel (n) ❖ εφοδιάζω με καύσιμα

2.187 convert (v) – *see* **2.67**

2.188 nutrient (n) – (C) chemical substance that provides nourishment and helps maintain life • *Vitamins, minerals, proteins, and carbohydrates are examples of ~s.* ➢ nutrition (n), nutritionist (n), nutritional (adj) ❖ θρεπτική ουσία

2.189 food web (n phr) – (C) network that involves eating and being eaten; similar to **food chain** • *Man, the ultimate predator, is always at the top of the ~.* ❖ τροφική αλυσίδα

2.190 grazing (n) → **graze** (v) – (of animals) eat grass • *We watched the cows and sheep ~ in the farmer's field.* ❖ βόσκω

2.191 predation (n) – (U) the act or process of one animal hunting and killing other animals for food • *P~ is the law of the jungle: to put it simply, life is a matter of "eat or be eaten."* ➢ predator (n), predatory (adj) ❖ αρπαγή

2.192 devour (v) – eat quickly • *The hungry boys ~ed the pizza in no time.* ❖ καταβροχθίζω. See also **2.225** for figurative meaning.

2.193 detritus (n) – (U) waste matter; also, (biology) organic matter produced by the decomposition of once living organisms • *Bacteria and worms feed on ~ such as rotting leaves and dead animals.* ❖ κατάλοιπα, αποσάθρωση οργανισμών

Word bank 2

2.194 bird of prey (n phr) – (C) large bird that hunt small animals for food • *The eagle is a ~, as are hawks and owls.* ❖ αρπακτικό πουλί

2.195 browser (n) – (C) (zoology) animal that feeds on grass or leaves • *Giraffes, cows, and sheep are examples of ~s.* ➢ browse (v) ❖ ζώο που βόσκει (τρώγοντας χορτάρι και φύλλα). 📖: e.g., an Internet ~, a ~ in a shop

2.196 hibernator (n) – (C) animal that enters into a deep sleep to survive winter food shortages • *The bear is a classic example of a ~ that sleeps through the winter.* ➢ hibernation (n), hibernate (v) ❖ ζώο που πέφτει σε χειμερία νάρκη

2.197 insectivore (n) – (C) animal or plant that preys on insects • *As you can tell from its name, the anteater is an ~.* ❖ εντομοφάγο ζώο/φυτό

2.198 migratory animal (n phr) – animal that **migrates** (i.e., moves from one place to another) according to the season, in search of suitable living conditions • *Some birds are ~s that move from north to south and back again in search of food and warmer climates.* ❖ αποδημητικό ζώο

2.199 predator (n) – (C) animal that attacks and kills other animals for food • *The zoo is home to lions, tigers, and other ~s of the African savanna.* ➢ predation (n), predatory (v) ❖ αρπακτικό ζώο

2.200 prey (n) – (U) animal(s) hunted for food • *The eagle flew overhead, hunting for field mice and other small ~.* ➢ prey on (phr v) ❖ λεία, βορά. See also **2.228** for figurative verb meaning.

2.201 scavenger (n) – (C) animal that feeds on the decaying meat/flesh of dead animals ➢ scavenge (v) ❖ ζώο που τρώει ψοφίμια

F A picture's worth a thousand words (page 51)
Word bank 1

2.202 fin (n) – *see* **2.159**

2.203 flank (n) – (C) one of the two sides (left or right) of an animal's body, usually between the ribs and the hips • *The rider kicked the horse in its ~s so that it would run faster.* ➢ flank (v) ❖ πλευρό, λαγόνα

2.204 foreleg (n phr) – (C) one of the two front legs of a four-legged animal • *The horse pawed the ground with its right ~.* ➢ Opp: hind leg (n phr) ❖ μπροστινό πόδι

2.205 gill (n) – *see* **2.157**

2.206 hind leg (n phr) – (C) one of the two back legs of a four-legged animal • *Frightened by the loud noise, the horse reared up on its ~s.* ➢ Opp: foreleg (n) ❖ πισινό πόδι

2.207 hoof (n) – (C) hard lower part of the foot of certain animals • *He gently picked up the horse's foot and pulled a thorn from its ~.* ➢ hooves (pl n), hoof it (idm) ❖ οπλή (ζώου). See also **2.227** for figurative verb meaning.

2 Flora and fauna

2.208 horn (n) – (C) one of usually two hard permanent outgrowths on the head of certain animals • *The legendary unicorn had only one ~, while animals like cows, bulls, and goats have two.* ➢ horny (adj) ❖ κέρατο

2.209 mane (n) – (C) long line of hair around the face of a lion or running down the neck of a horse • *The aging symphony conductor's hair was so long that it looked like a flowing white ~.* ➢ maned (adj) ❖ χαίτη

2.210 scale (n) – *see* **2.166**

2.211 tentacle (n) – (C) long, thin "arm/leg" of certain animals • *An octopus has eight ~s.* ❖ πλοκάμι

2.212 udder (n) – (C) the bag-like milk-producing organ of animals like cows, sheep, etc. • *The farmer showed us how to get the milk from the cow's ~.* ❖ μαστάρι

Word bank 2

2.213 antler (n) – (C) one of the two branched horns found on the head of certain animals (e.g., a deer or moose) • *The deer's ~s looked as if they had been cut from a tree and glued to its head.* ❖ κλαδωτό κέρατο

2.214 beak (n) – (C) the hard pointed or curved part of a bird's mouth • *The woodpecker used its ~ to make a hole in the tree bark.* ❖ ράμφος

2.215 bill (n) – a beak (*see* **2.214**) that is slender or flattened, such as those of web-footed birds or members of the pigeon family • *The duck pushed its head underwater and came up with a fish in its ~.* ➢ billed (adj) ❖ είδος ράμφους

2.216 breast (n) – (C) the chest area of a bird • *A robin is a bird that is easy to spot, as it has a bright reddish-orange ~.* ➢ breasted (adj) ❖ στήθος (πουλιού)

2.217 claw (n) – (C) one of a series of pointed nails on the feet of some animals • *The cat scratched me with its ~s.* ➢ claw (v), clawed (adj) ❖ νύχι (λιονταριού, γάτα. κλπ)

2.218 crest (n) – (C) small group of feathers or other growth on the top of a bird's head • *Atop the bird's head was a tiny red ~ of feathers, which looked like a small triangular hat from where we were standing.* ❖ λειρί (πουλιού). 📖: e.g., the ~ of a hill

2.219 mane (n) – *see* **2.209**

2.220 paw (n) – (C) the foot of an animal that has claws or nails • *Cats and dog have ~s, while hoofed animals like horses and goats do not.* ➢ paw (v) ❖ πόδι με νύχια (ζώου)

2.221 talon (n) – (C) strong pointed nails found on the feet of birds of prey; similar to **claw** (*see* **2.220**) • *The eagle flew off holding the mouse firmly in its ~s.* ❖ νύχι (πουλιού). **Note:** only bird nails are described as talons, not animal nails.

2.222 webbed (adj) – (of the feet of aquatic animals) connected by a membrane • *The children laughed when they saw the ducks waddling around on their ~ feet.* ➢ web (n) ❖ «νηκτικό» πόδι, μεμβρανώδες πόδι

2.223 wing (n) – (C) one of a pair of modified limbs that allow birds to fly • *The bird flapped its ~s.* ➢ wing (v), winged (adj) ❖ φτερό

G BEYOND ZOOLOGY: Speaking figuratively with animal language (page 51)

Word bank

2.224 cold-blooded (adj) – (fig) heartless, unfeeling • *The ~ murderer showed no emotion when he was sentenced to life in prison.* ❖ (μετ) ψυχρός, αναίσθητος. *See* **2.156** *for literal meaning.*

2.225 devour (v) – (fig) finish quickly and eagerly • *The child loves to read. She ~s every book she puts her hands on.* ❖ (μετ) καταβροχθίζω. *See* **2.192** *for literal meaning.*

2.226 digest (v) – absorb, take in • *There's are so many difficult words in this article that I find it difficult to ~.* ❖ (μετ) αφομοιώνω. *See* **2.135** *for literal meaning.*

2.227 hoof it (idm) – (fig – informal) walk (often quickly) • *My car's broken, so we'll just have to ~ to the supermarket.* ❖ (μετ) περπατώ. *See* **2.207** *for literal noun meaning.*

2.228 prey on (phr v) – (fig) trouble or distress greatly • *When she has a problem to solve, it can ~ her mind for days.* ❖ (μετ) βασανίζω. *See* **2.200** *for literal noun meaning.*

2.229 spawn (v) – (fig) produce (usually in large quantity), give birth to • *The industrial revolution has ~ed countless inventions that have improved our lives.* ❖ (μετ) γεννοβολώ, παράγω. *See* **2.177** *for literal meaning.*

2.230 voracious (adj) – (fig) eager and always hungry for more • *He's a ~ theater-goer. There isn't a Broadway play he hasn't seen.* ❖ (μετ) αχόρταγος. *See* **2.180** *for literal meaning.*

2.231 wing it (idm) – (fig – informal) improvise, speak or act without any preparation • *When the speaker came on stage, he realized he had lost his notes so he had to ~.* ❖ (μετ) αυτοσχεδιάζω, κάνω κτ πρόχειρα. *See* **2.223** *for literal noun meaning.*

Cloze Reference words (pages 53-54)

A Try it! (page 53)
Text 1

2.232 shrink – shrank – shrunk (irreg v) – become/cause to become smaller in size or amount • *Old age tends to ~ a person; my grandmother is several inches shorter than she used to be.* ➢ shrinkage, shrinking (adj), shrunken (adj) ❖ συρρικνούμαι, μικραίνω, μαζεύω

2.233 liver (n) – (C) large brownish-red organ on the right side of the body • *Cirrhosis and hepatitis are diseases of the liver.* ❖ συκώτι

2.234 fraction (of sth) (n) – (U) tiny part, amount, or proportion of sth • *The bullet missed him by just a ~ of an inch.* ➢ fractional (adj) ❖ μικρό μέρος, κλάσμα

Text 2

2.235 proximity (n) – 1. (U) nearness (e.g., in space or time) • *He rented the house because of its ~ to his office. / The two brothers have always been close, perhaps because of the ~ of their ages.* 2. **in close ~ (to sb/sth)** (prep phr) – near • *He lives in close ~ to his office.* ❖ 1. εγγύτητα, αμεσότητα 2. κοντά, πλησίον

2.236 arrangement (n) – agreement, understanding, relationship • *My friend in Athens and I have an ~ : I stay at her house when I'm in Athens, and she stays at my house when she's in New York.* ➢ arrange (v), arranged (adj) ❖ συμφωνία. 📖: e.g., a floral ~

2.237 nourishment (n) – (U) food or other substances necessary for health, growth, survival, etc. • *A young mammal receives ~ from its mother's milk.* ➢ nourish (v), nourishing (adj) ❖ τροφή, θρέψη

2.238 host (n) – (biology) animal or plant on which a parasite or other animal lives and gains a benefit • *A tapeworm lives in the intestines of its ~.* ➢ host (v) ❖ (βιολογία) ξενιστής

Flora and fauna 2

B CLOZE PRACTICE: Close encounters … (page 54)

2.239 encounter (n) – (C) unexpected meeting • *She had an uncomfortable ~ at the supermarket with her husband's ex-wife yesterday.* ➢ encounter (v) ❖ απροσδόκητη συνάντηση

STEP 2: Work through the text (page 54)
Paragraph 1

2.240 cove (n) – (C) small sheltered bay or inlet • *The coast was indented with tiny ~s that could only be reached with a boat.* ❖ ορμίσκος, λιμανάκι

2.241 binoculars (pl n) – instrument with two lenses, used for looking at things in the distance • *You use one eye to look through a telescope, but a pair of ~ requires the use of both eyes.* ❖ κυάλια

2.242 frolic – frolicked – frolicked (irreg v) – move about playfully • *Our three-year old doesn't know how to swim yet, but she enjoys ~ing in shallow water.* ❖ παιχνιδίζω, κάνω τρέλες

2.243 rush (n) – (C) (feeling) sudden, strong, wavelike feeling • *The skydiver felt a ~ of energy flow through his veins as he dropped through the air.* ➢ rush (v), rushing (adj) ❖ (αίσθηση) κύμα, ορμή

2.244 exquisite (adj) – strongly felt, beautiful, intense • *The team's victory left them with an ~ sense of triumph.* ➢ exquisitely (adv) ❖ έντονος, εξαίσιος

Paragraph 2

2.245 wager (v) – (formal) bet • *It's fun to place a friendly bet on a game once in while, but I would never ~ a month's salary on one.* ➢ wager (n) ❖ στοιχηματίζω

2.246 provoke (v) – cause sth, cause sb/sth to do sth or to react in a certain way • *The comedian's jokes ~d side-splitting laughter in the audience.* ➢ provocation (n), provoked (adj), provocative (adj), provocatively (adv) ❖ προκαλώ

2.247 chorus (n) – (C – used figuratively) sth said, shouted, or sung by many people (or in this case animals), concert • *She loves to wake up at dawn to the ~ of chirping birds.* ❖ (μετ) χορός, συναυλία

2.248 croaking (adj) – that **croaks** (i.e., makes a deep, hoarse sound like a frog) • *Those ~ frogs never stop! What a racket!* ❖ (για βάτραχους) που κοάζει «κουάκ-κουάκ»

2.249 fierce (adj) – angry, aggressive • *That ~ dog looks like he's going to bite the mail carrier.* ➢ ferocity (n), fiercely (adv) ❖ άγριος. *See also* **1.296**.

2.250 glare (n) – (C) angry look • *You could tell he was furious from the way he looked at her with a burning, penetrating ~.* ➢ glare (v), glaring (adj) ❖ άγριο, επίμονο βλέμμα

2.251 strut (v) – walk in a stiff, proud way • *The proud graduates ~ted across the stage to receive their diplomas.* ❖ περπατώ κορδωτά/καμαρωτά

2.252 boldly (adv) – bravely, with great courage • *The soldiers ~ moved forward to meet the enemy.* ➢ boldness (n), bold (adj) ❖ τολμηρά, θαρραλέα

Vocabulary (3) Animal language in action (page 58)

A Animal movements (pages 58-59)
Text 1 (page 58)

2.253 mound (n) – (C) mass of piled earth or soil that looks like a small hill • *The ~s in the farmer's field were made by ants and moles.* ❖ βουναλάκι, σωρός από χώμα, ανάχωμα

2.254 wildebeest (n/pl n) – (C) large antelope-like animal of southern Africa • *W~ are plentiful in the South African bush.* ❖ είδος αντιλόπης Νότιας Αφρικής

2.255 herd (n) – (C) group of animals of a single kind which live and feed together (e.g., cattle, elephants) • *The safari came across a pride of lions and several ~s of elephants, zebras, and giraffes.* ➢ herd (v) ❖ αγέλη

2.256 slink (v) – move quietly or secretly • *The burglar ~ed behind the house, hoping to enter it unseen.* ❖ περνώ/κουνώ κρυφά. **Note:** The verb can also be irregular: slink – slunk – slunk.

2.257 dart (v) – move suddenly and quickly • *The child ~ed into the street and was almost hit by an oncoming car.* ➢ darting (adj) ❖ ορμώ, ξεπετάγομαι

2.258 shaggy (adj) – (of hair, fur) long, thick, and messy • *The sheepdog's hair was so ~ that it was hard to see his eyes.* ❖ μαλλιαρός, τριχωτός

2.259 thunder (v) – move with a loud deep noise • *The elephants ~ed across the landscape.* ➢ thunder (n), thundering (adj), thunderous (adj) ❖ τρέχω με πάταγο. *See also* **1.283**.

2.260 ditch (n) – (C) narrow channel dug in the ground • *The car went off the road and landed in a ~.* ❖ χαντάκι, αυλάκι

2.261 leap – leapt – leapt (irreg v) – jump high or far • *Anyone who ~s from that high bridge will not survive the fall.* ➢ leap (n), leaping (adj) ❖ πηδώ

2.262 gorge (on sth) (v) – eat (sth) greedily, stuff oneself (on sth) • *After the long hike, the boys ~d themselves on pizza and ice cream as if they hadn't eaten in weeks.* ❖ τρώω λαίμαργα, καταβροχθίζω

2.263 prime rib (n phr) – (U) high-quality cut of beef • *It's not often we order ~, so we really enjoyed our meal.* ❖ είδος κρέατος άριστης ποιότητας

2.264 conspicuous (adj) – easily seen or noticed, attracting attention • *Having an open book on your desk is a rather ~ way of cheating, don't you think?* ➢ conspicuously (adj). Opp: inconspicuous (adj) ❖ καταφανής, εμφανής

2.265 stampede (v) – run wildly in a group • *The elephants ~d right through the safari camp. It's a miracle no one was crushed.* ➢ stampede (n), stampeding (adj) ❖ τρέπομαι σε άτακτη φυγή

2.266 coincidence (n) – (C/U) an instance of things happening by chance at the same time • *It was a ~ that the two old friends were staying at the same hotel. / They ran into each other by ~.* ❖ σύμπτωση

2.267 sprint (v) – run as fast as one can for a short distance • *The dog ~s to the front door as soon as he hears someone approaching.* ➢ sprint (n), sprinter (n) ❖ σπριντάρω, τρέχω ολοταχώς (σε μικρή απόσταση)

2.268 drive – drove – driven (irreg v) – force (sb/sth) to go a certain way or to do sth against their will • *It's the job of a sheepdog to ~ the herd up the mountain and back.* ❖ οδηγώ, εξωθώ

Text 2 (page 58)

2.269 cower (v) – bend over and move back in fear • *We found the lost child ~ing in fear at the back of the movie theater.* ➢ cowering (adj) ❖ ζαρώνω, μαζεύομαι (από φόβο)

2.270 quiver (v) – shake, tremble • *You could see she was nervous by the way her hands ~ed.* ➢ quiver (n), quivering (adj) ❖ τρέμω, τρεμουλιάζω

2 Flora and fauna

2.271 squat (v) – (animals) sit on one's back legs or heels (people) • *The frightened dog ~ted down and raised its front paws to its face.* ➤ squat (n), squatting (adj) ❖ (ζώα) κάθομαι στα πισινά πόδια

2.272 lick (v) – past the tongue over sth • *Cats ~ themselves to stay clean.* ➤ lick (n) ❖ γλείφω

2.273 flank (n) – see **2.203**

2.274 moisten (v) – make slightly wet, dampen • *She finds it easier to iron if she ~s the clothes first by spraying them with a bit of water.* ➤ moisture (n), moist (adj), moistened (adj) ❖ υγραίνω

2.275 grasp (v) – hold sth/sb tightly with one's hand • *She ~s her child's hand tightly whenever they cross a busy street.* ➤ grasp (n) ❖ πιάνω, σφίγγω

2.276 nibble (v) – take small light bites • *I could see she wasn't very hungry from the way she ~d at her food.* ➤ nibble (n) ❖ τσιμπώ ελαφρά, τσιμπολογώ

2.277 bat (v) – hit at sth lightly with a paw or one's open hand • *The kittens spent hours ~ting each other playfully.* ❖ χτυπώ

2.278 misgiving (n) – (C) (usually in plural) feeling of doubt, concern, or distrust • *She knew her parents had some ~s about her fiancé because he had trouble staying employed.* ❖ δισταγμός, επιφύλαξη

2.279 lumber (v) – move heavily or awkwardly • *Tired after a hard day, he ~ed up the stairs with heavy footsteps.* ➤ lumbering (adj) ❖ κινούμαι βαριά και με θόρυβο

2.280 squint (v) – look through partly closed eyes • *I know the sun is strong, but try not to ~ when I take your photo.* ➤ squint (n), squinting (adj) ❖ κοιτάζω με μισόκλειστα μάτια

2.281 stumble (v) – (lit) trip and almost fall • 1. *I ~d and almost fell as I ran down the street.* 2. **~ across** (phr v) – find by chance • *I ~d across my old tennis racket while cleaning out the attic.* ❖ 1. σκουντουφλώ, σκοντάφτω 2. βρίσκω τυχαία

2.282 launch (v) – put into action, start • *The general is planning to ~ the attack at sunrise.* ➤ launch (n) ❖ εξαπολύω (π.χ., επίθεση)

2.283 buck-toothed (adj) – having **buck teeth** (that is, front teeth that stick out over the lower lip) • *The ~ child couldn't wait to go to the orthodontist to get braces on his front teeth.* ❖ με μπροστινά δόντια που προεξέχουν πολύ

2.284 streak (v) – move quickly, like lightning • *The frightened cat ~ed across the room and hid under the sofa.* ❖ κινούμαι γρήγορα σαν αστραπή

2.285 perch (n) – (C) (fig) high place where sb/sth rests or sits; (lit) horizontal bar in a bird cage on which the bird rests or sits • *From our ~ at the top of the tree we could see the rooftops of the houses.* ❖ βίγλα ή κούνια (για πουλιά)

2.286 bare (v) → **~ one's teeth** (v phr) – show one's teeth (often in anger or as a threat) • *The dog growled and ~d its teeth.* ➤ bared (adj) ❖ δείχνω τα δόντια απειλητικά

2.287 nip (v) – bite sharply • *When the playful puppy ~ped my finger, I cried out in pain.* ❖ τσιμπώ, δαγκώνω κοφτά

2.288 gobble (v) – eat greedily and noisily • *The hungry children ~d down their hamburgers as if they hadn't eaten in weeks.* ❖ καταβροχθίζω, τρώω λαίμαργα

Text 3 (page 59)

2.289 soar (v) – rise fast and stay up high • *The eagle ~ed into the air and circled the field looking for prey.* ➤ soaring (adj) ❖ πετώ πολύ ψηλά

2.290 glide (v) – fly with minimal wing movement • *The hawk spent hours ~ing around in circles.* ❖ (πουλιά) πετώ στον άνεμο, με τεντωμένα φτερά

2.291 flap (v) – move up and down, often with a gentle noise • *The sea gulls flew so close to the boat that we could hear them ~ their wings.* ➤ flapping (n, adj) ❖ φτεροκοπώ

2.292 sustain (v) – keep sth going for a long time • *The teacher tried hard to ~ the interest of the class.* ➤ sustenance (n), sustained (adj) ❖ κρατώ (σε μεγάλη διάρκεια ή ένταση)

2.293 flit (v) – fly lightly from place to place • *The butterflies ~ted from one flower to another.* ❖ πετώ ανάλαφρα και φευγαλέα (από ένα μέρος στο άλλο)

2.294 hover (v) – remain in the air in one place • *The bee ~ed over the flower collecting its nectar. / The helicopter ~ed over the accident scene to see if anyone was hurt.* ❖ ζυγιάζομαι στον αέρα, παραμένω μετέωρος (σαν ελικόπτερο)

2.295 probe (v) – (lit) explore deep into a place that is difficult to reach • *The surgeon ~d the wound to see how deep the bullet had penetrated.* ➤ probe (n) ❖ ερευνώ βαθιά

2.296 nectar (n) – (U) sugary liquid secreted by plants to attract pollinators • *The hummingbird drank the flower's sweet ~ greedily.* ❖ νέκταρ

2.297 extensible (adj) – (technical) able to be extended • *The hummingbird has a long ~ tongue.* ➤ extension (n), extend (v), extensive (adj) ❖ εκτατός

Text 4 (page 59)

2.298 advance (on sth/sb) (v) – move forward aggressively • *As the enemy army ~d on the village, the villagers fled for their lives.* ➤ advancement (n), advancing (adj), advanced (adj) ❖ προχωρώ επιθετικά, προελαύνω

2.299 scamper (v) – run with quick light steps (usually out of fear or excitement) • *Mother screamed when she saw a mouse ~ across the kitchen.* ❖ τρέχω με γρήγορα ελαφρά βήματα

2.300 flop (v) – move or fall in an awkward, loose way • *Fish ~ around in the bottom of a boat. / A tired person ~s down on the couch. / Long hair ~s into your eyes.* ➤ flop (n), floppy (adj) ❖ τινάζομαι, κινούμαι, πέφτω, ρίχνω αδέξια ή με γδούπο

2.301 intruder (n) – (C) person/animal that enters a place without being invited, often with harmful intent • *Thanks to the family's burglar alarm, police caught the ~ as he was running from the house.* ➤ intrusion (n), intrude (v), intrusive (adj), intrusively (adv) ❖ παρείσακτος

2.302 lure (v) – tempt or trick sb/sth to go somewhere or do sth often by offering a tempting reward • *The kidnapper ~d the child into the car by offering to buy him ice cream.* ➤ lure (n) ❖ δελεάζω, παρασύρω

2.303 swoop (v) – fly down in a smooth curve, often with the intent to attack • *The eagle ~ed down and grabbed the mouse in its powerful talons.* ❖ εφορμώ, χιμώ (πετώντας)

2.304 blunder (v) – (fig) move awkwardly, as if blind • *When the lights went out, I ~ed into the coffee table and cut my leg.* ➤ blunder (n), blundering (adj) ❖ προσκρούω (σε εμπόδιο), σκοντάφτω

Flora and fauna 2

C Animal idioms (page 60)

GROUP 1

2.305 let sleeping dogs lie (idm) – avoid saying sth that will cause trouble • *I knew she didn't know the truth about her husband, but things were already so bad between them that I decided to ~.* ❖ μη θίγετε τα κακώς κείμενα, μην πας γυρεύοντας μπελάδες

2.306 take the bull by the horns (idm) – act decisively • *The boss expects his managers to ~ and show plenty of initiative.* ❖ ενεργώ αποφασιστικά / κεραυνοβόλα

2.307 birds of a feather flock together (idm) – (saying) people with like tastes attract each other • *They have all the same tastes, so I knew they'd like each other. B~.* ❖ όποιοι μοιάζουν συμπεθεριάζουν

2.308 night owl (idm) – person who likes to stay up late • *Most ~s have a hard time getting up for work in the morning, because they've stayed up half the night reading or watching TV.* ❖ ξενύχτης, νυχτοπούλι

2.309 as stubborn as a mule (idm) – extremely obstinate, pig-headed • *Her teenage son is ~ ; he does what he wants when he wants, and no one can get him to do anything else.* ❖ πεισματάρης σα μουλάρι

2.310 take to sth like a duck takes to water (idm) – display a natural talent for sth • *She loves downhill skiing, so I'm sure she'll take to snowboarding like a duck takes to water.* ❖ μαθαίνω κτ πολύ εύκολα

2.311 the black sheep of the family (idm) – family member who lives in disgrace • *Uncle Bob has been to prison a few times, so everyone considers him ~.* ❖ το μαύρο πρόβατο της οικογένειας

2.312 have/get butterflies in (sb's) stomach (idm) – have/get an unpleasant feeling in your stomach because you're nervous • *Every time I speak in public my hands shake and I get butterflies in my stomach.* ❖ έχω ανακατωσούρες στο στομάχι (από άγχος και αγωνία)

GROUP 2

2.313 be in the doghouse (idm) – (be) in disgrace, (fall) out of favor • *If she doesn't finish the report on time, she'll really be in the doghouse with the boss* ❖ (είμαι/πέφτω) σε δυσμένεια

2.314 let the cat out of the bag (idm) – reveal a secret • *I want this to be a surprise party so please don't ~.* ❖ μου ξεφεύγει ένα μυστικό

2.315 go to the dogs (idm) – fall into a bad state • *If the old chef leaves, this restaurant will really ~.* ❖ καταστρέφομαι, πάω κατά διαόλου

2.316 beat a dead horse (idm) – (Brit: **flog a dead horse**) insist on pursuing a hopeless goal • *Your husband is never going to help you with the housework. Why do you continue to ~ ?* ❖ (μετ) ματαιοπονώ

2.317 there are plenty more fish in the sea (idm) – (saying) there are lots of other people to fall in love with • *I wouldn't worry about John breaking up with you. T~ !* ❖ υπάρχουν κι αλλού πορτοκαλιές που κάνουν πορτοκάλια

2.318 have a frog in (sb's) throat (idm) – have a hoarse voice (e.g., due to laryngitis) • *John and Mary cheered so loudly at the game last night that they both have a frog in their throat.* ❖ είμαι βραχνιασμένος

2.319 get it straight from the horse's mouth (idm) – hear sth right from the person involved • *It's not a rumor. He told me himself, so I got it straight from the horse's mouth.* ❖ από πρώτο χέρι, κατευθείαν από την πηγή

Reading — Tracking down technical terms (pages 61-63)

Practice 1 (page 62)

2.320 plumage (n) – (U) all of the feathers covering a bird's body • *The ~ of male birds tends to be brighter and more colorful than the ~ of female birds.* ➢ plume (n) ❖ φτερά, πτέρωμα

2.321 ornamental (adj) – decorative, serving as decoration • *The flowering bushes in her garden are both ~ and functional: they are pretty but they also form a wall between her property and her neighbors'.* ➢ ornament (n), ornamentation (n) ❖ διακοσμητικός

2.322 plume (n) – (C) large decorative feather • *A peacock's tail is made up of long, beautiful ~s, which he opens into a fan-shaped display when excited.* ➢ plumage ❖ μεγάλο διακοσμητικό φτερό. 📖 : e.g., a ~ of smoke

2.323 influential (adj) – important, having an influence or effect on sth • *The businessman's generous donation was an ~ factor in the board's decision to build a new orphanage.* ➢ influence (n, v) ❖ σημαντικός, με επιρροή

2.324 mate (n) – (C) animal with which another animal produces young • *Impressive coloration is one way in which the male of a species attracts a ~.* ➢ mating (n, adj), mate (v) ❖ ταίρι

2.325 endure (v) – suffer or bear sb/sth for a long time • *The villagers ~d hunger and suffering throughout the war.* ➢ endurance (n), enduring (adj) ❖ αντέχω, υποφέρω

2.326 temperate (adj) – (of climate) mild, neither very hot nor cold • *She found the freezing winters of Canada very difficult to get used to after living in a ~ area for most of her life.* ➢ temperance (n), temper (v), temperately (adv) ❖ (για κλίμα) εύκρατος. See also **1.218**.

2.327 preening (n) → **preen** (v) – (birds) clean and smooth out the feathers with the beak • *Birds are very flexible to be able to ~ their tail feathers with their beak.* ❖ (για πουλί) καθαρίζω και στρώνω τα φτερά μου με το ράμφος. 📖 : e.g., (people) ~ oneself in front of a mirror

2.328 secrete (v) – (body, plants) produce a liquid substance (e.g., hormones, sweat, sap) • *The pancreas ~s insulin into the blood. / A tree ~s sap.* ➢ secretion (n) ❖ εκκρίνω. 📖 : e.g., ~ stolen money

B READING PRACTICE: Co-evolution (page 63)

STEP 2 : Text

Paragraph 1

2.329 joint (adj) – shared by or belonging to more than one person • *After they married, the couple opened a ~ bank account.* ➢ join (v), jointly (adv) ❖ κοινός

2.330 evolution (n) – see **2.24**

2.331 predator (n) – see **2.199**

2.332 prey (n) – see **2.200**

2.333 efficient (adj) – fast, effective, and competent • *The ~ secretary is not only fast but accurate as well.* ➢ efficiency (n), efficiently (adv). Opp: inefficient (adj) ❖ αποτελεσματικός, αποδοτικός

2 Flora and fauna

2.334 consume (v) – eat or drink • *It's amazing that he's so thin given the huge amounts of food he ~s.* ➢ consumption (n), consumer (v), consumable (adj) ❖ κατατρώγω, καταβροχθίζω. 📖 : e.g., ~ energy, goods, or a service

2.335 predation (n) – *see* **2.191**

2.336 thorn (n) – *see* **2.103**

2.337 spine (n) – (C) (plants, animals) hard, pointed protective structure usually longer and thinner than a thorn • *Many plants and animals have developed ~s as protection against predators: e.g., the cactus, porcupine, and hedgehog.* ❖ αγκάθι (κάκτου, σκατζόχειρου κλπ). *See also* **2.145**.

2.338 sap (n) – (U) sugary liquid that circulates through plants and trees • *The syrup that we put on pancakes is made from the ~ of a maple tree.* ❖ χυμός (δένδρου/φυτού)

2.339 deter (v) – prevent or discourage (sb from acting or sth from happening), especially by frightening or threatening • *They bought a fierce-looking dog to ~ burglars from breaking into their house.* ➢ deterrent (n), deterrence (n) ❖ αποτρέπω, εμποδίζω

2.340 would-be (adj) – trying or hoping to be sth (but perhaps not having the right qualities) • *The ~ writer refuses to give up even though he has received countless rejection letters.* ❖ επίδοξος

2.341 incorporate (into) (v) – combine or mix one or more things (e.g., ingredients) to create a mixture • *To make the sauce, slowly ~ the chicken broth into the mixture of flour and butter.* ❖ αναμειγνύω, ανακατώνω, ενσωματώνω/-ομαι. *See also* **5.122**.

2.342 tissue (n) – *see* **2.136**

2.343 employ (v) – use or apply sth • *Doctors are beginning to ~ the new surgical technique in hospitals throughout the country.* ➢ employment (n) ❖ χρησιμοποιώ. 📖 : e.g., ~ sb to do sth

2.344 mimicry (n) – (U) (animals, plants) the act or state of looking like sth else in nature, often as a means of camouflage against predators • *The chameleon's ability to change color is a form of protective ~.* ➢ mimic (n, v) ❖ (προστατευτικός) μιμητισμός, μιμητικότητα

2.345 natural selection (n) – (U) (biology) the process by which well-adapted organisms tend to survive and produce more young; similar to **survival of the fittest** • *It is widely believed that ~ is the process that underlies evolution.* ❖ φυσική επιλογή (η θεωρία του Δαρβίνου)

2.346 mimic (v) – (plants and animals) look like or act like another plant or animal (usually as protection) • *Chameleons avoid predation by changing color to ~ and thus blend in with their surroundings.* ➢ mimicry (n), mimic (n) ❖ απομιμούμαι, μιμούμαι

2.347 pattern (n) – (C) arrangement of lines, shapes, colors, or other decorative elements • *The zebra's stripes form a zigzag ~.* ❖ σχέδιο

2.348 unpalatable (adj) – not tasty or fit to eat; not pleasing to the **palate** (i.e., the upper part or roof of the mouth) • *We swore we would never go back to that restaurant as the service was dreadful and the food was totally ~.* ➢ palate (n). Opp: palatable (adj) ❖ με άσχημη/ δυσάρεστη γεύση

2.349 adaptation (n) – (C) change by which an organism becomes better suited to its environment; (U) the process of making such changes • *The chameleon's ability to blend change color is an effective ~ that has ensured its survival. / (U) A~ ensures that a species will survive by becoming better suited to its environment.* ➢ adapt (v), adaptable (adj) ❖ προσαρμογή

2.350 assume (v) – take on (e.g., a certain quality or characteristic), appear to be sth that you are not • *Some wetland birds can ~ a pose that makes them look like the tall, thin reeds in a marsh.* ➢ assumption (n), assumed (adj) ❖ προσποιούμαι, παριστάνω

2.351 obnoxious (adj) – (things) extremely unpleasant, irritating • *Some people insist that green peppers have an ~ taste; others find them pleasant.* ➢ obnoxiously (adv) ❖ αποκρουστικός, απαίσιος. *See also* **1.157**.

2.352 potential (adj) – possible, capable of being or becoming in the future • *If the new business succeeds, the ~ profits could be enormous.* ➢ potential (n), potentially (adv) ❖ πιθανός, ενδεχόμενος

Paragraph 2

2.353 association (n) – (C/U) relationship, connection • *Her mother disapproved of her ~ with an older man.* ➢ associate (n, v), associated (adj) ❖ συναναστροφή

2.354 fungi (pl n) – plural form of **fungus** (i.e., a multicelled plant-like organism that absorbs food from the soil it grows in) • *Like all ~, mushrooms absorb food from the soil rather than producing it by photosynthesis the way true plants do.* ❖ μύκητες

2.355 penetrate (v) – enter and pass into or through sth • *The bullet ~d the victim's heart, causing him to die instantly.* ➢ penetration (n), penetrating (adj) ❖ διαπερνώ, διατρυπώ

2.356 extend (v) – continue or stretch out over a certain distance • *It's a long, narrow lake that ~s for several miles.* ➢ extension (n), extent (n), extended (adj) ❖ απλώνομαι, εκτείνομαι. 📖 : e.g., ~ an offer

2.357 nutrient (n) – *see* **2.188**

2 Exam practice (pages 66–69)

Cloze (page 67)

The passage contains a number of plant-related words that appear in this unit. To review parts of a flower (e.g., *stamen, pistil, anther, stigma*) and other words related to the pollination process, *see entries* **2.98-2.114**.

Paragraph 1

2.358 external (adj) – coming from outside (not from within) • *The company uses an ~ accountant to oversee its finances; the person is under contract, but he is not an employee of the company.* ❖ εξωτερικός

2.359 agent (n) – (C) sb/sth that produces a particular effect • *Making bread requires the use of a rising ~ such as yeast. Technology is an ~ of change.* ➢ agency (n) ❖ μέσο, παράγοντας. 📖 : e.g., secret ~, real estate ~

2.360 grain (n) – (C) tiny piece of sth (e.g., salt, sand, gold, rice, pollen) • *When a bee lands on a flower, tiny ~s of pollen stick to its legs.* ❖ κόκκος, ψήγμα (χρυσού), σπυρί (ρυζιού). *See also* **5.35**.

Flora and fauna 2

2.361 unwittingly (adv) – without knowing or being aware of sth, by accident, unintentionally • *As the door closed behind me, I suddenly realized that I had ~ left my keys on the kitchen table.* ➢ unwitting (adj) ❖ ασυνείδητα, ασυναίσθητα, άθελα

Paragraph 2

2.362 beverage (n) – (C) a drink (especially one other than water) • *Examples of ~s include coffee, tea, beer, wine, and soda.* ❖ ποτό

Choices: Item 1

2.363 flowery (adj) – 1. full of, resembling, or smelling of flowers • *In spring the couple love to walk through ~ fields. / She wore a dress with a ~ pattern. / She likes perfumes with a ~ smell.* ❖ (χωράφι) ολάνθιστος, ανθισμένος · (φόρεμα ή άρωμα) λουλουδάτος, λουλουδένιος 2. (of speech or writing) full of rich and decorative language; same as **florid** • *The writer has a very ~ old-fashioned style which most people find hard to read.* ❖ διανθισμένος, φορτωμένος στολίδια

2.364 flowering (adj) – 1. that produces flowers • *Angiosperms is the technical term for ~ plants.* ❖ ανθοφόρος 2. in bloom • *It was a treat to see the ~ magnolias and lilac trees.* ❖ ανθισμένος

2.365 floral (adj) – 1. containing or made up of flowers • *The ~s decorations at the wedding were lovely.* ❖ λουλουδένιος 2. decorated with or depicting flowers • *She word a light summer dress with a lovely ~ pattern of lilies and orchids.* ❖ λουλουδάτος

2.366 flowered (adj) – decorated with or depicting flowers; same as **floral** (see **2.365**, meaning 2) • *For her birthday, I got her a box of stationery with a ~ border.* ❖ λουλουδάτος

Vocabulary (page 68)

All of the answer choices in questions 21-30 appear in previous entries in this unit. Consult the Alphabetical Word List at the back of the book to locate any words you wish to review.

Reading (page 69)

Paragraph 1

2.367 stimuli (pl n) – see **2.140**

2.368 sketchy (adj) – incomplete, not very detailed • *The witness's description was ~, so police are having a hard time finding the burglar.* ➢ sketch (n, v), sketchily (adv) ❖ πρόχειρος, σε γενικές γραμμές

2.369 predator (n) – see **2.199**

2.370 innately (adv) – natural, inborn • *Animals ~ know how to care for their young; they do not need to be taught how.* ➢ innately (adv) ❖ έμφυτα

2.371 begging call (n phr) – (C) the special cry or sound a young animal makes to signal its parents that it is hungry and wants food • *The ~s of the young chicks kept their parents busy hunting for food.* ❖ η συγκεκριμένη κραυγή ή κάλεσμα του νεαρού ζώου, για να ειδοποιήσει τους γονείς του ότι πεινάει και θέλει τροφή

2.372 tactile (adj) – that can be felt or perceived through one's sense of touch; of or related to the sense of touch • *We receive ~ sensations through the nerve endings in our skin.* ❖ απτός, της αφής

Paragraph 2

2.373 solitary (adj) – living or existing alone, without a companion • *Since his wife died, the old man has chosen to live a ~ life, cutting himself off from friends and family.* ➢ solitude (n) ❖ μοναχικός, ασυντρόφευτος

2.374 court (v) – (animals) behave in a way that is designed to attract another animal as a mate • *Peacocks ~ peahens by parading around with their brilliant tails.* ➢ courting (n, adj) ❖ (ζώα) ερωτοτροπώ, κορτάρω. 📖: e.g., (fig) ~ danger

2.375 rear (v) – care for a young animal or child until it is fully grown • *A tigress will ~ her young cubs for about two years until they can take care of themselves.* ➢ rearing (n) ❖ ανατρέφω, μεγαλώνω

2.376 potential (adj) – see **2.352**

2.377 unambiguous (adj) – clear, open to only one possible interpretation • *Her feelings were ~; she knew with all her heart that she wanted to marry him.* ➢ Opp: ambiguous (adj). ❖ σαφής, ξεκάθαρος, αναμφίβολος

2.378 facilitate (v) – make sth happen more easily • *The male's bright color ~s mating. / Foreign investment has ~d the development of the island's tourist industry.* ➢ facilitation (n), facility (n), facile (adj), facilely (adv) ❖ διευκολύνω

2.379 mating (n) – (animals) the act of coming together with a mate (see **2.324**) to produce young; also known as **breeding** • *Some animals precede ~ with a complex series of gestures, sounds, and movements resembling a strange dance.* ➢ mate (n, v), mating (adj) ❖ ζευγάρωμα, αναπαραγωγή

2.380 breeding (n/adj) – same as **mating** (see **2.379**). See also **2.79** and **2.123**.

2.381 provoke (v) – see **2.246**

2.382 trigger (v) – start, be the cause of sth • *The noisy students ~ed the teacher's anger.* ➢ trigger (n) ❖ προκαλώ

2.383 aggression (n) – (U) angry, violent, or attacking behavior • *Participating in sports is a good way to get rid of your hidden feelings of ~.* ➢ aggressor (n), aggressiveness (n), aggressive (adj) ❖ επιθετικότητα

2.384 posture (n) – (C) (animals) particular pose or position of the body • *When the bird senses danger, it assumes a straight-necked, vertical ~ that makes it look like the surrounding reeds.* ❖ στάση του σώματος. 📖: e.g., a political ~

2.385 swollen (adj) – (of part of the body) larger than normal in size, often due to the presence of excess liquid, eggs, etc. • *The cat's ~ belly was a clear sign that she was about to have kittens.* ➢ swelling (n), swell (v) ❖ πρησμένος

2.386 quiver (v) – see **2.270**

2.387 vibration (n) – (C/U) an instance of /the process of shaking or moving back and forth very rapidly • *As the train passed by, we could feel a ~ under our feet.* ➢ vibrate (v), vibrating (adj) ❖ δόνηση

2.388 fertilize (v) – (male animals) cause the beginning of new life by depositing sperm on one or more female egg cells • *The female fish spawn (i.e., lay their eggs in water), and male fish come along and ~ them.* ➢ fertilization (n), fertilized (adj) ❖ γονιμοποιώ. See also **2.81**.

2.389 latter (adj) – (U) the second of two people or things just mentioned; opposite of **former** • *John and Mary are siblings: the former [i.e., John] is a lawyer and the ~ [i.e., Mary] is a doctor.* ❖ ο δεύτερος (από δύο)

3 Health and medicine

Introduction First day of med school (pages 70-71)

A We've come a long way, baby (page 70)

3.1 **attribute (to)** (v) – (C) say (sth) is caused by • *The doctor ~d all of her health problems to smoking.* ➣ attribution (n), attribute (n) ❖ αποδίδω

3.2 **malevolent** (adj) – evil, intending harm • *There was something ~ in the way the two men looked at us that made our blood run cold.* ➣ malevolence (n), malevolently (adv) ❖ κακόβουλος, μοχθηρός

3.3 **charm** (n) – (C) object or saying that is said to bring good luck or have magical power. • *She carries a rabbit's foot on her keychain as a lucky ~.* ❖ μάγια, φυλακτό. 📖: e.g., a gentleman's ~, a ~ bracelet

3.4 **ward off** (v) – keep away, turn aside • *The villagers fought hard to defend themselves, but they were poorly armed and unable to ~ the invaders.* ❖ αποκρούω, αποτρέπω

3.5 **render** (v) – make, cause to become • *The blow to her head ~ed her unconscious.* ➣ rendering (n) ❖ καθιστώ, κάνω

3.6 **uninhabitable** (adj) – not fit to live in • *With a leaking roof and a basement full of rats, the old house was totally ~.* ➣ uninhabited (adj). Opp: inhabitable (adj) ❖ ακατοίκητος

3.7 **torture** (v) – cause (sb/sth) extreme physical pain (e.g., to punish sb or to force sb to confess) • *It is against the Geneva Convention to ~ prisoners.* ➣ torture (n), tortured (adj), torturous (adj) ❖ βασανίζω

3.8 **starve** (v) – 1. ~ **sb/sth** (v) – keep food away from sb/sth so they suffer from or die of hunger • *In Neolithic times, doctors thought they could cure patients by ~ing them.* 2. ~ (v) – suffer from or die of hunger • *Without food or fresh water, the children in the refugee camp will ~.* ➣ starvation (n), starving (adj), starved (adj) ❖ 1. στερώ το φαγητό (σε κάποιον), αναγκάζω κπ να λιμοκτονήσει 2. υποφέρω ή πεθαίνω από την πείνα

3.9 **expel** (v) – force to leave • *The principle was forced to ~ the poorly behaved student.* ➣ expulsion (n) ❖ αποβάλλω. 📖: e.g., ~ smoke/fumes

3.10 **potion** (n) – (C) any drink or liquid mixture used as a medicine, poison, or magic charm • *Whatever illness I have, my grandmother always recommends her favorite ~ : chamomile tea and honey.* ❖ ρόφημα, φίλτρο

3.11 **induce** (v) – produce, cause, bring about • *Hopefully, the sleeping pills the doctor gave me will ~ sleep.* ➣ inducement (n) ❖ προκαλώ, (επι)φέρω

3.12 **vomiting** (n) → **vomit** (v) – throw up (i.e., bring up matter from the stomach through the mouth) • *Every time they drive up the winding mountain road, she gets car sick and has to ~.* ➣ vomit (n) ❖ ξερνώ

3.13 **drill** (v) – make (a hole/holes) in sth using a tool called a drill • *Before we can hang the book shelves, we'll need to ~ holes in the wall.* ❖ τρυπώ (με τρυπάνι)

3.14 **drive out** (phr v) – similar to **expel** (see 3.9) ❖ διώχνω, εκδιώκω

3.15 **ancestor** (n) – (C) sb in former times who you are descended from, forefather • *His parents were born in the USA, but his great grandparents and other ~s were Russian.* ➣ ancestral (adj) ❖ πρόγονος

3.16 **fractured** (adj) – broken • *The X-ray will show whether or not you've got a ~ rib.* ➣ fracture (n, v) ❖ σπασμένος

3.17 **breakthrough** (n) – (C) important development • *Scientists have made continual ~s in cancer research over the last few decades.* ❖ αποφασιστικό βήμα, εντυπωσιακή ανακάλυψη

3.18 **physician** (n) – (C) medical doctor • *You need to see a ~ about that nasty cough. / The famous quotation "P~, heal thyself!" is attributed to Hippocrates.* ❖ γιατρός

3.19 **unsanitary** (adj) – unclean and unhealthy • *The restaurant owner received a heavy fine for allowing food to be prepared under ~ conditions.* ➣ Opp: sanitary (adj) ❖ ανθυγιεινός

B A sickness by any other name (page 71)
Word bank

3.20 **affliction** (n) – (C) sth that causes great physical or mental suffering • *Poverty is a terrible social ~.* ➣ afflict (v), afflicted (adj) ❖ βάσανο

3.21 **ailment** (n) – (C) minor illness • *The common cold is an ~ that does not compare in seriousness to diseases like cancer and hemophilia.* ➣ ail (v), ailing (adj) ❖ αδιαθεσία, αρρώστια

3.22 **disability** (n) – (C) injury, illness, or condition that restricts the way a person lives • *Luckily, her broken leg is healing well and will not leave her with a permanent ~.* ➣ disable (v), disabled (adj) ❖ αναπηρία, ανικανότητα

3.23 **disease** (n) – (C) specific illness that involves the improper functioning of an organ or system • *Malaria is a parasitic ~ spread by female Anopheles mosquitoes.* ➣ diseased (adj) ❖ αρρώστια, νόσος

3.24 **disorder** (n) – (C) disturbance of the normal workings of the body or mind • *Anorexia nervosa and bulimia are eating ~s.* ❖ διαταραχή

3.25 **illness** (n) – (C) 1. (U) the state of being ill • *Call your child's pediatrician at the first sign of ~.* 2. (C) a specific disease • *If not treated early, lung cancer is a life-threatening ~.* 3. a period of ill health • *He died after a long ~.* ➣ ill (adj) ❖ (ενς. 1-3) ασθένεια

3.26 **impairment** (n) – (U) the state of being damaged, injured, or weakened; (C) a specific condition or injury that prevents the proper functioning of one's eyes, ears, or brain • *(U) People who are partially blind suffer from vision ~. / (C) Nowadays cataracts are not considered to be serious visual ~s.* ❖ εξασθένηση, βλάβη

C What's up, doc? (page 71)
Word bank 1

3.27 **diagnose** (v) – identify the nature of sth by examining symptoms • *The doctor will need to run some tests before he can ~ your problem.* ➣ diagnosis (n), diagnostic (adj) ❖ κάνω διάγνωση

3.28 **fatigue** (n) – (U) extreme tiredness • *It's not like her to feel such ~ ; usually she's full of energy.* ➣ fatigue (v), fatigued (adj) ❖ κόπωση, εξάντληση

3.29 **fever** (n) – (U) higher than normal body temperature • *No wonder your forehead is so hot; you have a high ~.* ➣ feverish (adj), feverishly (adv) ❖ πυρετός

3.30 **fracture** (n) – (C) a crack or break in a hard object or material • *People with osteoporosis run the risk of bone ~s.* ❖ κάταγμα, θλάση, σπάσιμο

Health and medicine 3

3.31 **rash** (n) – (U) red spots on the skin • *He breaks out in a ~ every time he eats strawberries or tomatoes.* ❖ εξάνθημα

3.32 **swelling** (n) – (U) abnormal enlargement of part of the body (e.g., because of built-up fluid) • *The doctor recommended that he put ice on his sprained ankle to reduce the ~.* ➢ swell – swelled – swollen (irreg v), swollen (adj) ❖ πρήξιμο, φλεγμονή

3.33 **symptom** (n) – (C) a sign of the existence of sth (e.g., a disease) • *A runny nose, itchy eyes, and a cough are common ~s of an allergy to dust or pollen.* ➢ symptomatic (adj) ❖ σύμπτωμα

3.34 **tenderness** (n) – (U) soreness, pain • *If you experience ~ on the lower right side of your abdomen, you might have appendicitis.* ➢ tender (adj), tenderly (adv) ❖ πόνος, άλγος. 📖 : e.g., a mother's ~ toward her child

Word bank 2

3.35 **alleviate** (v) – reduce or lessen sth (e.g., pain, misery), making it easier to endure • *Hopefully, the pills the doctor gave me will ~ my pain.* ➢ alleviation (n) ❖ (για πόνο) ανακουφίζω

3.36 **anesthetize** (v) – (Brit: **anaesthetize**) make sb unconscious by giving them an **anesthetic** (i.e., a substance that makes you insensitive to pain) • *Just before the surgeon begins the operation, another doctor will ~ you so you sleep through the operation without feeling any pain.* ➢ anesthetic (n, adj) ❖ αναισθητοποιώ, ναρκώνω

3.37 **cure** (v) – bring about (sb's/sth's) full recovery • *The doctor knew he would not be able to ~ the patient, as the cancer was discovered too late.* ➢ cure (n), curative (adj) ❖ θεραπεύω (δηλ., επιφέρω πλήρη ανάρρωση). *See also* **5.304**.

3.38 **inject** (v) – give sb/sth a drug or medicine by using a syringe/needle • *The woman has diabetes and needs to ~ herself with insulin every day.* ➢ injection (n) ❖ κάνω ένεση

3.39 **operate** (v) – perform surgery • *The surgeon will ~ to repair the patient's blocked artery.* ➢ operation (n) ❖ χειρουργώ

3.40 **prescribe** (v) – (medical) recommend and give written authorization for a medicine or procedure • *The doctor ~d an antibiotic to get rid of my infection.* ➢ prescription (n), prescribed (adj), prescriptive (adj) ❖ διατάσσω

3.41 **preserve** (v) – maintain sth in its original condition • *~ sb's health, ~ wildlife and the wilderness, ~ a painting, ~ food in a fresh state* ➢ preservation (n), preservative (n, adj), preserved (adj) ❖ συντηρώ, διατηρώ

3.42 **set – set – set** (irreg v) – (of broken bones) put the pieces back in place so sth can heal properly • *The doctor carefully ~ the patient's arm and then put a cast on it so it the broken bone would stay in place.* ➢ setting (n) ❖ (κόκαλο) βάζω στη θέση του. 📖 : ~ the table, ~ a jewel in a ring

3.43 **stitch** (v) – (also **suture**) sew a wound closed with loops of thread known as **stitches/sutures** • *That's a nasty cut. The doctor will have to ~ it up for you.* ➢ stitch (n) ❖ (πληγή) ράβω, βάζω ράμματα

3.44 **treat** (v) – give medical care to • *After the fire, the doctors ~ed several burn victims.* ➢ treatment (n) ❖ υποβάλλω σε θεραπεία, περιθάλπω, νοσηλεύω. 📖 : e.g., ~ sb to a meal, ~ sth with a chemical

Writing (1) Paragraph development (page 73)

Warm-up (page 73)

3.45 **influenza** (n) – (U) common viral illness; same as **flu** • *Among the common symptoms of ~ are high fever, runny nose, sore throat, aching muscles, and a dry cough.* ❖ γρίπη

3.46 **germ** (n) – (C) microscopic organism that causes disease; same as **microbe** • *That cold may be catching. Why don't you stay home so you don't give your ~s to everyone at work?* ➢ germicide (n) ❖ μικρόβιο

3.47 **communicable** (adj) – (disease) able to be passed (or communicated) from one person to another • *The common cold and the flu are common ~ diseases.* ➢ communication (n), communicate (v) ❖ μεταδοτικός

3.48 **contagious** (adj) – catching, able to be spread by direct or indirect contact • *The flu virus that's going around is highly ~ ; half the school is out sick.* ➢ contagion (n) ❖ μεταδοτικός

Ⓐ Try it! (page 73)

3.49 **non-infectious** (adj) – not contagious (*see* **3.48**) • *Cancer is a ~ disease; it cannot be spread from one person to another.* ❖ μη μεταδοτικός

3.50 **mortality** (n) – (U) (in context) death, loss of life; also (U), the state of being mortal (able to die) • *After coming face to face with his own ~ during the car accident, he has a new appreciation of what it means to be alive.* ➢ mortal (n, adj), mortally (adv). Opp: immortality (n) ❖ θνησιμότητα

3.51 **industrialized** (adj) – having highly developed industries • *Japan and Germany are examples of ~ countries.* ➢ industry (n), industrialization (n), industrialize (v) ❖ βιομηχανοποιημένος

3.52 **exposure** (n) – (U) the state of being **exposed** to sth (i.e., open to being influenced by sth) • *Repeated ~ to the sun's ultraviolet rays may lead to skin cancer. / Most children have little or no ~ to classical music when they are growing up.* ➢ expose (v), exposed (adj) ❖ έκθεση

3.53 **susceptible (to)** (adj) – easily influenced, harmed, or affected by (sth) • *A sickly child is ~ to respiratory infections. / A lonely woman is ~ to the charms of a handsome man.* ➢ susceptibility (n) ❖ ευαίσθητος, ευπαθής, ευεπηρέαστος, ευάλωτος

3.54 **chronic** (adj) – (of illnesses) lasting for a long time or constantly recurring • *Sooner or later most smokers develop a ~ cough.* ❖ χρόνιος

3.55 **fatal** (adj) – ending in death or disaster • *a ~ traffic accident, a ~ mistake* ➢ fatality (n), fatally (adv) ❖ θανατηφόρος, μοιραίος

Vocabulary (1) Anatomy 101 (pages 74-77)

Ⓐ In the beginning (page 74)

The two texts in this section contain a number of anatomical/technical terms that are adequately explained in the course book. For the sake of brevity, the entries for these words are marked with a star symbol (★) and include only derivatives (where they exist) and Greek equivalents. For explanations in English, please consult the relevant text in the course book.

3 Health and medicine

Text 1

3.56 sum (n) – (C) combined total amount of sth when all its parts are added together • *It's a basic principle of geometry that the whole is equal to the ~ of its parts.* ➢ sum up (phr v) ❖ σύνολο

3.57 cell (n) – (C) smallest unit of living matter • *If you look at blood ~s and muscle ~s under a microscope, you can see how different they are. / An amoeba consists of only one ~.* ➢ cellular (adj) ❖ κύτταρο

3.58 fertilization (n) – (U) (animals) the action or process of a male sperm cell combining with the nucleus of a female egg cell • *After ~, a new life begins to develop.* ➢ fertilize (v), fertilized (adj), fertile (adj) ❖ γονιμοποίηση. 📖 : e.g. ~ of the soil

3.59 nucleus (n) – (C) the central part of sth (e.g., a cell, an atom) • *The ~ of an egg cell contains the female's genetic material. / The ~ of an atom contains neutrons and protons.* ➢ nuclei (pl n), nuclear (adj) ❖ πυρήνας

3.60 ★ sperm (n) – (C) ➢ sperm (pl n) ❖ σπέρμα, σπερματόζωο

3.61 ★ ovum (n) – (C) ➢ ova (pl n) ❖ ωάριο

3.62 ★ zygote (n) – (C) ❖ ζυγωτό

3.63 hereditary (adj) – related to **heredity** (i.e., the passing on of characteristics from parent to child); inherited, passed on • *A child's ~ characteristics are determined by the genes he gets from both his parents.* ➢ heredity (n) ❖ κληρονομικός

3.64 ★ chromosome (n) – (C) ❖ χρωμόσωμα

3.65 ★ gene (n) – (C) ➢ genetic (adj), genetically (adv) ❖ γονίδιο

3.66 incorporate (v) – (used passively in text) combine or mix one or more things (e.g., ingredients) to create a mixture • *To make the sauce, slowly ~ the chicken broth into the mixture of flour and butter* ❖ ενσωματώνω/-ομαι, αναμειγνύω, ανακατώνω. *See also* **5.122**.

3.67 blueprint (n) – (C) (used figuratively in the text) building plan, architectural drawing • *As my father was a freelance architect, we got used to him working at home with his massive ~s spread out all over the dining room table.* ❖ κυανοτυπία, πρωτότυπο, σχέδιο

Choices a–j

3.68 matter (n) – (U) material, substance • *There are three types of ~ : solids, liquids, and gases. / All living ~ contains DNA.* ❖ ύλη, ουσία

3.69 reproductive (adj) – related to **reproduction** (i.e., the process of producing young plants or animals) • *The human ~ system begins to function during adolescence (i.e., just before or during your teenage years).* ➢ reproduction (n), reproduce (v) ❖ αναπαραγωγικός

3.70 conception (n) – (U) (biology) the act of **conceiving** (i.e., becoming pregnant; forming a new life through the union of a female and male reproductive cells) • *In humans, the average pregnancy (from the moment of ~ to the moment of birth) lasts nine months.* ➢ conceive (v) ❖ σύλληψη

Text 2 (page 74)

3.71 hollow (adj) – empty, unfilled • *The old tree had a ~ space in its trunk where a bird had made its nest.* ➢ hollowness (n), hollowly (adv) ❖ κούφιος, κοίλος. 📖 : e.g., ~ cheeks, a ~ promise, a ~ victory

3.72 ★ blastula (n) – (C) ❖ βλαστίδιο

3.73 ★ uterus (n) – (C) ➢ uterine (adj) ❖ μήτρα

3.74 ★ embryo (n) – (C) ➢ embryonic (adj) ❖ έμβρυο (στα πρώτα στάδια της ανάπτυξης). 📖 : e.g., (fig) the ~ of an idea

3.75 ★ fetus (n) – (C) (Brit: **foetus**) fetal (adj) ❖ έμβρυο (στα προχωρημένα στάδια)

3.76 infant (n) – (C) very young child, up to about two years old • *Human ~s take roughly nine months to develop within their mother's body.* ➢ infantile (adj) ❖ βρέφο

3.77 ★ amniotic sac (n phr) – (C) ❖ αμνιακός σάκος

3.78 nourishment (n) – (U) food or other substances needed for health, growth, survival, etc. • *After birth, a young mammal receives ~ from its mother's milk.* ➢ nourish (v), nourishing (adj) ❖ θρέψη, τροφή

3.79 ★ umbilical cord (n phr) – (C) ❖ ομφάλιος λώρος

3.80 tissue (n) – (C) (anatomy) group of similar cells that perform the same function • *If the cancer cells spread, they will affect healthy ~ elsewhere in the body.* ❖ ιστός. 📖 : e.g., ~ paper, a box of ~s

3.81 bud (v) – appear and begin to develop • *On the ultrasound, you could clearly see that the embryo's arms and legs had begun to ~.* ➢ bud (n), budding (adj) ❖ πρωτοεμφανίζομαι και αρχίζω να αναπτύσσομαι

B All systems go! (page 75)

Word bank

3.82 circulatory (adj) – (biology) related to or affecting **circulation** (i.e., the flow of blood/sap through an animal/plant) • *The heart is the center of an animal's ~ system.* ➢ circulation (n), circulate (v) ❖ κυκλοφοριακός

3.83 digestive (adj) – (biology) related to or affecting **digestion** (i.e., the process by which food is broken up into simple chemical substances that nourish the body) • *The ~ process begins in the mouth when food is broken down by the teeth and mixes with saliva.* ➢ digestion (n), digest (v) ❖ πεπτικός

3.84 muscular (adj) – (biology) related to or affecting the **muscles** • *M~ dystrophy is a disease that causes the muscles to gradually become weak and waste away.* ➢ muscle (n) ❖ μυϊκός. 📖 : e.g., a ~ build

3.85 nervous (adj) – (biology) related to or affecting the **nerves** • *The brain and spinal cord are at the heart of the central ~ system.* ➢ nerve (n) ❖ νευρικός. 📖

3.86 respiratory (adj) – (biology) related to or affecting **respiration** (i.e., breathing) • *Asthma is a serious ~ condition which must be closely monitored by a doctor.* ➢ respiration (n), respirator (n), respire (v) ❖ αναπνευστικός

3.87 skeletal (adj) – (biology) related to or affecting the **skeleton** • *The ~ system is the framework of bone and other hard tissues that support and protect an animal's body.* ➢ skeleton (n) ❖ σκελετικός. 📖 : e.g., a ~ child

Texts 1–5 (pages 75–77)

The five texts in this section contain many anatomical/technical terms that are explained in the text. For the sake of brevity, the entries for these words are marked with a star symbol (★) and include only derivatives (where they exist) and Greek equivalents. For explanations in English, please consult the relevant text in the course book.

Health and medicine 3

Text 1 (page 75)

3.88 bind – bound – bound (irreg v) – (used passively in text) hold or fasten together, often with a rope • *Tough bands of tissue known as ligaments ~ the muscles together. / The kidnappers decided to ~ their captive's arms and legs to prevent him from escaping.* ➢ bond (n), bound (adj), binding (adj) ❖ δένω

3.89 ★ **ligament** (n) – (C) ❖ σύνδεσμος

3.90 ★ **joint** (n) – (C) ❖ άρθρωση

3.91 contraction (n) – (U) (biology – muscles) the process of **contracting** (i.e., becoming shorter and tighter); also, (C) a tightening or shortening of the muscle • *During childbirth a woman experiences painful ~s of the uterus.* ➢ contract (v). Opp: expansion (n) ❖ συστολή. 📖 : e.g., ~ of metal

3.92 ★ **tendon** (n) – (C) ➢ tendonitis (n) ❖ τένοντας

3.93 ★ **bone marrow** (n phr) – (U) ❖ μυελός, μεδούλι

3.94 ★ **blood corpuscle** (n phr) – (C) ❖ αιμοσφαίριο, αιμοκύτταρο

Text 2 (page 75)

3.95 network (n) – (C) large system of connected parts or pathways (e.g., nerves, wires, roads) that cross each other like the lines of a net • *The nervous system is a vast and complex ~.* ➢ network (v) ❖ δίκτυο

3.96 ★ **neuron** (n) – (C) (Brit: **neurone**) ➢ neurology (n), neurologist (n), neural (adj) ❖ νευρώνας, νευρικό κύτταρο

3.97 transfer (v) – move sth/sb from one place to another • *Our bodies are wired to ~ sensory messages to and from the brain via the nervous system. / The impulse ~s from one neuron to another.* ➢ transfer (n), transferable (adj) ❖ μεταφέρω/-ομαι

3.98 sensory (adj) – related to the **senses** or **sensation** • *The skin is our largest ~ organ.* ➢ sense (n, v), sensitivity (n), sensitive (adj) ❖ αισθητήριος

3.99 involuntary (adj) – (biology) done or occurring without conscious thought or intent; same as **automatic** • *Digestion and hormone production are ~ processes.* ➢ Opp: voluntary (adj) ❖ ακούσιος

3.100 process (n) – (C) series of natural actions that produce change or development • *the digestive ~, the evolutionary ~, the aging ~* ➢ process (v) ❖ διαδικασία, πορεία

3.101 digestion (n) – see **3.83**

3.102 ★ **central nervous system** (n phr) – (C) ❖ κεντρικό νευρικό σύστημα

3.103 ★ **spinal cord** (n phr) – (C) ❖ νωτιαίος μυελό

3.104 ★ **peripheral nervous system** (n phr) – (C) ❖ περιφερειακό νευρικό σύστημα

3.105 ★ **cerebrum** (n) – (C) ➢ cerebral (adj) ❖ εγκέφαλος

3.106 ★ **cerebral cortex** (n phr) – (C) ❖ εγκεφαλικός φλοιός

3.107 ★ **brain stem** (n phr) – (C) (also **brainstem**) ❖ στέλεχος εγκεφάλου

3.108 ★ **cerebellum** (n) – (C) ❖ παρεγκεφαλίδα

Text 3 (page 76)

3.109 dual (adj) – double, twofold (i.e., consisting of two parts or elements) • *Hybrid cars today have a ~ fuel system: a traditional gas-burning engine and an electric, battery-powered motor that operates at low speeds.* ➢ duality (n), dually (adj) ❖ διπλός

3.110 nutrient-laden (adj phr) – full of **nutrients** (i.e., chemical substances that provide nourishment and help maintain life) • *Young mammals survive on their mothers' ~ milk.* ❖ γεμάτος θρεπτικές ουσίες

3.111 four-chambered (adj) → **chamber** (n) – (C) (heart) one of four hollow areas that the heart is composed of • *Blood flows into and out of the heart through a series of four ~s called auricles and ventricles.* ❖ θάλαμος

3.112 pump (v) – force sth (e.g., a liquid or gas) to flow in a certain direction • *The heart ~s blood throughout the body's complex circulatory system.* ➢ pump (n), pumping (adj) ❖ αντλώ

3.113 ★ **lung** (n) – (C) ❖ πνεύμονας

3.114 ★ **blood vessel** (n phr) – (C) ❖ αιμοφόρο αγγείο

3.115 flow (v) – move freely in a steady, unbroken stream • *blood ~s through the body; a river ~s through the countryside; traffic ~s along a highway* ➢ flow (n), flowing (adj), flowingly (adv) ❖ ρέω, κυλώ

3.116 ★ **artery** (n) – (C) ➢ arterial (adj) ❖ αρτηρία

3.117 ★ **vein** (n) – (C) ➢ veiny (adj), venous (adj) ❖ φλέβα

3.118 oxygenation (n) – (U) the process of adding oxygen to sth • *O~ of the blood takes place in the lungs.* ➢ oxygen (n), oxygenated (adj) ❖ οξυγόνωση

3.119 ★ **capillary** (n) – (C) ❖ τριχοειδές αιμοφόρο αγγείο

Text 4 (page 76)

3.120 suck (v) – (used passively in text) draw/take in sth (e.g., air or a liquid) by creating a vacuum • *While swimming he accidentally ~ed water into his nose, which made him cough.* ❖ ρουφώ

3.121 ★ **trachea** (n) – (C) same as **windpipe** ❖ τραχεία (σωλήνας αέρος)

3.122 ★ **bronchus** (n) – (C) ➢ bronchi (pl n), bronchitis (n) ❖ βρόγχος

3.123 ★ **lung** (n) – see **3.113**

3.124 tube (n) – (C) long, hollow, cylindrical structure • *Blood flows through the body via specialized ~s known as arteries, veins, and capillaries.* ➢ tubular (adj) ❖ σωλήνας

3.125 ★ **bronchiole** (n) – (C) ❖ βρογχιόλιο

3.126 ★ **alveolus** (n) – (C) ➢ alveoli (pl n) ❖ κυψελίδα, φατνίο

3.127 ★ **capillary** (n) – see **3.119**

3.128 inhalation (n) – (U) the action of or (C) an act of **inhaling** (i.e., breathing in) • *The old man's lungs are so weak that each ~ is a struggle for him.* ➢ inhale (v). Opp: exhalation (n) ❖ εισπνοή

3.129 exhalation (n) – (U) the action of or (C) an act of **exhaling** (i.e., breathing out) • *During ~, we breathe out carbon dioxide.* ❖ εκπνοή

3.130 ★ **diaphragm** (n) – (C) ❖ διάφραγμα

Text 5 (page 77)

3.131 absorb (v) – (used passively in text) take/draw in, soak up • *The body's tissues ~ nutrients provided by food which has been broken down during the digestive process. / The dry soil quickly ~ed the falling rain.* ➢ absorption (n), absorbent (adj), absorbed (adj), absorbing (adj) ❖ απορροφώ

3 Health and medicine

3.132 ★ **saliva** (n) – (U) ❖ σάλιο
3.133 ★ **salivary gland** (n phr) – (C) ❖ σιελογόνοι αδένες
3.134 ★ **tongue** (n) – (C) ❖ γλώσσα
3.135 ★ **esophagus** (n) – (C) (Brit: **oesophagus**) ❖ οισοφάγος
3.136 ★ **stomach** (n) – (C) ❖ στομάχι
3.137 ★ **gastric acid** (n phr) – (U) ❖ γαστρικό οξύ
3.138 ★ **small intestine** (n phr) – (C) ❖ λεπτό έντερο
3.139 ★ **enzyme** (n) – (C) ❖ ένζυμο
3.140 ★ **liver** (n) – (C) ❖ συκώτι
3.141 ★ **abdominal cavity** (n phr) – (C) (same as **abdomen**) area of a vertebrate's body that contains the digestive organs • *The ~ contains the stomach, liver, and other digestive organs.* ❖ κοιλιακή χώρα
3.142 ★ **bile** (n) – (U) ❖ χολή
3.143 ★ **gall bladder** (n phr) – (C) ❖ χοληδόχος κύστη
3.144 ★ **pancreas** (n) – (C) ❖ πάγκρεας
3.145 **fluid** (n) – (C) liquid • *Since her stomach operation, the patient has only been allowed to drink ~s; solid food will be reintroduced next week.* ➢ fluidity (n), fluidly (adv) ❖ υγρό, ρευστή ουσία
3.146 **starch** (n) – (C) white tasteless substance found in plants like potatoes, rice, wheat, and other cereals • *Like sugar and cellulose, starch is a carbohydrate ($C_6O_{12}H_6$) and an important source of energy for humans and other animals.* ➢ starchy (adj) ❖ άμυλο
3.147 ★ **large intestine** (n phr) – (C) ❖ παχύ έντερο
3.148 **mineral** (n) – (C) inorganic substance that plants and animals need to stay healthy • *To ensure she gets all the nutrients she needs, she takes a multivitamin supplement that also includes ~s like zinc, iron, and phosphorous.* ❖ μεταλλικό στοιχείο
3.149 ★ **rectum** (n) – (C) ➢ rectal (adj) ❖ ορθό έντερο

C Other systems in brief (page 77)

Word bank

3.150 ★ **endocrine system** (n phr) – (C) ❖ ενδοκρινές σύστημα
3.151 ★ **immune system** (n phr) – (C) ❖ ανοσοποιητικό σύστημα
3.152 ★ **reproductive system** (n phr) – (C) ❖ αναπαραγωγικό σύστημα
3.153 ★ **urinary system** (n phr) – (C) ❖ ουροποιητικό σύστημα

Items 1-4

3.154 ★ **antigen** (n) – (C) ❖ αντιγόνο
3.155 ★ **phagocyte** (n) – (C) ❖ φαγοκύτταρο
3.156 ★ **macrophage** (n) – (C) ❖ μακροφάγο
3.157 **surround** (v) – be or exist all around sth/sb • *Rose bushes ~ the four sides of the house.* ➢ surroundings (pl n), surrounding (adj) ❖ περιβάλλω, (περι)κυκλώνω
3.158 ★ **lymphocyte** (n) – (C) ❖ λεμφοκύτταρο
3.159 ★ **antibody** (n) – (C) ❖ αντίσωμα
3.160 ★ **urine** (n) – (C) ❖ ούρα
3.161 ★ **kidney** (n) – (C) ❖ νεφρό
3.162 ★ **bladder** (n) – (C) ❖ κύστη
3.163 **expel** (v) – *see* **3.9**

3.164 **secrete** (v) – (body parts, plants) produce a liquid substance (e.g., hormones, sweat) • *glands ~ hormones; a tree ~s sap* ➢ secretion (n) ❖ εκκρίνω.
3.165 ★ **gland** (n) – (C) ➢ glandular (adj) ❖ αδένας
3.166 ★ **pancreas** (n) – *see* **3.144**
3.167 ★ **pituitary** (n) – (C) ❖ υπόφυση
3.168 ★ **thyroid** (n) – (C) ❖ θυρεοειδής αδένας
3.169 ★ **adrenal** (n) – (C) ➢ adrenaline (n) ❖ επινεφρίδιο

Cloze Easily confused words and word forms (page 81-83)

CLOZE PRACTICE (1): Easily confused word forms (page 82)
STEP 2: Text

3.170 **drove** (n) – (C) (often plural) (fig) very large number of people or animals • *D~s of tourists visit the Greek islands every year.* ❖ πλήθος κόσμου
3.171 **screen** (v) – test for the presence or absence of sth (e.g., a disease) • *The clinic in our neighborhood ~s patients for diabetes and high cholesterol.* ➢ screening (n) ❖ εξετάζω
3.172 **contract** (v) – (of diseases) catch, pick up • *Did you know that you can ~ AIDS from a contaminated blood transfusion?* ❖ προσβάλλομαι από, κολλάω. *See also* **2.137**.
3.173 **presumed** (adj) – supposed, probable, likely • *Mechanical problems are the ~ cause of the tragic plane crash.* ➢ presumption (n), presume (v), presumable (adj), presumably (adv) ❖ υποτιθέμενος
3.174 **eradicate** (v) – destroy completely, wipe out • *The world will be a better place if we ever manage to ~ crime, poverty, racism, and disease.* ➢ eradication (n) ❖ εξαλείφω, εξολοθρεύω, εξαφανίζω

Choices: Items 1-5
Item 2

3.175 **fatality** (n) – (C) an occurrence of death (usually as a result of war, accident, or disease); also, a victim of a war, accident, or disease • *In the latest outbreak of avian flu, health officials reported only one ~.* ➢ fatal (adj), fatally (adv) ❖ θάνατος, θύμα πολέμου, θανατηφόρου ατυχήματος ή αρρώστιας
3.176 **fatalistic** (adj) – believing in the idea that you have no control over what happens to you • *If you're unhappy with your job, you need to go out and find a new one. Sitting around and being ~ will get you nowhere!* ➢ fate (n), fated (adj) fatalistically (adv) ❖ μοιρολατρικός
3.177 **deathly** (adj) – like or suggesting death (i.e., very quiet or very pale) • *A ~ silence filled the room when the explosion was heard. / The doctor was concerned by the patient's ~ pallor (i.e., pale color caused by death, disease, or fear).* ➢ death (n), die (v), dead (adj), deadly (adj) ❖ νεκρικός
3.178 **deadly** (adj) – likely or able to cause death • *A pistol is a ~ weapon. / The policeman is said to be a good shot with ~ aim.* ➢ *see previous entry* ❖ θανατηφόρος, φονικός

Item 3
Note: Choices a, c, and d are derivatives of choice b:
3.179 **eradicate** (v) – *see* **3.174**

Item 4
3.180 **resurgence** (n) – (C/U) a fresh, strong reappearance of sth after a period of inactivity, unpopularity, etc. • *The actor made some bad movies over the last decade, but he is currently enjoying a ~ of popularity.* ➢ resurge (v), resurgent (adj) ❖ ξαναζωντάνεμα, επαναδραστηριοποίηση

Health and medicine 3

3.181 **resurgent** (adj) – occurring strongly again after a period of inactivity, unpopularity, etc. • *September 11th sparked a wave of ~ patriotism in many Americans.* ➢ see **3.180**
❖ αναδυόμενος, αναζωπυρούμενος

3.182 **stimulated** (adj) – active, energetic, full of life • *Action movies always leave her feeling ~.* ➢ stimulant (n), stimulation (n), stimulate (v), stimulating (adj) ❖ ζωηρός, ενεργητικός

3.183 **stimulation** (n) → from **stimulate** (v) – activate, arouse, excite, encourage sth to begin or to develop further • *A good teacher knows how to ~ interesting discussions. / Coffee contains caffeine, which ~s the body.* ➢ see previous entry
❖ κεντρίζω, παρακινώ, διεγείρω

Item 5
Note: Choices a, b, and c are derivative forms of choice d:

3.184 **withdraw – withdrew – withdrawn** (irreg v) → ~ **sb/sth (from sth)** – move or take sb/sth back or away • *a general ~s his defeated soldiers from the battlefield, a company ~s a product from the market, a bank client ~s money from an account* ➢ withdrawal (n), withdrawn (adj) ❖ αποσύρω, ανακαλώ, αποχωρώ

CLOZE PRACTICE (2): Easily confused words (page 83)
STEP 2: Passage

3.185 ★ **pertussis** (n) – (U) ❖ κοκίτης

3.186 **widespread** (adj) – found or distributed over a large area or number of people • *Health officials are taking measures to prevent the epidemic from becoming more ~. / The environmentalist is against the ~ use of chemicals in agriculture.* ❖ πλατιά διαδεδομένος

3.187 **vaccination** (n) – 1. (U) the practice of introducing a substance into the body to protect it against disease • *Many countries enforce mandatory ~ of school-age children.* 2. (C) an act of this • *Before traveling to Asia, check with the appropriate embassy to see if you need a typhoid, tetanus, or other ~.* ➢ vaccine (n), vaccinate (v), vaccinated (adj)
❖ 1. εμβολιασμός, 2. εμβόλιο

3.188 **immunity (to sth)** (n) – (U) the state of being protected or unable to be harmed or influenced by sth • *~ to disease, diplomatic ~* ➢ immunization (n), immune (adj)
❖ ανοσία, ασυλία

3.189 **low-grade fever** (n phr) – (usually singular) a fever that is slightly above normal • *The baby is running a ~ of 99.8° F; if it goes over 100°, call the doctor immediately.*
➢ χαμηλός πυρετός

3.190 **runny nose** (n phr) – (C) producing more mucus than normal • *A lot of people have ~s and itchy eyes in springtime.*
❖ μύτη που τρέχει, συνάχι

3.191 **render** (v) – see **3.5**

3.192 **contagious** (adj) – see **3.48**

Choices: Items 1-6
Item 1

3.193 **go back** (phr v) – return • *My Irish friend Michael is planning to ~ to Ireland in the spring.* ❖ γυρίζω πίσω

3.194 **go away** (phr v) – 1. disappear, fade, become weaker or less intense • *My uncle smoked a cigar in my house yesterday, and I can't get the smell to ~.* 2. get out, leave • *How dare you come into my room without knocking. G~!* 3. leave and go somewhere else (often for a short time – e.g., on a trip) • *Did you ~ last weekend?* ❖ 1. εξαφανίζομαι, εξασθενίζω 2. φεύγω 3. φεύγω (σε ταξίδι κλπ)

3.195 **go down** (phr v) – become less/lower • *Prices of prescription drugs always go up; they never ~.* ❖ μειώνομαι

3.196 **go off** (phr v) – 1. explode (e.g., bombs, fireworks) or fire (e.g., a gun) • *Don't touch the gun! It might be loaded and ~!* 2. deteriorate, spoil, go bad • *If you don't put the milk back in the refrigerator, it will ~.* ❖ 1. εκρήγνυμαι, σκάω 2. χαλώ.
📖: e.g., ~ (alarms)

Item 2

3.197 **resistant** (adj) – unaffected, able to stand up to or withstand sth/sb without being damaged or affected • *a ~ strain of bacteria, a vaccine which makes people ~ to a certain disease, a water-~ watch* ➢ resistance (n), resist (v), resistantly (adv) ❖ ανθεκτικός. 📖: e.g., be ~ to new ideas

3.198 **defiant** (adj) – disrespectful, challenging, rebellious • *He gave his mother a ~ look to show her that he did not intend to obey her.* ➢ defiance (n), defy (v), defiantly (adj). Opp: obedient (adj) ❖ προκλητικός, αψηφών

3.199 **consistent** (adj) – unchanging, steady • *He's a ~ student, who always scores around 85% in every subject.*
➢ consistency (n), consistently (adv) ❖ συνεπής, σταθερός

3.200 **persistent** (adj) – continuing non-stop, chronic • *a ~ cough, ~ rain, a ~ salesman, ~ questions* ➢ persistence (n), persist (v), persistently (adv) ❖ επίμονος, αδιάκοπος

Item 3

3.201 **infestation (of sth)** (n) – (C) invasion of large numbers of insects, small animals, or (fig) people in a place • *An ~ of termites forced them to find a new apartment. / In August, European beaches experience an ~ of tourists!* ➢ infest (v), infested (adj) ❖ προσβολή από πλήθος, εντόμων ή μικρών ζώων

3.202 **inflammation** (n) – (C/U) redness, swelling, and soreness in part of the body, especially due to infection • *If the ~ in your eye gets worse, you should see a doctor.* ➢ inflame (v), inflamed (adj) ❖ φλεγμονή

3.203 **infection** (adj) – (C) disease caused by harmful bacteria; also, (U/C) the action/an act of bacteria entering the body and causing disease ➢ infect (v), infectious (adj), infected (adj)
❖ μολυσματική ασθένεια, μόλυνση

3.204 **infraction** (adj) – (U/C) the action/an act of breaking a law or rule • *Parking illegally is a minor ~ of the law.*
❖ παράβαση, παραβίαση

Item 4

3.205 **wear out** (phr v) – become weak, thin, or useless • *jeans or shoes ~ and must be thrown away* ❖ φθείρω/-ομαι (σαν παλιά ρούχα)

3.206 **wear off** (phr v) – become ineffective, disappear • *When the effects of the anesthetic ~, you'll be in great pain.*
❖ περνάω, εξαφανίζω/-ομαι (σαν πόνος ή αναισθησία)

3.207 **wear away** (phr v) – become thin and hard to see • *The path up the mountain will ~ if so many people continue to use it.* ➢ worn-away (adj) ❖ φθείρω/-ομαι (σαν μονοπάτι)

35

3 Health and medicine

3.208 wear down (phr v) – become weak, tired, or strained • *If the doctors don't cure her soon, the disease will ~ the old woman. / If they keep up the air attack, the enemy forces will quickly ~ the defending army.* ❖ καταβάλλω, κάμπτω (την αντίσταση)

Item 5

3.209 on the wane (prep phr) – decreasing, becoming weaker or less • *Now that the scandal is public knowledge, the politician's popularity is definitely ~.* ❖ στη χάση, σε παρακμή

3.210 on the verge of (prep phr) – at or close to the point where sth is about to begin or happen • *countries ~ war / scientists ~ a new discovery* ❖ στο χείλος, στα πρόθυρα

3.211 on the rise (prep phr) – increasing, becoming stronger or more • *Gas prices are ~ again, so I'm thinking of selling my car and getting a bicycle!* ❖ σε άνοδο

3.212 on the move (prep phr) – 1. moving, in motion • *The general has given the order to attack and the army is ~.* ❖ σε κίνηση 2. constantly in motion • *Cell phones are designed for people who are always ~.* ❖ διαρκώς σε κίνηση

Item 6

3.213 unvaccinated (adj) – not immunized • *The doctors rounded up all the ~ children, and made sure they received a dose of polio vaccine.* ➤ see **3.187** ❖ που δεν έχει εμβολιαστεί

3.214 irresistible (adj) – charming, attractive • *Finding the handsome young man ~, she gladly agreed to go out with him.* ❖ ακατανίκητος, ακαταμάχητος

3.215 resisting (adj) – opposing, fighting back • *The ~ forces are putting up a good fight; it looks like they may win the battle.* ➤ resistance (n), resist (v), resistant (adj) ❖ που αντιστέκεται

3.216 inoculated (adj) – immunized, vaccinated (i.e., protected against disease after having received a **vaccination** – see **3.187**) ➤ inoculation (n), inoculate (v) ❖ εμβολιασμένος

Vocabulary (2)   In sickness and in health … (pages 84-86)

A Sicknesses and symptoms (pages 84-85)
Word bank

The starred (★) entries below are diseases that are explained at length in the text. For the sake of brevity, the entries for these words include only derivatives, where they exist, and Greek equivalents. For explanations in English, please consult the relevant texts in the course book.

3.217 ★ arteriosclerosis (n) – (U) ❖ αρτηριοσκλήρωση

3.218 ★ epilepsy (n) – (U) ➤ epileptic (adj) ❖ επιληψία

3.219 ★ hemophilia (n) – (Brit: **haemophilia**) ➤ hemophiliac (n) ❖ αιμοφιλία

3.220 ★ sinusitis (n) – (U) ➤ sinus (n) ❖ ιγμορίτιδα

3.221 ★ sleeping sickness (n phr) – (U) ❖ ασθένεια του ύπνου (τρυπανοσωμίαση)

3.222 ★ stroke (n) – (C) ➤ strike (n), stricken (adj) ❖ εγκεφαλικό, εγκεφαλική συμφόρηση. 📖 : e.g., *a ~ of luck, a ~ on the head, the ~ of a brush*

Text 1 (page 84)

3.223 afflicted (pp) → **be ~ with** (v phr) – be made to suffer from sth terrible (e.g., trouble, pain, disease) • *He was ~ with cancer for ten long years.* ➤ affliction (n), afflict (v) ❖ βασανίζομαι · υποφέρω από, βασανίζομαι από

3.224 grim (adj) – depressing, gloomy, extremely unpleasant • *The news in the Middle East is ~ again; there's been another suicide bombing. / The forecast calls for a ~ weekend: rainy and cold.* ❖ δυσοίωνος, ζοφερός, απαίσιος

3.225 toll (n) – (U) number killed or injured • *The number of victims is still unknown. Officials fear that the ~ from yesterday's earthquake may reach two thousand or more.* ❖ (μετ) φόρος αίματος. 📖 : e.g., *pay a bridge/highway ~*

3.226 rank (v) – classify or put in a certain group or order (e.g., of importance or preference) • *The teacher put the names of three countries on the board and asked us to ~ them in order of size.* ➤ rank (n), (high-/low-)ranking (adj) ❖ κατατάσσω, ιεραρχώ

3.227 numbness (n) – (U) loss of physical feeling • *She experiences ~ in her fingers and toes whenever it's cold outside.* ➤ numb (v, adj) ❖ μούδιασμα

3.228 dimness (n) – (U) lack of brightness • *D~ of vision could be a sign of serious illness. / The ~ of the cloudy day depressed her.* ➤ dim (v, adj), dimly (adv). Opp: brightness (n) ❖ θολούρα, θαμπάδα

3.229 dizziness (n) – (U) light-headed, spinning feeling • *A wave of ~ suddenly came over her; she felt as if the room were spinning out of control.* ➤ dizzy (adj), dizzily (adv) ❖ ζαλάδα

3.230 coordination (n) – (U) ability to control arms and legs • *It takes almost a year before babies have enough ~ to begin to walk.* ➤ coordinator (n), coordinate (v), (un)coordinated (adj) ❖ συντονισμός. 📖 : e.g., *the ~ of a meeting*

Text 2 (page 84)

3.231 seizure (n) – (C) (same as **convulsion**) sudden attack of epilepsy • *In many cases, epileptic ~s can now be controlled with medication.* ➤ seize (n) ❖ σπασμός. 📖 : e.g., *the ~ of one's property*

3.232 underlying (adj) – (fig) basic, fundamental; also (lit) hidden beneath the surface • *If you look deeper, you'll see the ~ motive for the murder was simply greed.* ➤ underlie (v) ❖ βαθύτερος

3.233 lesion (n) – (C) (medical) wound, injury, sore • *The MRI showed that the patient had several ~s on the brain.* ❖ κάκωση, αλλοίωση

3.234 consciousness (n) – (U) state of being awake and aware; knowing what is happening around you • *When the anesthetic wears off, the patient will regain ~.* ➤ conscious (adj), consciously (adv). Opp: unconsciousness (n) ❖ συναίσθηση, το να έχω τις αισθήσεις (μου). 📖 : e.g., *national ~*

3.235 jerking (n) – (U) sudden quick movement • *If you feel a ~ on the line, it means you've caught a fish.* ➤ jerk (v), jerky (adj), jerkily (adv) ❖ τράνταγμα, τίναγμα, απότομη κίνηση

3.236 manifestation (n) – (C) clear indication • *A gift is a ~ of sb's kindness. / A symptom is a ~ of a disease.* ➤ manifest (v. adj), manifestly (adv) ❖ εκδήλωση

3.237 abnormal (adj) – uncommon, unnatural, unusual • *The doctor was concerned about the ~ amount of sugar in the child's blood.* ➤ abnormality (n), abnormally (adv). Opp: normal. ❖ αντικανονικός, αφύσικος ανώμαλος

3.238 excessive (adj) – much more than is reasonable or necessary • *The police were criticized for using ~ force in their attempt to quiet the protest.* ➤ excess (n), exceed (v), excessively (adv) ❖ υπέρμετρος, υπερβολικός

3.239 discharge (n) – (C) emission (i.e., sth sent out or emitted) • *As the cut begins to heal, you can expect to see a bloody ~ on the bandage.* ➤ discharge (v) ❖ εκροή

Health and medicine 3

Text 3 (page 84)

3.240 scourge (n) – (C) thing that causes great suffering • *AIDS is one of the great ~s of the 20th century.* ❖ (μετ) μάστιγα, πληγή

3.241 transmit (v) – pass sth from one person to another • *~ a disease/a message* ➤ transmission (n) ❖ μεταδίδω, διαβιβάζω

3.242 agonizing (adj) – causing great suffering • *It was hours before we found out who had been killed; the wait was ~.* ➤ agony (n), agonize (v) ❖ σπαρακτικός

3.243 foe (n) – (C) enemy • *The two politicians have been ~s for years; they dislike each other intensely.* ❖ εχθρός

3.244 immune system (n phr) – see **3.151**

3.245 inflame (v) – cause swelling, pain, redness • *The bacteria will ~ the lining of your stomach.* ➤ inflammation (n), inflamed (adj) ❖ ερεθίζω

3.246 weird (adj) – strange, odd • *He hasn't call us in weeks. What do you think is causing his ~ behavior?* ➤ weirdness (n), weirdly (adv) ❖ αλλόκοτος, ακατανόητος

3.247 lapse (v) – pass/fall (into a worse state) • *After six months of not being able to find a job, she ~d into a state of depression.* ➤ lapse (n), lapsed (adj) ❖ πέφτω.
📖 : e.g. a membership ~s

Text 4 (page 85)

3.248 inflammation (n) – see **3.202**

3.249 congestion (n) – (U) (medical) the state of being blocked/full • *C~ in the nose is a common symptom of the common cold.* ➤ congest (v), congested (n), congestive (adj) ❖ συμφόρηση

3.250 cavity (n) – (C) empty space in sth solid • *The stomach and other digestive organs are located in the abdominal ~.* ❖ κοιλότητα

3.251 cranium (n) – (C) skull, head bone • *The ~ houses and protects the brain.* ➤ cranial (adj) ❖ κρανίο

3.252 lingering (adj) – slow to leave; drawn-out • *She has a ~ cold that has lasted more than three weeks.* ➤ linger (v) ❖ μακροχρόνιος

3.253 strain (n) – (C) kind, type, breed (e.g., of a germ, plant, or other life form) • *In recent years several new ~s of the virus have appeared that do not respond to antibiotics.* ❖ είδος, ράτσα. 📖 : e.g., the ~ of modern life, muscle ~

3.254 resistance (to sth) (n) – 1. (U) the power to stand or endure sth without damage or harm • *the body's ~ to infection/disease, a germ's ~ to antibiotics* ➤ resist (v), resistant (adj)
2. (U) opposition; the ability to fight or oppose sth • *I was surprised when my parents offered no ~ to the idea of my going to college in the USA.* • resist (v), resistant (adj) ❖ (ενς. 1-2) αντίσταση

3.255 recurrent (adj) – repeated, reappearing, occurring again and again • *Since the birth of her son, she's suffered from ~ headaches.* ➤ recurrence (n), recur (v) ❖ επαναλαμβανόμενος

3.256 hallmark (n) – (C) distinctive characteristic, trait • *Quality and reliability are the company's ~s.* ❖ διακριτικό γνώρισμα

Text 5 (page 85)

3.257 hereditary (adj) – see **3.63**

3.258 clot (v) – thicken, form lumps • *It's a deep cut, so it may take a few minutes before the blood ~s and you stop bleeding.* ➤ clot (n), clotting (n), clotted (adj) ❖ πήζω

3.259 massive (adj) – enormous, huge • *There was no hope of him surviving such a ~ heart attack. / You need to see the Great Pyramids in person to appreciate just how ~ they are.* ➤ mass (n), massively (adv) ❖ πολύ ισχυρός, ογκώδης

3.260 insufficiency (of sth) (n) – (U) shortage, inadequate amount • *People with anemia have an ~ of red blood cells.* ➤ insufficient (adj), insufficiently (adv). Opp: sufficiency (n) ❖ ανεπάρκεια

3.261 excessive (adj) – see **3.238**

3.262 bruising (n) – (U) the appearance of dark, purplish marks on the skin as a result of injury • *People who take blood-thinning medication often have ~ on their arms and legs.* ➤ bruise (n, v), bruised (adj) ❖ μελάνιασμα

3.263 persistent (adj) – see **3.200**

3.264 hemorrhaging (n) → from **hemorrhage** (v) – bleed in large amounts • *After being shot in the heart, the soldier ~d to death.* ❖ αιμορραγώ

3.265 advent (of) (n) – (U) arrival of sth important, the act of coming into existence for the first time • *the ~ of spring, the ~ of a cure for cancer, the ~ of the computer* ❖ έλευση, ερχομός

Text 6 (page 85)

3.266 deposit (n) – (C) layer of built-up matter • *The surgeon found thick ~s of plaque on the walls of his aorta. / The scientists are studying mud ~s from the bottom of the river.* ➤ deposit (v) ❖ εναπόθεση, ίζημα. 📖 : e.g., a bank ~, ~s of gold/oil in the ground

3.267 plaque (n) – (U) hard substance that forms at various places in the body (e.g., arteries, brain, teeth) • *High cholesterol causes ~ to build up in the arteries. / Alzheimer's disease is caused by ~ in the brain. / Regular brushing helps minimize the amount of ~ that builds up on your teeth.* ❖ (για αρτηρίες ή εγκέφαλο) πλάκα, (για δόντια) οδοντική πλάκα, πέτρα

3.268 restrict (v) – limit, confine • *Since his heart attack, he has had to ~ the amount of exercise he does.* ➤ restriction (n), restricted (adj), restrictive (adj) ❖ περιορίζω

3.269 obstruct (v) – block, impede • *A build-up of plaque will ~ the arteries and could lead to a stroke or heart attack.* ➤ obstruction (n), obstructed (adj) ❖ εμποδίζω, φράζω

3.270 obstruction (n) – blockage • *The stroke was caused by an ~ in his carotid artery.* ➤ see **3.269** ❖ στένωση, φράξιμο (αρτηριών)

3.271 lodge (v) – become stuck • *The bullet ~d in his shoulder, narrowly missing his lung and heart.* ❖ σφηνώνω/-ομαι, χώνω/-ομαι

3.272 undergo – underwent – undergone (irreg v) – experience, be put through (usually sth unpleasant or difficult) • *Medical students ~ extensive training before they can practice medicine.* ❖ υφίσταμαι, περνώ

3.273 rehabilitation (n) – (U) recovery; the act of restoring sb to good health • *The stroke victim's ~ included physical therapy as well as speech therapy.* ➤ rehabilitate (v), rehabilitated (adj) ❖ αποκατάσταση

3.274 recurrence (n) – (C) repetition, the act of sth happening again • *He's been healthy since the heart attack; there has been no ~ of his previous symptoms.* ➤ recur (v), recurrent (adj) ❖ επανεμφάνιση

3 Health and medicine

B Routine check-up (preposition and particle practice) (page 86)

3.275 come down with (phr v) – get sick, catch an illness
• School children frequently ~ colds that they catch from their classmates. ❖ αρρωσταίνω

3.276 susceptible (to) (adj) – easily influenced, harmed, or affected by (sth) • A sickly child is ~ to respiratory infections. / A lonely woman is ~ to the charms of a handsome man. ➢ susceptibility (n) ❖ ευαίσθητος, ευπαθής, ευεπηρέαστος, ευάλωτος

C Anatomical idioms (page 86)

3.277 chest (n) → **get it off (sb's) ~** (idm) – confess, speak openly about sth that is troubling you • Tell me what's wrong. You'll feel better if you get it off your ~. ❖ ξαλαφρώνω την καρδιά μου (συζητώντας)

3.278 ear (n) → **be all ~s** (idm) – be eager to hear sb's news • Tell me what happened! I'm all ~s! ❖ είμαι όλος αυτιά

3.279 elbow (v) → **~ (sb's) way through/to** (a place) (idm) – clear people out of the way by pushing them with your elbow(s) • There were so many people at the stadium that I had to ~ my way through the crowd to get to the restroom! ❖ ανοίγω δρόμο (σε πλήθος) σπρώχνοντας με τους αγκώνες

3.280 finger (n) → **have (sb) wrapped/twisted around (sb's) little ~** (idm) – get sb to do whatever you want • Just wait and see. The boss will let her take an extra week off again. She has him wrapped around her little ~. ❖ κάνω κπ ότι θέλω

3.281 head (n) → **two ~s are better than one** (idm) – (saying) two people working together can solve a problem more easily or achieve more than one working alone • If you need help deciding, call me. Two ~s are always better than one. ❖ δύο άνθρωποι βρίσκουν τη λύση πιο εύκολα από έναν

3.282 lung (n) → **scream at the top of (sb's) ~s** (idm) – yell very loudly; same as **scream (sb's) head off** • As the rollercoaster went up and around the big loop, we all screamed at the top of our ~s. ❖ ξεφωνίζω/ουρλιάζω με όλη μου τη δύναμη

3.283 nose (n) → **~ out (sth/sb)** (idm) – find or discover sth/sb by searching carefully (e.g., like a dog sniffing around for sth) • He managed to ~ out his old girlfriend by Googling her on the Internet. ❖ (μετ) ξετρυπώνω κτ (ψάχνοντας)

3.284 stomach (v) → **can't ~ (sb/sth)** (idm) – not be able to tolerate or stand sb/sth; same as **have no ~ for (sb/sth)** • I can't ~ the way she brags about her rich husband. ❖ (μετ) δε χωνεύω

3.285 shoulder (n) → **cry on (sb's) ~** (idm) – tell your problems to sb • Poor Nick! I spent the whole weekend crying on his ~ about what happened at the office. ❖ λέω τον πόνο μου σε κπ

3.286 thumb (n) → **be all ~s** (idm) – be very clumsy or awkward • I'm afraid I'm all ~s when it comes to digital cameras. I never know which buttons to press. ❖ είμαι πολύ αδέξιος

Vocabulary (3) Daunting developments (pages 90-91)

The four exercises in this section contain a number of technical/medical terms, most of which are explained in the texts. As in previous sections, these entries are marked with a star (★) and include only derivatives (where they exist) and Greek equivalents. For explanations in English, please consult the relevant text in the course book.

A The conquest of disease (page 90)

3.287 stunning (adj) – extremely impressive and/or surprising; also, surprisingly beautiful • a ~ defeat/victory, ~ accomplishments, a ~ woman in a ~ dress ➢ stun (v), stunned (adj), stunningly (adv) ❖ καταπληκτικός, έξοχος

3.288 ★ **life expectancy** (n phr) – (U) ❖ πιθανή διάρκεια ζωής

3.289 decline (n) – (C/U) a decrease or drop in quantity or quality • Many people say that there has been a general ~ in the quality of schools in recent years. ➢ decline (v), declining (adj) ❖ πτώση, μείωση

3.290 ★ **infant mortality** (n phr) – (U) ❖ παιδική θνησιμότητα

3.291 eradicate (v) – see **3.174**

3.292 ★ **smallpox** (n) – (U) ❖ ευλογιά

3.293 ★ **bubonic plague** (n phr) – (U) ❖ βουβωνική πανούκλα

3.294 decimate (v) – kill or destroy a large part or amount of sth • The Black Plague ~d close to 25% of Europe's population from 1337 to 1341. ➢ decimation (n), decimated (adj), decimating (adj) ❖ αποδεκατίζω

3.295 segment (n) – (C) section or part of sth • The body of a worm is divided up into different ~s. / A major ~ of the village's population was killed in the earthquake. ❖ τμήμα, τεμάχιο

3.296 sanitation (n) – (U) conditions and procedures related to cleanliness • Western standards of ~, especially with regard to the disposal of garbage and sewage, have improved greatly in the last fifty years. ➢ sanitize (v), sanitary (adj) ❖ υγιεινή

3.297 ★ **sewage system** (n phr) – (C) ➢ sewage (n/adj), sewer (n) ❖ αποχετευτικό σύστημα

3.298 immunology (n) – (U) the study of how the immune system (see **3.151**) protects the body against disease ➢ immunity (n), immunize (v), immunized (adj) ❖ ανοσολογία

3.299 ★ **mass immunization** (n phr) – (U) ❖ μαζική ανοσοποίηση

3.300 vaccinate (v) – protect sb/sth against disease by giving them (orally or by injection) a special substance known as a **vaccine**; similar to **inoculate** • The vet ~s hundreds of dogs a year against rabies. ➢ vaccination (n), vaccine (n), vaccinated (adj) ❖ εμβολιάζω

3.301 combat (v) – fight against (e.g., an enemy or problem) • Despite the government's efforts to ~ unemployment, many people are still jobless. ➢ combat (n), combatant (n), combative (adj), combatively (adv) ❖ πολεμώ, καταπολεμώ, μάχομαι

3.302 foe (n) – see **3.243**

3.303 ★ **cancer** (n) – (U) ❖ καρκίνος

3.304 abnormal (adj) – see **3.237**

3.305 resurgence (n) – see **3.180**

3.306 resistance (n) – see **3.254**

B Diagnostic technology (page 90)
Word bank

3.307 ★ **angiogram** (n) – (C) ❖ αγγειογραφία

3.308 ★ **biopsy** (n) – (C) ❖ βιοψία

3.309 ★ **electrocardiogram** (n) – (C) ❖ ηλεκτροκαρδιογράφημα

3.310 ★ **electroencephalogram** (n) – (C) ❖ ηλεκτροεγκεφαλογράφημα

Health and medicine 3

3.311 tumor (n) – (C) (Brit: **tumour**) an abnormal growth (i.e., excess mass of cells) in the body • *A biopsy will determine whether a ~ is cancerous or not.* ➤ tumorous (adj) ❖ όγκος

3.312 benign (adj) – (of tumors) harmless in effect, not cancerous • *She was relieved when the doctor informed her that the tumor was ~ and would not require chemotherapy.* ➤ benignly (adv) ❖ (για όγκους) καλοήθης. See also **5.335** and 📖: e.g., a ~ ruler

3.313 malignant (adj) – (tumors/growths) that cannot be controlled, cancerous • *Everyone was relieved when the growth turned out not to be ~.* ➤ malignancy (n), malign (v), ❖ (για όγκους) κακοήθης. 📖: e.g., a ~ spirit/power

3.314 sophisticated (adj) – (of procedures, technology, ideas) complex, advanced • *The hospital has invested millions of dollars in ~ new diagnostic equipment.* ➤ sophistication (n) ❖ περίπλοκος, προηγμένος. See also **1.213**.

3.315 ★ **ultrasound** (adj) – ❖ υπερηχητικός

Text

3.316 precision (n) – (U) the quality of being precise (i.e., exact, accurate) • *The delicate surgery requires absolute ~ ; one wrong move and the patient could be paralyzed for life.* ➤ precise (adj), precisely (adv) ❖ ακρίβεια

3.317 impulse (n) → **electrical ~** (n phr) – (C) (nervous system) short pulsation or current of energy that causes a reaction in a muscle, gland, or other part of the body • *Electrocardiograms record the electrical ~s of the heart.* ❖ νευρική διέγερση, παλμός. See also **5.44** and 📖: e.g., do sth on ~.

3.318 ★ **Computerized Axial Tomography** (n phr) – (U) same as **CAT/CT scan** ❖ υπολογιστική αξονική τομογραφία

3.319 ★ **Nuclear Magnetic Resonance Imaging** (n phr) – (U) same as **MRI or NMRI** ❖ μαγνητική τομογραφία

C Surgical advances (page 91)
Word bank

3.320 bloodless (adj) – (surgery) causing little or no bleeding • *B~ surgical procedures are much less invasive than traditional procedures, which means faster recovery time for the patient.* ➤ blood (n), bleed (v), bloody (adj), bleeding (n, adj) ❖ αναίμακτος

3.321 ★ **bypass** (n) – (C) ➤ bypass (v) ❖ μπάι πας

3.322 ★ **cataract** (n) – (C) ❖ καταρράκτης (ματιού). 📖: e.g., a ~ in the mountains

3.323 incision (n) – (C) cut made by a sharp instrument, esp. the cut made by a surgeon during an operation • *The surgeon made a five-inch ~ on the patient's abdomen.* ❖ τομή

3.324 ★ **microsurgical** (adj) – ➤ microsurgery (n) ❖ μικροχειρουργικός

3.325 ★ **prosthetic** (adj) → **~ device** (n phr) – same as **prosthesis** and **artificial limb** ➤ prosthetics (n) ❖ προσθετική συσκευή (π.χ., τεχνητό μέλος)

3.326 severed (adj) – completely cut off or cut into two pieces • *The surgeons were able to reattach the ~ finger to his hand. / A ~ rope was the cause of the climbing accident.* ➤ sever (v) ❖ ακρωτηριασμένος, αποκομμένος

3.327 ★ **transplant** (n/adj) – (C) ➤ transplant (v), transplanted (adj) μεταμόσχευση, μεταμοσχευτικός

Text

3.328 procedure (n) – (C/U) set way of doing sth, established method • *If you need surgery, you must call your health insurance provider and find out what ~s they require you to follow. / A liver transplant is a difficult surgical ~.* ➤ proceed (v), procedural (adj) ❖ διαδικασία

3.329 technique (n) – (C) method of doing or performing sth; also, (U) the ability to use such methods • *Laser surgery for cataracts is no longer a new ~. / The musician performed the piece with flawless ~.* ➤ technical (adj), technically (adv) ❖ τεχνική

3.330 artificial limb (n phr) – (C) mechanical arm or leg that is used to replace a patient's own arm or leg that has had to be surgically removed • *It will take several months of physical therapy before the patient is able to walk comfortably with his artificial limb.* ❖ τεχνητό μέλος

3.331 segment (n) – *see* **3.295**

3.332 stride (n) → **make great ~s** (v phr) – make great progress • *Everyone expects medical science to make great ~s in the 21st century.* ❖ σημειώνω μεγάλη πρόοδο

3.333 tumor (n) – *see* **3.314**

D Reproductive medicine (page 91)
Word bank

3.334 ★ **amniocentesis** (n) – (U) αμνιοκέντηση

3.335 ★ **artificial insemination** (n phr) – (U) τεχνητή γονιμοποίηση

3.336 conceiving (n) → **conceive** (v) – become pregnant • *Women who can't ~ children on their own now have the option of trying to become pregnant via artificial insemination.* ➤ conception (n) ❖ μένω έγκυος, συλλαμβάνω

3.337 ★ **congenital** (adj) – εκ γενετής, έμφυτος

3.338 ★ **fertility** (n) – (U) ➤ fertilization (n), fertilize (v), fertile (adj). Opp: infertility (n) ❖ γονιμότητα

3.339 ★ **oral contraceptive** (n phr) – (C) ➤ contraception (n) ❖ αντισυλληπτικό χάπι

Text

3.340 old hat (idm) – (U) sth that is old-fashioned and/or no longer interesting • *In the early 1990s e-mail was an exciting novelty. Now it seems a bit ~.* ❖ ξεπερασμένος

3.341 faulty (adj) – not perfect, containing errors or mistakes • *Smoking and drug abuse during pregnancy may contribute to ~ fetal development.* ➤ fault (n, v). Opp: faultless (adj) ❖ ελαττωματικός

3.342 ★ **cloning** (n) – (U) ➤ clone (n, v), cloned (adj) ❖ κλωνοποίηση

3.343 feat (n) – (C) impressive and difficult achievement • *Climbing Mount Everest is an impressive ~.* ❖ κατόρθωμα, άθλος

3.344 come into its (one's) own (idm) – show (one's) true capabilities; receive the credit, recognition, or fame that one deserves • *Since the hospital began doing robotic surgery, it has really begun to ~. Last year it received several awards for medical excellence.* ❖ δείχνω τι αξίζω, τυχαίνω της οφειλόμενης αναγνώρισης

3 Health and medicine

Reading Visualizing metaphors (pages 93-95)

B READING PRACTICE (1): Drug abuse (page 93)
Text
Paragraph 1

3.345 eradicate (v) – *see* **3.174**

3.346 abuse (n) – (U) 1. illegal, improper, or harmful use of sth • *Drug ~ involves the excessive and/or habitual use of narcotics such as heroin or cocaine. / Appointing a friend to a government post is an ~ of political power.* ➣ abuse (v), abusive (adj), abusively (adv) ❖ κατάχρηση. 📖: e.g., physical/mental ~

3.347 sustained (adj) – continuing for a long time • *S~ financial problems can put a great strain on a couple's relationship.* ➣ sustenance (n), sustain (v) ❖ συνεχής, παρατεταμένος

3.348 misleading (adj) – intended to create a false impression, deceiving • *When the truth about the scandal came out, the government was criticized for releasing ~ information.* ➣ mislead (irreg v) ❖ παραπλανητικός

3.349 overwhelming (adj) – so great, strong, large, or complete that one is left feeling weak, surprised, powerless, or unable to act • *The heat is so ~ that I refuse to leave my air-conditioned house. / The team suffered an ~ defeat in the championship match.* ➣ overwhelm (v), overwhelmed (adj) ❖ συντριπτικός, ακατανίκητος

3.350 wage war (v phr) – begin and continue a war against sb/sth • *The government continues to ~ on drugs and terrorism.* ❖ κάνω πόλεμο

3.351 addicted (adj) – 1. totally dependent on sth • *If you continue to use those painkillers, you'll become ~ to them.* 2. (in context) **the ~** (pl n) – people who are addicted to (i.e., totally dependent on) drugs • *The ~ have psychological as well as medical needs.* ➣ addict (n), addictive (adj), addicted (adj) ❖ 1. εξαρτημένος, εθισμένος 2. οι εξαρτημένοι, οι εθισμένοι

Paragraph 2

3.352 appropriate (adj) – suitable, proper, apt, fitting • *Jeans and a T-shirt are not ~ clothing for a wedding. Don't you have a suit?* ➣ appropriately (adv). Opp: inappropriate (adj) ❖ κατάλληλος

3.353 conceptual (adj) – of or related to a general or specific concept/idea • *Studying history involves more than facts and dates; it helps you develop a deeper, ~ understanding of how the world has got to where it is today.* ➣ concept (n), conceptualize (v) ❖ εννοιολογικός

3.354 framework (n) – (C) (fig) basic structure that gives shape or support to sth (e.g., a building, an idea, a text) • *Compositions should have a clear ~ of ideas, just as buildings need a strong ~ to keep them standing.* ❖ δομή, σκελετός

3.355 proposition (n) – (C) task, situation, problem, or matter that must be dealt with • *Waging war on terrorism is a difficult ~.* ➣ propose (v), proposed (adj) ❖ επιχείρηση, πρόβλημα. 📖: e.g., a business ~ ; the ~ that all men are created equal

3.356 mobilization (n) – (U) the act of organizing and setting sb/sth into motion • *The two countries are on the brink of war; both sides have given the order for the immediate ~ of troops.* ➣ mobilize (v). Opp: immobilization (n) ❖ κινητοποίηση, επιστράτευση

3.357 check (v) – stop or slow down the progress of sth • *Police are on hand to ~ any violence that might break out at the stadium tonight.* ❖ αναχαιτίζω, σταματώ. 📖: e.g., ~ your work

3.358 consequence (n) – (C) result, effect • *He's a conscientious worker who always considers the ~s of his actions.* ➣ consequential (adj), consequentially (adv) ❖ συνέπεια

3.359 prognosis (n) – forecast or prediction of how sth will turn out (e.g., an illness, a match) • *The heart attack was mild, so the patient's ~ for recovery is good.* ➣ prognostic (adj) ❖ πρόγνωση

3.360 resistance (n) – *see* **3.254(2)**

3.361 compassion (n) – (U) sympathy and understanding for sb's suffering • *His cruel remarks showed a distinct lack of ~ for the poor.* ➣ compassionate (adj), compassionately (adv) ❖ οίκτος, συμπόνια

3.362 will (n) – (U) strong desire • *Doctors are convinced that the patient's ~ to live is what saved her life.* ❖ will (v), willing (adj), willingly (adv) ❖ θέληση

C READING PRACTICE (2): Commando viruses to the rescue (pages 94-95)
STEPS 2-3 (page 94)

For unknown vocabulary in these two sections, see the paragraph-by-paragraph analysis of the reading passage in the following section.

STEP 4 (page 95): Passage
Title and paragraph 1

3.363 virus (n) – (C) kind of tiny, disease-causing life form; also, a disease caused by such a life form • *Antibiotics can fight diseases that are caused by bacteria, but they are no help against ailments like the flu and common cold, both of which are caused by ~es.* ➣ viral (adj) ❖ ιός

3.364 ruthless (adj) – cruel, without mercy • *The ~ dictator thought nothing of making his enemies "disappear."* ➣ ruthlessness (n), ruthlessly (adv) ❖ αδίστακτος, ανελέητος, άσπλαχνος

3.365 inflict mayhem (v phr) – cause disorder, chaos, destruction • *Disorderly soccer fans ~ wherever they go.* ❖ προκαλώ ταραχή, χάος, καταστροφή

3.366 commando (n) – (C) soldier specially trained to conduct sudden sneak attacks (i.e., raids) • *Rambo is the prototypical ~.* ❖ καταδρομέας

3.367 infiltrate (v) – (military troops, spies) enter secretly • *The soldiers were ordered to ~ the enemy camp at dawn and take as many prisoners as possible.* ➣ infiltration (n) ❖ (για στρατεύματα) διεισδύω, εισχωρώ

3.368 commandeer (v) – (military – used figuratively in text) take possession of sth for military use • *The Germans took over the village and ~ed a large house to use as their headquarters.* ❖ επιτάσσω, κατάσχω (για στρατιωτική χρήση)

3.369 wreak havoc (on sth) (v phr) – create disorder/chaos; compare **play havoc (with sth)** (*see* **4.360**) • *The flood ~ed havoc on the area, leaving thousands of people homeless.* ❖ προκαλώ μεγάλη ζημιά, καταστρέφω

3.370 wart (n) – (C) small, hard, flesh-colored growth of skin • *That growth on your finger is nothing to worry about. It's just a ~.* ❖ κρεατοελιά

Health and medicine 3

Paragraph 2

3.371 twist (n) – (C) sudden, unexpected development • *A good mystery has so many ~s that it keeps you guessing till the last chapter.* ➢ twist (v) ❖ διαστροφή, κτ που δεν περιμέναμε

3.372 recruit (v) – persuade to join (e.g., the military, a company, or club) • *In large corporations, the Human Resources Department ~s new employees.* ➢ recruit (n), recruitment (n), recruiter (n), recruiting (adj) ❖ στρατολογώ

3.373 special forces (n phr) – (used as adj in text) any elite group of soldiers specializing in commando tactics; also, **Special Forces** – an elite commando unit in the U.S. Marines • *After watching all the Rambo films, the young boy's dream was to become a member of the S~ F~.* ❖ ειδικές δυνάμεις

3.374 ★ cystic fibrosis (n phr) – (U) ❖ κυστική ίνωση

3.375 emerge (v) – (lit) appear, come to the surface; (fig, as in text) rise up and become important • *divers ~ from the sea, a figure ~s from the shadows, a plan ~s from months of discussion* ❖ εμφανίζομαι, αναδύομαι

3.376 enlisted (pp) → **enlist (sb)** (v) – (military) (used passively and figuratively in text) sign sb up, make sb join the army, navy, etc. • *The army recruiter ~ed dozens of college students last year.* ➢ enlistment (n), enlisted (adj) ❖ στρατολογώ. 📖 : e.g., ~ sb's help

3.377 slip (v) – move quietly, secretly • *Without Mom noticing, we managed to ~ into the kitchen and raid the cookie jar.* ❖ γλιστρώ, πηγαίνω στα κρυφά

3.378 deploy (v) – use, employ, send into action • *The police have ~ed new DNA techniques to combat crime. / The general gave the order to ~ more soldiers to the front line.* ➢ deployment (n), deployed (adj) ❖ παρατάσσω/-ομαι

Paragraph 3

3.379 elaborate (adj) – complicated, detailed • *Big weddings usually involve ~ plans that take months to execute. / The inventor's new creation is an ~ device.* ➢ elaboration (n) elaborate (v), elaborately (adv) ❖ περίπλοκος, λεπτομερής

3.380 faulty (adj) – *see* **3.341**

3.381 headway (n) → **make ~** (v phr) – make progress despite difficulty • *She hasn't finished writing the novel, but she's made excellent ~. She's only got two more chapters to do.* ❖ σημειώνω πρόοδο

3.382 acquired disease (n phr) – (C) a disease one develops/ acquires after birth (as opposed to a genetic or inherited disease) • *Cancer is often an ~.* ❖ επίκτητη αρρώστια

3.383 stem (from) (v) – (always in 3rd person) be caused by, come from, happen as a result of • *Hemophilia ~s from genetic causes. / Your composition problems ~ from the fact that you translate word for word from Greek.* ❖ προέρχομαι, κατάγομαι

3.384 ★ recombinant DNA technology (n phr) – (U) ❖ τεχνολογία του ανασυνδυασμένου DNA

3.385 ★ replicate (v) – ❖ αυτοδιπλασιάζομαι

3.386 rogue (n/adj) – (fig) dangerous and destructive (e.g., like a lone, angry elephant who attacks everything it sees) • *The ~ elephant thundered into the village and began destroying everything in sight. / The ~ protein deposits itself in the brain in the form of a sticky plaque.* ❖ (μετ) επικίνδυνος και καταστρεπτικός. 📖 : e.g., a romantic ~

3.387 viral (adj) – caused by a **virus** (*see* **3.363**) • *The common cold is a ~ disease that cannot be cured by antibiotics.* ❖ ιογενής

3 Exam practice (pages 98-101)

Cloze (page 99)

Paragraph 1

3.388 microbe (n) – (C) tiny disease-causing life form; same as **germ** • *Bacteria are ~s.* ❖ μικρόβιο

3.389 resurgent (adj) – *see* **3.181**

3.390 slum (n) – (C) (often in plural) poor, overcrowded area of a city with old or badly constructed buildings • *The social worker's dream is to fight poverty and crime in the ~ where she grew up.* ❖ φτωχογειτονιά

3.391 resistant (adj) – *see* **3.197**

3.392 strain (n) – *see* **3.253**

3.393 plague (n) – (U) a disease that spreads rapidly and kills many people • *the Black P~, bubonic ~* ➢ plague (v) ❖ πανούκλα. 📖 : e.g., (C) the seven ~s of Egypt

3.394 unwitting (adj) – unaware of what is happening, innocent • *The ~ passengers had no idea that the man with the briefcase was carrying a bomb.* ❖ χωρίς επίγνωση

Paragraph 2

3.395 widespread (adj) – *see* **3.186**

3.396 sanitation (n) – *see* **3.296**

3.397 ★ smallpox (n) – *see* **3.292**

3.398 vanquish (v) – (formal, literary) defeat, conquer • *The Spanish forces ~ed the local population and made slaves of the Indians.* ❖ (υπερ)νικώ κατανικώ, καταβάλλω

3.399 ★ tuberculosis (n) – (U) ❖ φυματίωση

3.400 vaccination (n) – *see* **3.187**

3.401 transition (n) – (C/U) change from one form or state to another • *the ~ from winter to spring, the ~ from childhood to adulthood, a company in ~* ❖ μεταβολή αλλαγή

3.402 shift (sth) (v) – move (sth) from one place, position, etc., to another • *a person ~s his weight from one foot to another, a politician ~s his loyalty from one party to another, winds ~ from one direction to another* ➢ shift (n), shifting (adj), shifty (adj). shiftily (adv) ❖ αλλάζω (θέση ή κατεύθυνση), μετατοπίζω, μετακινώ

3.403 resistant (adj) – *see* **3.197**

3.404 follow suit (idm) – do what sb/sth else has just done • *When his friend bought a digital camera, he wanted to ~, but his parents made him wait till his next birthday.* ❖ κάνω το ίδιο, μιμούμαι

3.405 ★ malaria (n) – (U) ❖ ελονοσία

3.406 mosquito-borne (adj) – (of diseases, microbes) carried or transferred by mosquitoes; from **bear – bore – borne** (irreg v), meaning "to carry" • *Malaria is a ~ disease, while the flu or common cold is often air-borne.* ❖ που μεταφέρεται από κουνούπια

Vocabulary (page 100)

All of the answer choices in questions 21-30 appear in previous entries in this unit. Consult the Alphabetical Word List at the back of the book to locate any words you wish to review.

3 Health and medicine

Reading (page 101)

Paragraph 1

3.407 resist (v) – 1. (drugs, medicine) remain unaffected by • *The new strain of bacteria ~s antibiotics.* 2. oppose, put up a fight against • *A healthy diet helps the body ~ disease. / A teenager ~s the authority of his parents.* ➢ resistance (n), resistant (adj) ❖ (evs. 1-2) ανθίσταμαι, αντιστέκομαι.
📖 : e.g., ~ temptation

3.408 thrive (v/irreg v) – grow strong and healthy • *Children ~ on love, just as plants ~ on rich soil, water, and sunlight.* ❖ ευδοκιμώ, ευημερώ. **Note:** the verb has both regular and irregular forms: *thrive – thrived – thrived* or *thrive – throve – thriven.*

3.409 keep up with (phr v) – progress or develop at the same rate as, not fall behind • *The new drug is selling so well that the pharmaceutical firm is unable to ~ the demand.* ❖ συμβαδίζω με

3.410 wake (n) → **in the ~ of (sth)** (prep phr) – (also **in sth's wake**) as a result of (sth); following (sth), subsequent to (sth) • *In the ~ of the burglary, we finally decided to install a burglar alarm.* ❖ αμέσως μετά, σαν συνέπεια

3.411 alarming (adj) – disturbing, frightening, distressing • *Everyone is concerned about the ~ increase in crime in the area.* ➢ alarm (n, v), alarmingly (adv) ❖ ανησυχητικός

3.412 compound (n) – (C) (chemistry) combination of two or more substances • *Sulfur dioxide is a ~ of sulfur and oxygen.* ➢ compound (v) ❖ (χημεία) ένωση

3.413 agent (n) – (C) sb/sth that produces a particular effect • *Making bread requires the use of a rising ~ such as yeast. / Technology is an ~ of change.* ➢ agency (n) ❖ μέσο, παράγοντας. 📖 : e.g., secret ~, real estate ~

Paragraph 2

3.414 dwell (v) – (formal) live in, reside in • *The first humans ~ed in caves.* ➢ dweller (n), dwelling (n) ❖ κατοικώ, διαμένω. **Note:** derivatives of *dwell* are used in compounds: e.g., *Worms are soil-dwelling animals. / The first humans were cave-dwellers.*

3.415 content (to do sth) (adj) – satisfied, quietly happy • *Tired from a hard week at work, she was ~ just to stay at home and watch TV.* ➢ contentment (n), contentedly (adv). Opp: discontented (adj) ❖ ικανοποιημένος, ευχαριστημένος

3.416 reside (v) – live, inhabit, make one's home in a place • *He ~s in Rome, where his children also live.* ➢ resident (n), residence (n), residential (adj) ❖ κατοικώ, διαμένω

3.417 encounter (v) – find, meet with, come face to face with (ofen by chance) • *It's natural for students to ~ difficulties during their first year of university. / I went into the kitchen and ~ed a burglar.* ➢ encounter (n) ❖ βρίσκω, συναντώ, έρχομαι αντιμέτωπος με

3.418 breeding ground (n phr) – (C) place where animals mate • *Salmon swim upstream to their ~.* ❖ τόπος αναπαραγωγής

3.419 burrow (v) – (animals) dig a tunnel or hole in sth • *Large mounds of soil marked the places where the rabbits had ~ed into the farmer's field.* ➢ burrow (n), burrowing (adj) ❖ ανοίγω λαγούμι, τρυπώνω, σκάβω, ανοίγω τρύπα

3.420 hapless (adj) – unlucky, unfortunate • *We felt sorry for the ~ tourists whose flight was cancelled due to the bad storm.* ❖ άτυχος, κακόμοιρος

3.421 furiously (adv) – (fig) wildly, with uncontrolled energy, anger, or speed • *The eager student waved her hand fast and ~ whenever she knew the answer. / They drove ~, hoping to arrive at the hospital before the baby was born.* ➢ fury (n), furious (adj) ❖ ασυγκράτητα, μανιασμένα, εξαγριωμένα

Paragraph 3

3.422 intrigue (v) – fascinate, arouse sb's curiosity or interest • *Something about the woman ~d him and made him want to know her better.* ➢ intrigue (n), intrigued (adj), intriguing (adj), intriguingly (adv), intrigue (n) ❖ κινώ την περιέργεια ή το ενδιαφέρον

3.423 frenzy (n) – (C/U) state of uncontrollable excitement or emotion • *The excited fans left the stadium in a ~ after their team won the championship.* ❖ φρενίτιδα, λύσσα, οργή

3.424 dump (v) – throw down carelessly (e.g., in a heap or a mass) • *He came in from school and ~ed his jacket on the floor.* ❖ ρίχνω, πετώ, ξεφορτώνω. 📖 : e.g., ~ trash, ~ sb

3.425 pest (n) – (C) insect or small animal that causes damage to crops or food supplies • *mice and other pests* ➢ pesticide (n), pester (v) ❖ επιβλαβές φυτό ή ζώο, παράσιτο

3.426 isolate (v) – (chemistry) separate out a chemical or biological material from sth else in order to identify and/or study it • *Forensic scientists can ~ DNA from a blood or saliva sample.* ➢ isolation (n), isolated (adj) ❖ (χημεία) διαχωρίζω. 📖 : e.g., ~ sb with a contagious disease, ~ oneself from society

3.427 petri dish (n phr) – (C) ❖ δίσκος καλλιέργειας μικροβίων (τρυβλίο)

3.428 application (n) – (C) practical use • *the ~s of a computer program, a theory and its ~s* ➢ apply (v), applied (adj) applicable (adj) ❖ εφαρμογή, χρήση. 📖 : e.g., job ~, study with great ~, the ~ of glue to a surface

4. Environmentalism 101

Introduction — In the beginning ... (pages 102-106)

As in units 2 and 3, this unit contains a number of scientific and technical terms, most of which are explained in the course book or are English words derived from Greek (e.g., *chasm* – χάσμα). For the sake of brevity, the entries for these words are marked with a star symbol (★) and include only derivatives (where they exist) and Greek equivalents.

A The biosphere and the forces that helped to shape it (pages 102-103)

STEP 2: Text (page 102)

Paragraphs 1-2

4.1 ★ **biosphere** (n) – (C) ❖ βιόσφαιρα

4.2 **condense** (v) – 1. become/make sth become denser, more compact • *Over time the cloud of cosmic dust ~d into a thick hot substance which eventually cooled into a spherical planet. / She ~d the 100-page report into a five-page summary.* 2. (of a gas) change (from vapor) to liquid form • *The water vapor ~d into droplets of water.* ➢ condensation (n), condensed (adj) ❖ 1. συμπυκνώνω/-όμαι 2. υγροποιώ

4.3 **impact** (n) – 1. (C) crash, collision; also, (U) the force with which one objects hits or collides into another • *(C) The moon's craters are the result of meteorite ~s. / (U) The ~ of the meteorite hitting the earth was so great that it left a huge crater in the area.* 2. (C) strong effect or influence • *Renewed terrorism in the area is bound to have a negative ~ on tourism.* ➢ impact (v) ❖ 1. (C) σύγκρουση, (U) δύναμη σύγκρουσης 2. επίδραση, αντίκτυπος

4.4 ★ **radioactive decay** (n phr) – (U) ❖ ραδιενεργός διάσπαση

4.5 **molten** (adj) – in a hot, thick, melted state • *As the volcano rumbled, ~ lava streamed down its slopes.* ❖ λειωμένος, χυτός

4.6 ★ **crust** (n) – (C) ❖ εξωτερικός φλοιός της γης

4.7 ★ **mantle** (n) – (C) ❖ μανδύας

4.8 ★ **core** (n) – (C) ❖ πυρήνας της γης

4.9 **radiate** (v) – come out in rays, be emitted • *Heat and light ~ from the sun.* ➢ radiator (n), radiation (n), radiant (adj), radiantly (adv) ❖ (θερμότητα) εκπέμπω/-ομαι · (φως) ακτινοβολώ/-ούμαι

4.10 **volatile** (adj) – (of a substance) changeable, unstable; easily evaporated at normal temperatures; • *If you've ever spent time at a gas station and got dizzy from the fumes, you know that liquid petroleum is highly ~.* ❖ πτητικός, που έχει την ιδιότητα να εξατμίζεται. 📖 : e.g., *a ~ personality*

4.11 ★ **vapor** (n) – (U) ❖ ατμός

4.12 **condense** (v) – *see* **4.2(2)**

Paragraph 3

4.13 ★ **tectonic plate** (n phr) – (C) ❖ τεκτονική πλάκα

4.14 ★ **continent** (n) – (C) ➢ continental (adj) ❖ ήπειρος

4.15 **drift** (v) – be carried along on (or as if on) a current (e.g., of air or water or by life) • *She let go of the balloon and watched it ~ upwards. / He ~s through life expecting everyone else to take care of him.* ➢ drift (n), drifter (n), drifting (adj) ❖ παρασύρομαι (π.χ., από ρεύμα νερού ή αέρος)

4.16 **collide** (v) – crash into • *The driver lost control of the car and ~d into a tree.* ➢ collision (n), colliding (adj) ❖ συγκρούω

4.17 ★ **fault** (n) – (C) ❖ τεκτονικό ρήγμα

4.18 **mountain chain** (n phr) – (C) connected series of mountains; same as **mountain range** • *The Rocky Mountains are a ~ located in the western United States.* ❖ οροσειρά

4.19 ★ **plateau** (n) – (C) ❖ οροπέδιο

4.20 **erosion** (n) – (U) slow wearing away of soil or rock by natural forces (e.g., water, wind) ➢ erode (v), erosive (adj). ❖ διάβρωση. *See also* **2.125** *for figurative meaning.*

4.21 ★ **cliff** (n) – (C) ❖ γκρεμός

4.22 ★ **beach** (n) – (C) ❖ παραλία, ακτή

4.23 ★ **glacier** (n) – (C) ➢ glacial (adj) ❖ παγετώνας

4.24 **carve** (v) – (geology) produce sth (e.g., a certain landform) by means of erosion (*see* **4.20**) • *Over millions of years, glaciers and rivers have ~d out valleys, canyons, and other landforms.* ➢ carving (n), carved (adj) ❖ σμιλεύω, λαξεύω, χαράζω

4.25 ★ **valley** (n) – (C) ❖ κοιλάδα

4.26 ★ **ravine** (n) – (C) ❖ φαράγγι, λαγκάδα, ρεματιά

4.27 ★ **gorge** (n) – (C) ❖ φαράγγι, λαγκάδα

4.28 ★ **canyon** (n) – (C) ❖ φαράγγι, βαθιά χαράδρα

4.29 **eventually** (adv) – in the end, after some time has passed • *They don't have the money to buy a house right now, but they'll do so ~.* ➢ event (n), eventuality (n), eventual (adj) ❖ τελικά, με τον καιρό

4.30 ★ **sediment** (n) – (U) ➢ sedimentary (adj) ❖ ίζημα

4.31 ★ **topsoil** (n) – (U) ❖ επιφανειακό στρώμα εδάφους

4.32 **fertile** (adj) – (soil, land) able to sustain the growth of healthy and plentiful plant life • *the rich, ~ soil of the Nile Delta* ➢ fertility (n), fertilizer (n), fertilization (n), fertilize (v), fertilized (adj) ❖ γόνιμος. *See also* **2.131** *for figurative meaning.*

4.33 ★ **plain** (n) – (C) ❖ πεδιάδα, κάμπος, στέπα

4.34 **advance** (v) – (of sb's/sth's position) move forward • *As the huge glacier ~d, it eroded the soil and rock underneath it.* ➢ advancement (n), advancing (adj), advanced (adj) ❖ προχωρώ. *See also* **2.298** *and* 📖 : e.g., *~ sb's career, ~ sb money*

4.35 **retreat** (v) – move back or away from sth, withdraw • *Realizing that the battle was lost, the army ~ed to a safe place behind the front line.* ➢ retreat (n) ❖ υποχωρώ

4.36 **erode** (v) – (geology) gradually wear away or destroy sth • *The heavy rains have completely ~d the soil on the slope of the mountain.* ➢ erosion (n), erosive (adj), eroded (adj) ❖ διαβρώνω. *See* **2.125** *for figurative meaning.*

Text 1 (page 104)

4.37 **praise** (n) – (U) admiration, approval • *The excellent performance won the high ~ of all the drama critics.* ➢ praise (v), praiseworthy (adj) ❖ έπαινος

4.38 **wax** (v) → **~ eloquent** (v phr) – (formal) express oneself in beautiful, poetic language • *The famous travel writer loved to ~ eloquent about the many beautiful places he has visited.* ❖ εκφράζομαι με λυρικό τρόπο. 📖 : e.g., *the moon ~es and wanes*

Paragraph 1

4.39 ★ **plain** (n) – *see* **4.33**

43

Environmentalism 101

4.40 kneel (v) – get down on one's knees • *Rising from the table, he ~ed, took her hand in his, and asked her to marry him.* ➢ knee (n), kneeling (adj) ❖ γονατίζω. **Note:** In American English both **kneeled** and **knelt** are acceptable as past tense and past participle forms.

4.41 sweep – swept – swept (irreg v) – move with grace or great force • *The queen swept through the room and seated herself on the throne. / The storm swept through the area leaving a path of destruction in its wake.* ❖ διασχίζω, σαρώνω. 📖 : e.g., ~ a floor, (sports) ~ a series of games

4.42 landscape (n) – (C) scenery, what you see when you look at a place (e.g., hills, water, plant life) • *Snow-capped mountains and beautiful green valleys are characteristic of the ~ in the Swiss alps.* ➢ landscape (v) ❖ τοπίο

4.43 jagged (adj) – with a rough, uneven edge or surface, often with sharp points • *~ mountains, a ~ piece of glass* ❖ οδοντωτός, πριονωτός, ακανόνιστος

4.44 ooze (n) – (U) soft, slimy mud • *The children laughed as they felt their feet sink into the ~ on the shore of the lake.* ➢ ooze (n), oozing (adj) ❖ ιλύς, λάσπη, βόρβορος

4.45 scoop (v) – (often with **up/out**) move, lift, or remove with a curving, upward movement, as if using a scoop (i.e., a tool/utensil used to pick up flour, sugar, ice-cream, etc.) • *The children used their cupped hands to ~ up sand for their sand castle.* ➢ scoop (n) ❖ μαζεύω, φτυαρίζω

4.46 ★ **ridge** (n) – (C) ❖ κορυφογραμμή (λόφων/βουνών)

4.47 ★ **dome** (n) – (C) ❖ εδαφικός σχηματισμός σε μορφή θόλου, τρούλου

4.48 palette (n) – (C) (painting) range of colors used by an artist in a particular picture; (C) also, the thin, often rounded board on which a painter mixes his paints • *In his later years, the artist used a much darker ~ of blacks, browns, and grays; the color scheme of his earlier paintings was much brighter and more optimistic.* ❖ (ζωγραφική) παλέτα

4.49 rival (v) – be as good as or as important as sth/sb else, compare favorably with • *The college's research library ~s the great libraries of Harvard and Yale.* ➢ rival (n), rivalry (n) ❖ συναγωνίζομαι, συγκρίνομαι

4.50 ★ **bluff** (n) – (C ❖ απότομος γκρεμός

4.51 ★ **spire** (n) – (C) ❖ εδαφικός σχηματισμός σε μορφή οβελίσκου

4.52 ★ **arch** (n) – (C) ➢ arched (adj) ❖ αψίδα, καμάρα

4.53 dappled (adj) – marked or spotted with light and dark patches • *a ~ pony, the floor of a forest ~ with sunlight* ❖ παρδαλός, διάστικτος

4.54 muted (adj) – (color) soft, not bright • *She prefers ~ watercolors to bright oil paintings.* ➢ mute (n, v) ❖ (χρώμα) απαλός. 📖 : e.g., (sound) ~ voices, (fig) ~ disagreement

Paragraph 2

4.55 howling (adj) – making a long, loud, sad cry • *The ~ wind was so strong that it kept us up most of the night. / The ~ wolf sounded as if he were in great pain.* ➢ howl (n, v) ❖ που λυσσομανά

4.56 grandeur (n) – (U) impressive beauty, majestic appearance or style • *She'll never forget the ~ of the Palace of Versailles. / The photos of the Grand Canyon had a breathtaking ~ about them.* ➢ grand (adj), grandly (adj) ❖ μεγαλείο

4.57 coexist (v) – (also **co-exist**) exist/be together at the same time or place • *The couple reached a point where they found it impossible to ~ under the same roof.* ➢ coexistence (n) ❖ συνυπάρχω

4.58 invade (v) – enter and spread throughout sth, often to gain control or exert a harmful influence • *soldiers ~ a foreign country, insects ~ a farmer's field, flood waters ~ a valley* ➢ invasion (n), invasive (adj), invasively (adv) ❖ εισβάλλω. 📖 : e.g., ~ sb's privacy

4.59 countless (adj) – very many, too many to be counted or mentioned • *I've told her ~ times that he can't be trusted, but she still doesn't believe me.* ❖ αναρίθμητος

4.60 ★ **limestone** (n) – (U) ❖ ασβεστόλιθος

4.61 ★ **sand dune** (n phr) – (C) ❖ αμμόλοφος

4.62 ★ **harsh** (adj) – ❖ τραχύς, δριμύς, άγριος, σκληρός

4.63 eons (pl n) – (Brit: **aeons**) indefinitely long period of time (in context, millions of years) • *E~ of erosion have carved out the U-shaped valleys. / I haven't seen him for ~. What's he up to?* ❖ αιώνες (δηλ. χιλιάδες χρόνια)

4.64 fossilize (v) – harden into or become preserved as (or in) stone; become a **fossil** • *If I bury this rose in the ground, how long do you think it will take to ~?* ➢ fossil (n), fossilized (adj) ❖ απολιθώνω/-ομαι

Text 2 (page 105)
Paragraph 1

4.65 shove (v) – push sb/sth roughly • *He ~d his way through the crowd, trying to find a police officer.* ➢ shove (n) ❖ σπρώχνω δυνατά

4.66 deposit (n) – (C) layer of built-up matter (e.g., rock, soil, cholesterol) • *The scientists are studying mud ~s from the bottom of the river. / The surgeon found thick ~s of plaque on the walls of his aorta.* ➢ deposit (v) ❖ εναπόθεση, ίζημα, κοίτασμα. 📖 : e.g., a bank ~, ~s of gold/oil in the ground

4.67 bluff (n) – see **4.50**

4.68 haunting (adj) – beautiful yet sad, making a strong impression that remains in your thoughts • *The ~ melody stayed in her mind for days after the concert.* ❖ που δε φεύγει από το νου

4.69 bind – bound – bound (irreg v) – (chemistry) hold together by a chemical process • *In arts and crafts, glue is used to ~ various substances together, such as wood, paper, or plastic.* ➢ binding (n, adj). ❖ συνδέω. *See also* **3.88**.

4.70 dissolve (v) – cause sth solid to break down, become mixed with a liquid and disappear • *Over the years the groundwater in the cave has begun to ~ the limestone walls, creating interesting patterns.* ❖ διαλύω. 📖 : e.g., hopes ~, ~ Parliament

4.71 ★ **gully** (n) – (C) ❖ χαντάκι

4.72 ★ **void** (n) – (U) ❖ κενό

4.73 sculptor (n) → sb/sth whose job is to **sculpt** (v) – give shape or form to sth • *The sea ~s the shoreline like an artist ~s marble into a statue.* ➢ sculpture (n), sculpt (v), sculpted (adj) ❖ σμιλεύω, λαξεύω, χαράζω

4.74 enlist (v) → **~ the help of (sb/sth)** (v phr) – get sb/sth to provide help • *The children's charity has ~ed the help of local businessmen to build a new orphanage.* ❖ εξασφαλίζω την βοήθεια κάποιου/κάτι

4.75 surreal (adj) – having the qualities of **surrealism** (e.g., strange landscapes, objects with bizarre, distorted shapes) • *The photo had a weird, ~ quality about it, like the melting clocks in some of Salvador Dalí's paintings.* ➢ surrealism (n), surrealistic (adj) ❖ σουρεαλιστικός

Environmentalism 101

4.76 **bewildering** (adj) – amazing yet puzzling/confusing • *She looked at the ~ mass of files on her desk and didn't know where to begin.* ➢ bewilderment (n), bewilder (v), bewildered (adj) ❖ που φέρνει σύγχυση, ζάλη · αμηχανία

4.77 **array** (n) – (C) variety, assortment, collection • *The natural history museum has an impressive ~ of butterfly and moth specimens.* ❖ διάταξη

4.78 **rubble** (n) – (U) bits of broken rock, stone, concrete, brick, etc. • *The unused piece of land has become a dumping ground for the local builder's ~.* ❖ χαλάσματα, μπάζα

C Enter *Homo sapiens* ... and let the real damage begin (page 106)

4.79 **retreat** (n) – (U/C) the action or an act of moving back or withdrawing when faced with danger or difficulty • *Realizing the battle was lost, the general ordered a ~ to prevent losing more soldiers.* ➢ retreat (v), retreating (adj) ❖ υποχώρηση. 📖: e.g., a weekend ~

4.80 **vicious cycle** (n phr) – (C) (also **vicious circle**) ongoing situation in which one problem leads to another, making everything worse • *Fighting terrorism leads to more and more people becoming terrorists; it's a ~.* ❖ φαύλος κύκλος

4.81 **modify** (v) – change slightly, often (but not always) to improve • *Most scientists now believe that global warming has ~ied worldwide weather patterns.* ➢ modification (n), modified (adj) ❖ τροποποιώ

4.82 **degrade** (v) – ruin the quality of • *On the one hand, humans have made great technological progress; on the other, we have dangerously ~d the environment.* ➢ degradation (n), degraded (adj), degrading (adj) ❖ υποβιβάζω, εξευτελίζω. 📖: e.g., ~ sb with rude comments

4.83 **domestication** (n) – (U) the action of getting an animal used to living with or near people • *the ~ of wild animals into farm animals and pets* ➢ domesticate (v), domestic (adj) ❖ εξημέρωση

4.84 **herding** (n) → **herd** (v) – keep or look after a large group of animals • *His ancestors ~ed sheep on the mountain where he now has a summer home.* ➢ herd (n) ❖ φυλάω κοπάδι ζώων

4.85 ★ **overgrazing** (n) – (U) ➢ overgraze (v) ❖ (ζώα) υπερβοσκή

4.86 **eliminate** (v) – get rid of, remove • *The new law will help reduce prejudice in the workplace, but it will not ~ it completely.* ➢ elimination (n), eliminated (adj) ❖ εξαλείφω

4.87 **vegetation** (n) – (U) plant life (considered collectively) • *She was amazed at how dense the ~ was in the tropical rain forest.* ➢ vegetable (n, adj), vegetate (v), vegetative (adj) ❖ βλάστηση

4.88 **deplete** (v) – greatly reduce a supply of sth • *If you ~ your savings by buying that expensive car, how will you pay your rent?* ➢ depletion (n), depleted (adj) ❖ εξαντλώ, μειώνω

4.89 **denude** (v) – make bare, strip • *The slopes of the mountain were once covered with trees, but over the past two decades, the logging industry has completely ~d it.* ❖ απογυμνώνω

4.90 **slaughter** (v) – (of animals) kill for food, butcher; also, (of animals, people) kill in a needlessly cruel manner • *The fur trade ~s tens of thousands of beavers, foxes, and seals each year.* ➢ slaughter (n), slaughtered (adj) ❖ σφαγιάζω, σφάζω

4.91 **pest** (n) – (C) insect or small animal that causes damage to crops or food supplies • *mice and other ~s* ➢ pesticide (n), pester (v) ❖ επιβλαβές φυτό ή ζώο, παράσιτο

4.92 **predator** (n) – (C) animal that attacks and kills other animals for food • *The zoo is home to lions, tigers, and other ~s of the African savanna.* ➢ predation (n), predatory (adj) ❖ αρπακτικό ζώο

4.93 **in earnest** (prep phr) – seriously, with strong determination and intention • *He realizes he needs a good grade on the final exam to pass the course, so he's been studying ~ for the past two weeks.* ➢ earnest (adj), earnestly (adv) ❖ στα σοβαρά, για καλά

4.94 **exploit** (v) – use to gain a fair or unfair advantage • *If we want to win the game, we must ~ the opposition's weaknesses. / The workers went on strike, charging that the company was ~ing them.* ➢ exploitation (n), exploited (adj), exploitative (adj), exploitable (adj) ❖ εκμεταλλεύομαι

4.95 **reserve** (n) – (C/U) an amount or supply that is kept for later use • *(C) The country has large ~s of water and natural gas. / (U) The miser has plenty of money in ~.* ❖ απόθεμα. 📖: e.g., nature ~, military ~s, ~ (character trait)

4.96 **resource** (n) – (C) (usually plural) sth that can be used as a means of help or support • *the earth's natural ~s, a person's financial/mental ~s* ❖ πόρος

4.97 **ravage** (v) – cause great damage to • *Severe flooding has ~d the area, leaving death and destruction everywhere.* ➢ ravages (pl n), ravaged (adj) ❖ καταστρέφω, ρημάζω

4.98 **accelerating** (adj) → **accelerate** (v) – go faster, pick up speed; also, cause sth to go faster or pick up speed • *Drivers ~ on an open highway. / Cars ~ when drivers step on the gas. / Fertilizers ~ plant growth.* ➢ acceleration (n), accelerator (n), accelerated (adj), accelerating (adj) ❖ επιταχύνω, επισπεύδω

4.99 **decline** (n) – (C/U) a decrease or drop in quantity or quality • *Many people say that there has been a general ~ in the quality of schools in recent years.* ➢ decline (v), declining (adj) ❖ πτώση, μείωση

D Verbs to nouns (page 106)

Text

4.100 **objection (to)** (n) – (C) statement or feeling of dislike or disapproval of sth • *As usual, the boss raised strong ~s to the idea of spending more money on employee benefits.* ➢ object (v), (un)objectionable (adj) ❖ αντίρρηση

4.101 **proactive** (adj) – taking charge of a situation by causing change (rather than reacting to sth that has happened) • *If companies had been less profit-oriented and more ~, the environment would be in better shape today.* ➢ proactively (adv). Opp: reactive (adj) ❖ προδραστικός (δηλ. που ενεργεί προληπτικά)

4.102 **upgrade** (v) – (of equipment, services) to improve so as to enable sth to do more things or be more efficient • *~ medical facilities, ~ a computer's memory* ➢ upgrade (n) ❖ αναβαθμίζω, βελτιώνω

4.103 **pollutant** (n) – (C) substance which pollutes the environment (e.g., fumes or chemicals from industrial waste) • *There would be less ~s in the air if more of us rode bicycles or walked to work.* ❖ ρυπαντική ουσία

4.104 **discharge** (v) – give or send out (e.g., a liquid, gas, or electrical current) • *The factory was fined for ~ing dangerous chemicals into the air.* ➢ discharge (n) ❖ βγάζω, εκβάλλω, εκρέω. 📖: e.g., ~ a patient/soldier, ~ one's duties

4 Environmentalism 101

Writing (1) Paragraph development (page 107)

A Which is better: objective or imaginative?

4.105 objective (adj) – detached and dispassionate, influenced by reason and facts rather than feelings or opinions
• *Journalists must be ~ and report only what they observe.*
➢ objectivity (n), objectively (adv). Opp: subjective (adj)
❖ αντικειμενικός

4.106 imaginative (adj) – creative, inventive, having or showing **imagination** • *His plan is an ~ solution to the problem.*
➢ imagination (n), imagine (v), imaginatively (adv). Opp: unimaginative (adj) ❖ ευφάνταστος, επινοητικός, εφευρετικός

4.107 wake (n) → **in sth's ~ / in the ~ of (sth)** (prep phr) – as a result of, following, subsequent to • *In the burglary's ~, we finally decided to install a burglar alarm.* ❖ αμέσως μετά, σαν συνέπεια

4.108 assessment (n) – evaluation or judgment about the quality, value, or worth of sth • *The teacher's ~ was that the class had made excellent progress.* ➢ assessor (n), assess (v), assessed (adj) ❖ αξιολόγηση

4.109 orbiting (adj) → from **orbit** (v) – move around sth in an **orbit** (i.e., a curved path that goes all the way around sth)
• *The earth ~s the sun, and the moon ~s the earth.*
➢ orbit (n, v) ❖ κινούμαι σε τροχιά

B Try it! (page 107)
Topics 1 and 2

4.110 fossil fuel (n phr) – (C) fuel produced by the very slow decaying of animals or plants over millions of years
• *Examples of ~s include coal, petroleum, and natural gas.*
❖ ορυκτό καύσιμο

4.111 ban (v) – forbid, disallow, prohibit • *Many cities have ~ned smoking in public places such as government offices and hospitals.* ➢ ban (n), banned (adj) ❖ απαγορεύω

Vocabulary (1) Pandora's box (pages 108-111)

A Global warming (page 108)
1. Causes (page 108)

4.112 trap (v) – prevent the escape of • *Hunters ~ animals with the use of a trap. / Carbon dioxide ~s the sun's heat in the atmosphere.* ➢ trap (n), trapper (n), trapped (adj)
❖ παγιδεύω

4.113 reflect (v) – send or bounce back • *Mirrors ~ light.*
➢ reflection (n), reflector (n), reflective (adj), reflectively (adv)
❖ καθρεφτίζω, αντανακλώ. 📖 : e.g., ~ on a problem

4.114 greenhouse effect (n phr) – (U) natural phenomenon in which water vapor and other gases in the atmosphere keep in the sun's heat and help warm the planet • *Without the ~, the earth would be a cold planet unable to support life.*
❖ φαινόμενο του θερμοκηπίου

4.115 habitable (adj) – fit to live in • *The house is more ~, now that they've put in central air-conditioning and heating.*
➢ Opp: uninhabitable (adj) ❖ κατοικήσιμος

4.116 deforestation (n) – (U) the act of cutting down huge areas of trees to make room for industrial development • *D~ in the Amazon basin has endangered hundreds of species in the area.* ❖ καταστροφή δασών, αποψίλωση

4.117 exacerbate (v) – make worse (e.g., a pain, problem, situation)
• *Smoking ~s a cough. / Financial difficulties ~ problems in a marriage* ➢ exacerbation (n), exacerbating (adj), exacerbated (adj) ❖ επιδεινώνω

4.118 denude (v) – *see* **4.89**

4.119 absorb (v) – take/draw in, soak up (e.g., what roots do to water) • *The soil was dry and quickly ~ed the falling rain.*
➢ absorption (n), absorbent (adj), absorbed (adj), absorbing (adj) ❖ απορροφώ

4.120 magnify (v) – make more intense or bigger • *An alarmist ~ies a problem. / Telescopes and microscopes have special lenses that ~ objects to many times their normal size.*
➢ magnification (n), magnified (adj), magnifying (adj)
❖ μεγεθύνω μεγαλοποιώ

4.121 global warming (n phr) – (U) the slow rise in the earth's temperature (caused by too much carbon dioxide in the earth's atmosphere) • *Scientists believe that ~ is already causing the ice caps at the North and South Pole to begin melting.* ❖ υπερθέρμανση του πλανήτη

2. Effects (page 108)

4.122 curb (v) – control, restrain • *Eating plenty of fruits and salads helps ~ your appetite when you're dieting.*
❖ συγκρατώ, χαλιναγωγώ

4.123 emit (v) – send out (e.g., a gas or liquid) • *The sun ~s heat and light. / A factory ~s toxic fumes.* ➢ emission (n)
❖ εκπέμπω, αναδίνω

4.124 inundate (v) – flood, swamp, cover over with water • *The river overflowed its banks and ~d several towns in the area.*
➢ inundation (n), inundated (adj) ❖ πλημμυρίζω, κατακλύζω.
📖 : e.g., be ~d with work

4.125 drought (n) – (C/U) long period without rain, dry spell • *(C) Crops wither and die during a long ~. / (U) Years of ~ have led to famine and starvation.* ❖ ξηρασία

4.126 ★ **flash flooding** (n phr) → **flash flood** (n phr) – (C)
❖ ξαφνικός χείμαρρος

4.127 proliferate (v) – multiply and spread • *Mosquitoes ~ in summertime. Our town is near a lake, and it seems like they're everywhere!* ➢ proliferation (n), proliferating (adj)
❖ εξαπλώνομαι ταχύτατα, πολλαπλασιάζομαι

4.128 linger (v) – remain, stay on in a place • *The smell of the forest fire ~ed in the air for weeks after it was put out. / Most guests left at midnight, but a few of the hosts' close friends ~ed until two in the morning.* ➢ lingering (adj)
❖ (παρα)μένω, δείχνω απροθυμία να φύγω

4.129 ★ **heat stroke** (n phr) – (U) ❖ θερμοπληξία

4.130 ailment (n) – (C) minor illness • *An ~ like the common cold does not compare in seriousness to a disease like cancer.*
➢ ail (v), ailing (adj) ❖ αδιαθεσία, αρρώστια

4.131 aggravate (v) – make worse, exacerbate (*see* **4.117**)
• *Air pollution ~s respiratory problems.* ➢ aggravation (v), aggravated (adj), aggravating (adj) ❖ επιδεινώνω

B Declining air quality (page 109)
1. Smog

4.132 emit (v) – *see* **4.123**

4.133 fumes (pl n) – unhealthy smoke/gas given off by vehicles, factories, etc. • *The horrible car ~ make it impossible for her to cycle in the city's heavy traffic.* ❖ καυσαέρια, αναθυμιάσεις

4.134 toxic (adj) – poisonous • *The government decided to bury the ~ waste in a lead container deep underground.* ➢ toxin (n).
Opp: non-toxic (adj) ❖ τοξικός

Environmentalism 101

4.135 consequence (n) – (C) result, effect • *He's a conscientious worker who always considers the ~s of his actions.*
➢ consequential (adj), consequentially (adv) ❖ συνέπεια

4.136 emission (n) – (C) sth **emitted** or sent out into the air (e.g., gas, light, heat, matter) • *Strict clean-air laws have been passed to reduce the toxic ~s from cars and factories.*
➢ emit (v) ❖ εκπομπή (αερίου, φωτός κλπ)

4.137 smog (n) – (U) mixture of fog, smoke, and toxic chemicals that hangs over big cities or industrial areas • *As they looked down onto the city from the top of the mountain, they could see a layer of yellow ~ covering the valley.* ➢ smoggy (adj)
❖ το νέφος

4.138 irritate (v) – cause to be red or sore • *Working all day on a computer can ~ your eyes.* ➢ irritation (n), irritant (n), irritating (adj), irritated (adj) ❖ ερεθίζω. 📖 : e.g., ~ your parents

4.139 prolonged (adj) – lengthy, extended, drawn out • *After a ~ engagement lasting over eight years, the couple finally decided to get married.* ➢ prolongation (n), prolong (v)
❖ παρατεταμένος

4.140 stagnant (adj) – not moving, still • *The farmer decided to drain the ~ pond on his land.* ➢ stagnation (n), stagnate (v)
❖ στάσιμος, λιμνάζων

4.141 humid (adj) – full of water vapor ❖ (για κλίμα και αέρα) υγρός

2. Acid rain (page 109)

4.142 prevalent (adj) – common, widespread • *Columbus challenged the ~ belief that the world was flat.*
➢ prevalence (n), prevalently (adv) ❖ που κυριαρχεί, που επικρατεί

4.143 devastating (adj) – extremely destructive or damaging
• *The ~ earthquake leveled all the houses in the village.*
➢ devastation (n), devastate (v) ❖ καταστρεπτικός, ολέθριος

4.144 billow (v) – flow out in clouds or waves • *Smoke ~ed from the burning building in great black clouds. / As the wind came up, we watched the flags ~ing in the breeze.*
➢ billow (n), billowing (adj) ❖ ρέω/κινούμαι σε σύννεφα ή κύματα, κυματίζω

4.145 moisture (n) – (U) dampness, wetness (usually in the form of tiny drops of water on a surface or in the air) • *The humidity is so high that you can feel the ~ in the air on your skin.* ➢ moisten (v), moist (adj) ❖ υγρασία

4.146 component (n) – (C) part of sth (e.g., of a chemical compound, a system) • *Hydrogen and oxygen are the main ~s of water.* ➢ compose (v) ❖ συστατικό μέρος

4.147 ★ acid rain (n phr) – (U) ❖ όξινη βροχή

4.148 contaminate (v) – pollute, make impure • *Dumping toxic waste into a lake or river will ~ it.* ➢ contamination (n), contaminant (n), contaminated (adj) ❖ μιαίνω, μολύνω

4.149 deteriorate (v) – slowly fall apart, crumble, decay, break down • *The forces of wind and water can cause rock to ~. / Air pollution is causing the surface of the monuments to ~.*
➢ deterioration (n), deteriorated (adj) ❖ φθίνω, φθείρομαι, εκφυλίζομαι. 📖 : e.g., a situation/one's health ~s

3. Ozone (page 109)

4.150 ★ ultraviolet (adj) – ❖ υπεριώδης

4.151 radiation (n) – 1. (U) heat or energy sent out in the form of rays; the act of sending out heat or energy in the form of rays
• *Without the warmth of the sun's ~, life on earth would not be possible. / No one knows for sure what effects the ~ from cell phones will have on us.* 2. (U) powerful and dangerous rays sent out from radioactive substances; similar to **radioactivity**
• *R~ from nuclear explosions can cause widespread damage.*
➢ radiate (v), radiant (adj), radiantly (adv) ❖ 1. ακτινοβολία 2. ραδιενέργεια

4.152 detrimental (adj) – harmful, dangerous • *Excessive sunbathing may have a seriously ~ effect on your skin.*
➢ detriment (n) ❖ επιβλαβής, επιζήμιος

4.153 ★ ozone layer (n phr) – (U) ❖ στρώμα του όζοντος

4.154 ★ refrigerant (n) – (C) ❖ ψυκτικό (υγρό)

4.155 ★ aerosol spray (n phr) – (C) ❖ αερόλυμα, αεροζόλ

4.156 deplete (v) – see **4.88**

4.157 compromise (sth/sb) (v) – (health) put at risk, endanger
• *Abusing substances like tobacco and alcohol can seriously ~ your health.* ➢ compromise (n), compromising (adj)
❖ (υγεία) εκθέτω, διακινδυνεύω. 📖 : e.g., ~ with sb, reach a ~, ~ one's reputation

4.158 haze (n) – (U) thin warm-weather fog • *In summer a thick yellow ~ known as smog hangs over the city.* ➢ haze (v), hazy (adj), hazily (adv) ❖ αχλή, ελαφριά ομίχλη, καταχνιά

4.159 exacerbate (v) – see **4.117**

C Declining water quality (page 110)

1. Water pollution (page 110)

4.160 waste (n) – (U) useless material • *We can cut down on ~ by recycling glass, aluminum, and paper.* ➢ waste (v), wasteful (adj), wastefully (adv) ❖ απόβλητα, απορρίμματα

4.161 agricultural (adj) – related to **agriculture** (i.e., farming)
• *Many immigrants to Greece earn their living as ~ workers, picking olives, fruit, and other crops.* ➢ agriculture (n), agriculturist (n) ❖ γεωργικός

4.162 ★ waste disposal (n phr) – (U) ❖ διάθεση απορριμμάτων/ αποβλήτων

4.163 overburden (v) – demand more work of sb/sth than can be handled • *Unfortunately, it's natural for bosses to ~ their best employees.* ➢ overburdened (adj) ❖ παραφορτώνω

4.164 sewer (n) – (C) large underground channel that carries water and waste away from buildings • *The prisoner was bitten by a rat as he tried to escape through the ~ under the prison.*
➢ sewage (n, adj) ❖ υπόνομος

4.165 ★ raw sewage (n phr) – (U) ❖ ακατέργαστα λύματα

4.166 grease (n) – (U) thick, oily substance used to help machines run smoothly • *The floor of the mechanic's garage was covered in ~.* ➢ grease (v), greasy (adj) ❖ γράσο, λιπαντικό

4.167 ★ pesticide (n) – (C) ❖ φυτοφάρμακο (π.χ., εντομοκτόνο, ζιζανιοκτόνο)

4.168 ★ runoff (n) – (U) ❖ βρόχονερο που δεν απορροφάται από το έδαφος

4.169 ingest (v) – take into the body (e.g., by swallowing) • *If someone in your family ~s poison, call the local poison center immediately.* ➢ ingestion (n), ingested (adj)
❖ τρώγω, καταπίνω

4.170 ★ shellfish (n) – (U) ❖ θαλασσινά, οστρακοειδή

Environmentalism 101

4.171 fertilizer (n) – (C) substance that enriches the soil and helps plants grow • *Organic vegetables are grown without pesticides and artificial ~s.* ➤ fertilization (n), fertilize (v), fertilized (adj) ❖ λίπασμα

4.172 nutrient (n) – (C) chemical substance that provides nourishment and helps maintain life • *Vitamins, proteins, and carbohydrates are examples of ~s.* ➤ nutrition (n), nutritionist (n), nutritional (adj) ❖ θρεπτική ουσία

4.173 trigger (v) – start, be the cause of sth • *The noisy students ~ed the teacher's anger.* ➤ trigger (n) ❖ προκαλώ

4.174 abnormal (adj) – uncommon, unnatural, unusual • *The doctor was concerned about the ~ amount of sugar in the child's blood.* ➤ abnormality (n), abnormally (adv). Opp: normal (adj) ❖ αντικανονικός, αφύσικος, ανώμαλος

4.175 algae (pl n) → **alga** (n) – (C) simple form of plant life that grows in water • *The water of the pool is specially treated to prevent the growth of slimy, green ~ on the sides of the pool.* ❖ άλγη

4.176 oil spill (n phr) – (C) accident in which a large quantity of oil spills (i.e., pours out of) a vehicle, ship, container, etc. • *An ~ can have a disastrous effect on sea and coastal life.* ❖ διαρροή μεγάλης ποσότητας πετρελαίου

4.177 leakage (n) – (U) gas or liquid that escapes from a crack, hole, etc. • *L~ from a gas stove may lead to an explosion.* ➤ leak (n, v), leaking (adj) ❖ διαρροή, διαφυγή

4.178 ★ refinery (n) – (C) ➤ refinement (n), refine (v), refined (adj) ❖ διυλιστήριο

4.179 ★ offshore oil rig (n phr) – (C) ❖ πλατφόρμα (άντλησης πετρελαίου)

4.180 devastating (adj) – *see* **4.143**

4.181 impact (n) – *see* **4.3(2)**

2. Depletion of freshwater resources (page 110)

4.182 ★ groundwater (n) – (U) ❖ υπόγεια ύδατα

4.183 potable (adj) – drinkable • *The drought caused a serious shortage of ~ water.* ➤ potability (n) ❖ πόσιμος

4.184 irrigation (n) – (U) the act of supplying water to land that is usually dry • *The ~ of desert areas can be accomplished by digging canals and constructing a vast network of pipelines for carrying water.* ➤ irrigate (v), irrigated (adj) ❖ άρδευση

4.185 ★ aquifer (n) – (C) ❖ υδροφόρο πέτρωμα

4.186 seep (v) – leak, flow slowly and in small quantities • *blood ~s out of a wound and through a bandage, oil ~s out of the ground* ➤ seepage (n), seeping (adj) ❖ διαρρέω, διαποτίζω

4.187 rural (adj) – concerning life in the countryside or a village • *He grew up on a farm in a ~ area, hundreds of miles from a big city.* ➤ Opp: urban (adj) ❖ αγροτικός, εξοχικός

4.188 urban (adj) – related to life in a large town or city • *You can't fully appreciate the term "rat race" until you've lived in a major ~ area like New York or London.* ➤ urbanization (n), urbanize (v), urbanized (adj). Opp: rural (adj) ❖ αστικός

4.189 access (n) – (U) right or opportunity to use or benefit from sth • *The nation's poor people have little or no ~ to health care or education.* ➤ accessibility (n), access (v), accessible (adj) ❖ πρόσβαση. 📖 e.g., wheelchair ~, ~ to a mountain village

4.190 scarcity (n) – (U) lack, shortage • *The war-torn country is suffering from a serious ~ of food and medical supplies.* ➤ scarce (adj), scarcely (adv) ❖ έλλειψη

4.191 poverty (n) – (U) state of being very poor • *He grew up in a poor neighborhood surrounded by crime, drug abuse, and other symptoms of ~.* ➤ impoverish (v), poverty-stricken (adj), impoverished (adj). Opp: wealth (n) ❖ φτώχεια

Vocabulary (2) Disasters wrought by ... (pages 114-116)

A word about *wrought* – As an adjective, *wrought* means "made or shaped in a skillful or decorative way" (e.g., *wrought iron*). As a verb form, *wrought* usually means "made" or "done." It is an archaic past tense/past participle of the verb *work*, which in formal modern usage usually has the meaning of "made" or "done" as in the phrases "disasters wrought by nature" (p. 114) and "disasters wrought by man" (p. 120), or Samuel Morse's first telegraph message: What hath God wrought?" (p. 135). A more common modern usage is the adjective *overwrought*, meaning "worked up, extremely upset and agitated": e.g., "I've never seen her so overwrought before. Did something terrible happen?"

STEP 1 (page 114)

For general reference, here is an alphabetical listing of natural disasters that you should be familiar with, along with their Greek equivalents.

4.192 ★ avalanche (n) – (C) ❖ χιονοστιβάδα
4.193 ★ blizzard (n) – (C) ❖ χιονοθύελλα
4.194 ★ deluge (n) – (C) ❖ κατακλυσμός
4.195 ★ drought (n) – (C) ❖ ξηρασία
4.196 ★ earthquake (n) – (C) ❖ σεισμός
4.197 ★ famine (n) – (C) ❖ λιμός
4.198 ★ flood (n) – (C) ➤ flooding (n), flood (v), flooded (adj) ❖ πλημμύρα
4.199 ★ hurricane (n) – (C) ❖ τυφώνας (στον Ατλαντικό)
4.200 ★ landslide (n) – (C) ❖ κατολίσθηση
4.201 ★ tornado/cyclone/twister (n) – (C) ❖ κυκλώνας
4.202 ★ typhoon (n) – (C) ❖ τυφώνας (στον Ειρηνικό)
4.203 ★ volcano (n) – (C) ➤ volcanic ❖ ηφαίστειο

STEP 3 (page 114)
Text 1 (page 114)
Paragraph 1

4.204 ferocious (adj) – fierce, violent, savage • *The letter carrier refused to deliver letters to any house with a ~ dog in the yard.* ➤ ferocity (n), ferociously (adv). Opp: gentle (adj) ❖ άγριος, θηριώδης

4.205 tremor (n) – (C) (of the ground) moving or shaking • *There have been a number of minor ~s recently. I hope it isn't a sign that an earthquake is coming.* ❖ (σεισμική) δόνηση

4.206 rage (v) – continue violently • *storms and fires ~ , battles ~, angry people ~* ➤ rage (n), raging (adj) ❖ λυσσομανώ

4.207 funeral (n) – (C) ceremony that precedes the burial or cremation of a dead person • *Political leaders from all over the world attended the ~ of the assassinated president.* ➤ funereal (adj) ❖ κηδεία

4.208 sheer (adj) – absolute, complete, utter • *There is only one reason that he failed his exams, and that is ~ laziness.* ❖ απόλυτος

4.209 displace (v) – force sb to leave one's home or normal location • *The war has ~d thousands of families.* ➤ displacement (n), displaced (adj) ❖ μετατοπίζω, εκτοπίζω

Environmentalism 101 4

4.210 **topple** (v) – (with object) cause (sth) to fall over or collapse; (without object) fall over • *A hurricane can ~ houses. / (fig) A scandal may ~ a government. / A pile of books can ~ onto the floor.* ➢ toppled (adj) ❖ (με αντικείμενο) γκρεμίζω, (μετ) ανατρέπω, (χωρίς αντικείμενο) σωριάζομαι

4.211 **twist** (v) – bend out of shape, distort • *The crash ~ed the hood of the car into a crumpled mass.* ➢ twist (n), twisted (adj), twisting (adj) ❖ στραβώνω, στρεβλώνω, παραμορφώνω. ▭ : e.g., ~ in your seat, ~ the truth, ~ sb's arm

4.212 **sever** (v) – cut completely through • *He ~d his hand in a boating accident last year.* ➢ severance (n), severed (adj) ❖ αποκόπτω

Paragraph 2

4.213 **give way** (phr v) – collapse, cave in • *The wooden house was so old and run down that we were afraid that the steps would ~ if we tried to go upstairs.* ❖ καταρρέω. ▭ : e.g., ~ to sb's demands

4.214 **crumble** (v) – break into pieces • *There was so much rust on the body of the car that wherever he touched it, pieces just ~d away.* ➢ crumb (n), crumbled (adj), crumbling (adj) ❖ θρυμματίζω/-ομαι, τρίβω/-ομαι

4.215 **elevated** (adj) – raised above the ground • *One of New York City's interesting features is that in some areas the subway trains run on elevated bridges known as "els" high above the city streets.* ➢ elevation (n), elevator (n), elevate (v), elevating (adj) ❖ εναέριος (π.χ., δρόμος, τρένο)

4.216 **sway** (v) – move from side to side • *The slender trees ~ed in the strong breeze.* ➢ sway (n), swaying (adj) ❖ κινούμαι. ▭ : e.g., ~ sb's opinion

4.217 **buckle** (v) – collapse, cave in • *Before she fainted, she remembers feeling her knees ~ and then everything went black.* ➢ buckled (adj) ❖ καταρρέω, υποχωρώ. ▭ : e.g., ~ your seatbelt

4.218 **incongruous** (adj) – out of place, inappropriate • *Can you imagine how ~ a fifty-story skyscraper would look in the village square?* ➢ incongruity (n), incongruously (adv) ❖ αταίριαστος, άτοπος

4.219 **charred** (adj) – burnt and blackened • *We left the steaks on the grill for too long, and wound up with ~ lumps of inedible meat!* ➢ charcoal (n), char (v) ❖ καρβουνιασμένος, μαυρισμένος

4.220 **smoldering** (adj) – (Brit: **smouldering**) smoking or burning without flame • *After the flames had died down, the ~ logs in the fireplace continued to give off heat for an hour or so.* ➢ smolder (v) ❖ που κρυφοκαίει

4.221 **calamity** (n) – (C) disaster, tragedy • *The terrorist attack on the World Trade Center was a ~ of tragic proportions.* ➢ calamitous (adj), calamitously (adv) ❖ πανωλεθρία, συμφορά

4.222 **humble** (v) – make sb feel that they are low or common • *An overwhelming defeat in an election would ~ even the most arrogant politician.* ➢ humble (adj), humble (adv) ❖ ταπεινώνω

Text 2 (page 115)
Paragraph 1

4.223 **scalding** (adj) – boiling, steaming hot • *The water in the pot is ~, so make sure you use a potholder.* ➢ scald (v) ❖ ζεματιστός

4.224 ★ **magma** (n) – (U) ❖ μάγμα

4.225 ★ **chasm** (n) – (C) ❖ χάσμα

4.226 **fiery** (adj) – (lit) burning strongly and brightly, like fire • *Temperatures on the sun's ~ surface exceed 9,300° F.* ❖ φλογισμένος, πύρινος. ▭ : e.g., (fig) a ~ temper

4.227 **medieval** (adj) – of or related to the Middle Ages (c. AD 1100-1500) • *The wall surrounding the city was built in early ~ times, more than eight hundred years ago.* ➢ medievalist (n), medievalism (n) ❖ μεσαιωνικός

4.228 ★ **glacial** (adj) – ❖ παγετώδης

4.229 **cauldron** (n) – (C) (also **caldron**) large deep metal pot with handles, used for cooking over an open fire • *Her favorite scene in Shakespeare's* Macbeth *is the one where the three witches stand over a boiling ~ , chanting "Double, double, toil and trouble. Fire burn, and ~ bubble."* ❖ καζάνι, κακκάβι

4.230 **rumble** (v) – make a low, deep rolling sound (e.g., like thunder) • *He was so hungry that you could hear his stomach ~.* ➢ rumble (n), rumbling (n, adj) ❖ βροντώ υπόκωφα

4.231 **billow** (v) – see 4.144

4.232 **elemental** (adj) – related to the four **elements** of nature (i.e., earth, wind, fire, water) • *If you've ever been out at sea in a tiny fishing boat in the middle of a huge thunder, lightning, and wind storm, you'll understand what it means to witness an ~ battle.* ➢ element (n) ❖ των στοιχείων της φύσης

4.233 **clash** (v) – (C) meet in combat, fight • *Government and rebel forces ~ed again yesterday in a bloody fight for the capital city.* ➢ clash (n), clashing (adj) ❖ συγκρούομαι

4.234 **thermal** (adj) – related to or caused by heat or a change in temperature • *A thermostat is a ~ control that turns a machine on or off at specific temperatures.* ➢ thermal (n) ❖ θερμικός. ▭ : e.g., ~ underwear

4.235 **well up** (phr v) – rise up and overflow (i.e., spill over) • *Paralyzed by fear, she could feel a scream ~ from deep within her.* ❖ αναβλύζω

4.236 ★ **bedrock** (n) – (U) ❖ βραχώδες υπόστρωμα

4.237 **collapse** (v) – fall in, give way • *If there's a heavy snowstorm, the roof of that old house will surely ~.* ➢ collapse (n), collapsible (adj) ❖ καταρρέω, σωριάζομαι

4.238 **shatter** (v) – break into small pieces • *The plate dropped and ~ed into a thousand pieces. / He ~ed the window with a brick.* ➢ shattered (adj) ❖ θρυμματίζω/-ομαι

4.239 **torrent** (n) – strong, fast stream (e.g., of water or of words) • *As the rain continued to pour down, a ~ of water ran through the streets. / The television station received a ~ of complaints about the new show.* ➢ torrential (adj) ❖ χείμαρρος

4.240 **surge** (v) – move forward in strong waves • *electricity ~s through a wire, flood waters ~ through a valley* ➢ surge (n), surging (adj) ❖ κινούμαι σαν κύμα

4.241 ★ **geothermal** (adj) – ❖ γεωθερμικός

4.242 **crater** (n) – (C) round hole or indentation in the ground made by sth that has fallen or exploded • *The surface of the moon is full of ~s made by falling meteorites. / Magma welled up deep within the volcano's ~.* ❖ κρατήρας

49

Environmentalism 101

Paragraph 2

4.243 peak (v) – reach a high point/level • *temperatures ~ in the summer, retail sales ~ before Christmas* ❖ κορυφώνω, ανυψώνω στον ανώτερο βαθμό

4.244 bursting (n/ger) → **fill (sth) to ~** (v phr/idm) – fill sth until it is ready to explode or spill over • *We ate so much at Christmas dinner that everyone was filled to ~.*
❖ παραφουσκώνω

4.245 prompt (v) – cause sb to do sth • *It was his son's illness that ~ed the poor man to rob the bank. / The devastating earthquake ~ed officials to strengthen the building code.*
➢ prompt (n), prompting (n) ❖ παρακινώ

4.246 imminent (adj) – about to happen • *Judging from the black clouds and thunder rumbling in the distance, a storm was ~.* ➢ imminence (n), imminently (adv) ❖ επικείμενος, αναμενόμενος

4.247 deluge (n) – *see* **4.194**

4.248 anticipation (n) – (C) expectation, the feeling (e.g., of excitement or anxiety) that sb gets when they are waiting for sth to happen • *Some people await Christmastime with eager ~; others await it with a sense of anxious ~, knowing they will be alone or with people they won't enjoy.*
❖ αναμονή, προσδοκία, προαίσθημα

4.249 wane (v) – gradually decrease, become weaker or less intense • *As the sunlight gradually ~d, the bathers picked up their belongings and headed for home.* ➢ on the ~ (prep phr), waning (adj) ❖ εξασθενίζω, ελαττώνομαι

4.250 pent-up (adj phr) – stored-up, ready to burst • *a bride and groom experience ~ emotion on their wedding day, children have ~ energy when they can't go out to play*
❖ συγκρατημένος

4.251 spew (v) → **~ forth** (v phr) – (formal, literary) come out in a strong stream • *A wave of humanity ~ed forth from the stadium at the end of the match.* ❖ ξερνώ

Text 3 (page 115)

4.252 resident (n) – (C) sb who lives in a place • *The village has just under two thousand ~s.* ➢ residence (n), reside (v), residential (adj) ❖ κάτοικος

4.253 evacuate (v) – leave to avoid danger; also, help/make people leave to avoid danger • *As soon as they heard the fire alarm, everyone ~d the building. / Firefighters and police officers were sent to ~ the office workers from the burning building.* ➢ evacuation, evacuee (n), evacuated (adj)
❖ εκκενώνω

4.254 ensue (v) – follow, come after • *Everyone had been expecting a mild tropical storm rather than a full-blown hurricane, so nobody was prepared for the devastation that ~d.* ➢ ensuing (adj) ❖ επακολουθώ, προκύπτω

4.255 shred (n) – (C) ripped or torn-off piece of sth (e.g., of material or meat) • *After the balloon burst, we found ~s of it everywhere!* ❖ κομματάκι (πχ, από ύφασμα, κρέας)

4.256 lodge (v) – become stuck • *The bullet grazed his shoulder and ~d in the wall in back of him.* ❖ σφηνώνω/-ομαι, χώνω/-ομαι

4.257 topple (v) – *see* **4.210**

4.258 uproot (v) – 1. (trees, plants) pull out of the ground, together with the roots • *The tornado was so powerful that it ~ed all the trees in our yard.* 2. (people) leave or make sb leave a place where s/he has lived for a long time (i.e., displace – *see* **4.209**) • *refugees ~ed by war* ❖ (ενς. 1-2) ξεριζώνω

4.259 debris (n) – (C) ruined bits of sth that has been destroyed • *After the World Trade Center was destroyed, wrecking crews took several months to remove all the ~ from the area.* ❖ συντρίμματα, χαλάσματα

4.260 rubble (n) – *see* **4.78**

4.261 blessed (adj) – (in context) fortunate to be under the protection and/or favor of a divine power • *After years of wanting a child, she felt ~ when she gave birth to a healthy baby boy.* ➢ blessing (n), bless (v). Opp: cursed (adj)
❖ ευλογημένος

4.262 demolish (v) – (of buildings and other large structures) destroy, usually by knocking it down or causing it to explode • *A wrecking crew arrived to ~ the run-down hotel. / The commandoes used explosives to ~ the bridge.*
➢ demolition(s) (n), demolished (adj) ❖ κατεδαφίζω

4.263 wake (n) → **in sth's/sb's ~** (prep phr) – *see* **4.107**

4.264 restrospect (n) → **in ~** (prep phr) – looking back on a past event or situation • *In ~, it was clear that the marriage would not last.* ➢ retrospection (n), retrospective (adj), retrospectively (adv) ❖ εκ των υστέρων, αναδρομικά

4.265 pale (v) – (fig) appear weak or insignificant when compared to sth else • *Her old apartment was nice, but it ~s before the one she lives in now. You should see the river view she has!* ➢ paleness (n), pale (adj) ❖ (μετ) ωχριώ μπροστά σε κτ /σε σύγκριση με κτ

4.266 brunt (n) → **the ~ of sth** (idm) – the full force (or weight) of sth • *Most people think Anna is sweet, but they soon change their mind when they taste the ~ of her anger.*
❖ ορμή, κύριο βάρος

4.267 aftermath (n) → **in the ~ (of sth)** (prep phr) – during the period immediately following an unpleasant event; similar to **in the wake of sth** (*see* **4.107**). • *In the ~ of the earthquake, rescue teams spent days searching for survivors.* ❖ ως επακόλουθο

4.268 inundate (v) – *see* **4.124**

Cloze Linking words (pages 117-119)

Skills focus: Finding "missing links" … (page 117)

4.269 missing link (n phr) – (lit) sth that is needed in order to complete a series or provide complete continuity in sth ❖ ο ελλείπων κρίκος. **Note:** As usual, Michigan Mama is playing with words here. By putting the phrase "missing links" in quotation marks, she's signaling that she wants her readers to make a connection between "missing linking words" in a cloze passage and "the missing link" between humans and apes that anthropologists are still trying to find. Hopefully, ECPE candidates will have better luck than anthropologists have had!

4.270 train of thought (n phr) – (fig) logical series or sequence of ideas • *He tried to concentrate on the test, but the slightest sound made him lose his ~.* ❖ ειρμός των σκέψεων μου

CLOZE PRACTICE (1): Establishing relationships … (page 118)

1. Describing a sequence of events (page 118)

Paragraph 1

4.271 glint (v) – give off small flashes of light • *The rippled surface of the river ~ed in the strong sunlight.* ➢ glint (n)
❖ σπιθίζω, αστράφτω

Environmentalism 101

4.272 **bustle (with)** (v) – (of a place) be alive with (or full of) movement or busy activity • *New York City is hardly a relaxing place to spend time; the streets are always ~ing with traffic and people, even in the middle of the night.* ➢ bustle (n), bustling (adj) ❖ κινούμαι εδώ κι εκεί, είμαι γεμάτος κίνηση, θόρυβο και ζωντάνια

4.273 **gasp** (v) – struggle to breathe • *By the time we reached the top of the steep hill, we were ~ing for air.* ❖ gasp (n), gasping (adj) ❖ ασθμαίνω, αγκομαχώ

Paragraph 2

4.274 **flop** (v) – move or fall in an awkward, loose way • *fish ~ around in the bottom of a boat, a tired person ~s down on a bed, long hair ~s into your eyes* ➢ flop (n), floppy (adj) ❖ τινάζομαι, χτυπιέμαι · ρίχνω ή πέφτω αδέξια ή με γδούπο

4.275 **glisten** (v) – shine brightly, especially with light reflected from a wet or polished surface • *Wet grass ~s in the sun, as does a new car or a diamond ring.* ➢ glistening (adj) ❖ λαμποκοπώ, γυαλίζω

4.276 **corpse** (n) – (C) dead body (usually of a human being) • *Police are still trying to identify the ~ that washed up on the beach last night.* ❖ πτώμα. **Note:** for animals the word **carcass** is usually used.

4.277 ★ **seagull** (n) – (C) ❖ γλάρος

4.278 **perch** (v) – come to rest or balance unsteadily on sth thin or high (e.g., a bird on a branch or a house on a cliff) • *My kitten is fond of jumping up onto my back and ~ing herself bird-style on my shoulder.* ➢ perch (n), perched (adj) ❖ κουρνιάζω, κάθομαι

4.279 **massacre** (n) – (C/U) mass killing, slaughter • *The battle between the rebels and government forces turned into a ~, with both sides suffering heavy losses.* ➢ massacre (v), massacred (adj) ❖ μακελειό

2. Emphasizing and convincing (page 118)

4.280 **consumption** (n) – (U) (in context) the using up or expenditure of sth • *The global ~ of electrical power has increased greatly over the past hundred years.* ➢ consumer (n), consume (v), consumable (adj) ❖ κατανάλωση. 📖 : e.g., food ~

4.281 **sufficient** (adj) – enough, adequate • *If he had ~ money in the bank, he'd buy a new car.* ➢ sufficiency (n), suffice (v), sufficiently (adv). Opp: insufficient (adj) ❖ αρκετός, επαρκής

4.282 **unevenly** (adv) – (in context) not equally • *Workaholics divide their time ~ between work and their family, with work receiving the greater emphasis.* ➢ unevenness (n), uneven (adj) ❖ άνισος

4.283 **distributed** (pp) → **distribute** (v) – (used passively in text) give or pass sth out to a number of people • *To earn extra money, the teenagers ~d supermarket leaflets in their neighborhood.* ❖ μοιράζω, διανέμω, κατανέμω

4.284 **access** (n) – see **4.189**

4.285 **irrigation** (n) – see **4.184**

4.286 **account (for)** (v) – explain • *They were supposed to get married next week. Can anyone ~ for their sudden break-up?* ❖ εξηγώ

4.287 **forecast** (v) – predict, say in advance what is expected to happen • *The weather report ~s rain for tomorrow.* ➢ forecasting (n), forecaster (n) ❖ προβλέπω

4.288 **leak** (n) – (C) flow of liquid or gas that gets in or out of a hole or crack in sth; the hole or crack from which such a flow escapes • *Get a bucket, quick! There's a ~ in the roof!* ❖ διαρροή. 📖 : e.g., an information ~

4.289 **tap** (n) – (C) part of a sink, bathtub, hosepipe, etc., that one turns to control the flow of water • *Old-fashioned sinks had two ~s: one for hot water and another for cold.* ➢ tap (v) ❖ βρύση. 📖 : e.g., wire/phone ~

4.290 **dire** (adj) – terrible, urgent • *After the accident the passengers were in ~ need of immediate medical attention.* ➢ direness (n) ❖ τρομερός, έσχατος

4.291 **sanitary** (adj) – related to **sanitation** (i.e., conditions and procedures related to public health, cleanliness, and hygiene) • *A city's ~ facilities include services such as the provision of healthy drinking water, sewage treatment, garbage disposal, and public food inspection.* ➢ sanitation (n), sanitize (v). Opp: unsanitary (adj) ❖ υγιεινός

4.292 **untreated** (adj) – raw, unprocessed (i.e., not having been treated with a process or substance to improve, protect, or preserve sth) • *The cruise ship company was fined for dumping ~ waste into the sea.* ➢ Opp: treated (adj) ❖ ακατέργαστος

4.293 **lethal** (adj) – deadly, able to kill or cause great damage • *We are polluting our rivers and seas with ~ chemicals.* ➢ lethality (n), lethally (adv) ❖ φονικός, θανατηφόρος

CLOZE PRACTICE (2): Finding missing links … (page 119)
Paragraph 1

4.294 **bulk (of)** (n) – (U) greatest or major part of sth • *"Your sister is too young to know right from wrong, so the ~ of the blame for what happened lies with you! You're grounded!"* ❖ το κύριο μέρος. 📖 : e.g., the sheer ~ of sth, a person's ~

4.295 **associated** (adj) – related • *The college offers programs in criminal justice and ~ subjects such as law enforcement and courtroom reporting.* ➢ association (n), associate (v) ❖ συγγενής, ομοειδής

4.296 **factor** (n) - (C) sth that causes or influences a result • *The boss based his decision on financial ~s.* ❖ παράγοντας

4.297 **drive – drove – driven** (irreg v) – force (sb/sth) to go a certain way or to do sth against their will • *If we're lucky, the strong winds will ~ the oil spill away from the shore. / It's the job of a sheepdog to ~ the herd up the mountain and back.* ❖ οδηγώ, εξωθώ

4.298 **whip** (v) – beat sth into a froth (or foam) • *She ~ped the cream until it formed stiff peaks.* ❖ χτυπώ

Paragraph 2

4.299 **robust** (adj) – strong and healthy • *a ~ young man in the prime of life, a ~ environment that recovers quickly from an oil spill* ➢ robustness (n), robustly (adv) ❖ ρωμαλέος, γερός

4.300 **diverse** (adj) – varied, showing variety • *Big cities are often populated by people of ~ ethnic backgrounds.* ➢ diversity (n), diversify (v), diversified (adj) ❖ ποικίλος, διαφορετικός

4.301 **resilient** (adj) – able to recover quickly from illness, injury, or other misfortune • *It often takes a great tragedy for people to show how ~ they really are.* ➢ resilience (n), resiliently (adv) ❖ ανθεκτικός, ευπροσάρμοστος

4 Environmentalism 101

4.302 coincide (v) – (events) happen at the same time or during the same time as sth else • *Luckily, the two birthday parties don't ~, so we can go to both of them!* ➤ coincidence (n), coincidental (adj), coincidentally (adv) ❖ συμπίπτω

Vocabulary (3) Disasters ... man (pages 120-121)

STEP 3: Vocabulary retrieval (page 120)

Text 1 (page 120)

Paragraph 1

4.303 debris (n) – *see* **4.259**

4.304 particle (n) – (C) very small piece of sth • *~s of dust in the air, subatomic ~s* (e.g., electrons, protons, neutrons) ❖ μόριο

4.305 swath (n) – (C) (Brit: **swathe**) – (C) broad strip or area, often of plants, land, or water • *In order to build the new highway, it was necessary to cut a ~ through the forest.* ❖ δρεπανιά (χόρτου κλπ), πλατιά λωρίδα

4.306 infiltrate (v) – enter secretly (e.g., like Special Forces soldiers or spies) • *The soldiers were ordered to ~ the enemy camp at dawn and take as many prisoners as possible.* ➤ infiltration (n) ❖ (για στρατεύματα) διεισδύω, εισχωρώ

4.307 seep (v) – *see* **4.186**

Paragraph 2

4.308 insidious (adj) – spreading silently but harmfully, without anyone noticing how much damage or harm is being done • *the ~ effect of nuclear fall-out* ❖ ύπουλος, επίβουλος

4.309 toll (n) – **take (a/its) ~ (on sth)** (idm) – have a harmful effect on sth/sb • *Too much work and improper sleep will eventually take its ~ on your health.* ❖ έχω βαριές επιπτώσεις

4.310 chilling (adj) – causing a cold, frightening feeling, as if one's blood has suddenly gone cold • *The televised scenes of the disaster were among the most ~ she had ever seen.* ➤ chill (n, v) ❖ τρομακτικός, που σου παγώνει το αίμα

4.311 trigger (v) – *see* **4.173**

4.312 aberration (n) – (C) abnormal or unusual change • *Years of abusing drugs can cause ~s in an addict's personality.* ➤ aberrant (adj), aberrantly (adv) ❖ ανωμαλία, παρεκτροπή

Paragraph 3

4.313 refugee (n) – (C) person displaced by war or other catastrophe • *Since the early 1990s Western Europe has been swamped with ~s from former Communist nations like Bulgaria, Romania, and Albania.* ➤ refuge (n) ❖ πρόσφυγας

4.314 long-term (adj) – lasting for a long time • *Diplomatic efforts have failed to achieve ~ peace in the troubled area.* ➤ Opp: short-term (adj) ❖ μακροπρόθεσμος

4.315 contamination (n) – (U) the quality or act of being **contaminated** (i.e., impure or polluted with substances that are dangerous or undesirable) • *The factories in the area are all partly responsible for the ~ of local water sources.* ➤ *see* **4.148** ❖ μίασμα, μόλυνση

4.316 irreparable (adj) – unable to be repaired or corrected • *The earthquake caused ~ damage to the city's ancient monuments.* ➤ irreparably (adv). Opp: repairable (adj) ❖ ανεπανόρθωτος

4.317 amok (adv) → **run ~** (v phr) – go wild, lose control • *The investigation showed that the killer was a quiet student who suddenly began to run ~.* ❖ παθαίνω αμόκ

Text 2 (page 121)

4.318 sprawling (adj) – spread out over a wide area • *Modern Athens is a ~ metropolis, much larger than the ancient city.* ➤ sprawl (n, v) ❖ που απλώνεται ακατάστατα

4.319 shanty (n) – 1. (C) crudely built shed or shack • *It was difficult to believe that ten people lived within the walls of the tiny tin-roofed shanty.* ❖ παράγκα 2. **~town** (n) – (C) poor area made up of small dwellings known as ~ies, usually on the outskirts of a town or city; a type of slum *(see **4.325** below)* • *The ~-towns of Latin America are places of extreme poverty.* ❖ παραγκούπολη

4.320 stench (n) – (U) terrible smell • *the ~ of rotting garbage* ❖ απαίσια βρώμα, δυσωδία

4.321 snarled (adj) – knotted, tangled; used figuratively in text to mean congested or blocked • *Her long hair is always ~ when she wakes up in the morning. / It took us two hours to get home in the ~ traffic.* ➤ snarl (n, v) ❖ που μπλέκεται (μετ) με κυκλοφοριακή συμφόρηση

4.322 noxious (adj) – harmful, very unpleasant • *When the wind blew eastward, you could smell the ~ fumes of the plastics factory to the west.* ❖ επιβλαβής

4.323 exhaust fumes (pl n phr) – smoke and gases produced by cars and other vehicles that burn oil and gas • *She looks forward to the weekends, when she can get out of the city and away from the choking smell of ~.* ❖ καυσαέρια

4.324 squalid (adj) – (of a place or one's surroundings) extremely dirty and unpleasant due to neglect or poverty • *The teacher was shocked by the ~ conditions in which some of her students lived.* ➤ squalor (n) ❖ βρώμικος, άθλιος

4.325 slum (n) – (C) very poor neighborhood • *The social worker's dream is to fight poverty and crime in the ~ where she grew up.* ➤ slumlord (n) ❖ φτωχογειτονιά

4.326 eke out a living (v phr) – earn and exist on very little money • *Fast food workers can barely ~ on the low wages they are paid.* ❖ τα βγάζω πέρα με μεγάλη δυσκολία

4.327 municipal (adj) – related to city or town government • *The town mayor is hoping to be re-elected in the ~ elections next year.* ➤ municipality (n) ❖ δημοτικός

4.328 sanitation (n) – (U) conditions related to public health, cleanliness, and hygiene • *Western standards of ~, especially with regard to the disposal of garbage and sewage, have improved greatly in the last fifty years.* ➤ sanitize (v), sanitary (adj) ❖ υγιεινή (π.χ., αποχέτευση κλπ)

4.329 ★ malaria (n) – (U) ❖ ελονοσία

4.330 ★ asthma (n) – (U) ❖ άσθμα

4.331 ★ tuberculosis (n) – (U) ❖ φυματίωση

4.332 ★ gastroenteritis (n) – (U) ❖ γαστρεντερίτιδα

4.333 rampant (adj) – widespread and out of control • *Crime and unemployment are ~ in the city's slums.* ❖ αχαλίνωτος, οργιαστικός

Text 3 (page 121)

4.334 contain (v) – hold in, keep in one place or under control • *A rescue crew ~s an oil spill by putting a sea wall around it. / Police ~ a riot by surrounding the area where it occurs. / A widow tries to ~ her emotions at her husband's funeral.* ➤ containment (n), container (n), contained (adj) ❖ αναχαιτίζω, συγκρατώ. 📖 : e.g., *a report ~s vital information*

Environmentalism 101

4.335 oil slick (n phr) – (C) thick patch of oil on the sea • *Oil poured out of the side of the wrecked ship, and the helicopter crew watched in horror as the ~ grew larger and larger.* ❖ πετρελαιοκηλίδα

4.336 scatter (v) – cause to spread out or spread out in all directions • *The wind ~ed puddles of oil over the surface of the sea. / The crowd ~ed as soon as the police officers appeared.* ❖ διασκορπίζω/-ομαι

4.337 puddle (n) – (C) small pool of liquid • *The body was found in a ~ of blood. / By noon, the ~s left from last night's rainstorm had disappeared.* ➢ puddle (v), puddle (adj)
❖ λιμνούλα (υγρού)

4.338 detergent (n) – (U/C) dirt remover, cleanser • *Of course your clothes are still dirty. You forgot to put ~ in the washing machine.* ❖ απορρυπαντικό

4.339 foil (v) – prevent (sth) from succeeding • *Thanks to accurate information from a police informer, police were able to ~ the terrorist attack before it occurred.* ➢ foiled (adj)
❖ ματαιώνω, αποτρέπω, προκαλώ αποτυχία

4.340 cargo (n) – (C) load of goods or a substance that is transported from one place to another (e.g., on a ship, plane, truck) • *It took dock workers several days to unload all of the ~ from the huge ship.* ❖ φορτίο

4.341 hemorrhage (v) – bleed, (fig, as in text) flow out freely • *A person ~s when a vein or artery is cut, just as an oil tanker ~s if it runs into a rocky reef.* ➢ hemorrhage (n), hemorrhaging (adj) ❖ αιμορραγώ

4.342 pristine (adj) – pure, unspoiled, in its original condition • *Thirty years ago the island was still ~ ; now it has become a popular tourist resort.* ❖ πρωτόγονος, παρθένος

4.343 drift (v) – see **4.15**

4.344 plant (n) – (C) factory, any place where an industrial or manufacturing process takes place • *The steel ~ in our town employs over 2,000 people.* ❖ εργοστάσιο

4.345 clog (v) – block with sth thick or sticky • *Don't pour oil down the drain; it will ~ the sink, and you'll have to get the plumber to unblock it.* ➢ clog (n), clogged (adj) ❖ βουλώνω

4.346 draw – drew – drawn (irreg v) – pull out, take • *In the old days the villagers used to ~ water from the well in the village square.* ❖ βγάζω, τραβώ. 📖 : e.g., ~ a cart, ~ a picture, ~ the curtains

Reading Coping with texts ... (pages 125-127)

READING PRACTICE: What's an El Niño
STEP 3: Vocabulary retrieval

For unknown vocabulary in this two section, see the paragraph-by-paragraph analysis of the reading passage in the following section.

STEP 4: Tackle the questions (page 127)
Text
Paragraph 1

4.347 temper tantrum (n phr) – childish display of anger • *The child throws a ~ every time his parents say "no" to him.*
❖ παροξυσμός, υστερία, (μετ) μπουρίνι

4.348 disruptive (adj) – disturbing, upsetting • *She needs absolute silence when she works; the least bit of noise breaks her concentration and is very ~.* ➢ disruption (n), ❖ διασπαστικός

Paragraph 2

4.349 shift (v) – change direction or position; also, move (sth) from one place, position, etc., to another • *Winds ~ from one direction to another. / A person ~s his weight from one foot to another. / A politician ~s his loyalty from one party to another,* ➢ shift (n), shifting (adj), shifty (adj), shiftily (adv)
❖ αλλάζω (θέση ή κατεύθυνση), μετατοπίζω/-ομαι, μετακινώ/-ούμαι

4.350 trigger (v) – see **4.173**

4.351 nourish (v) – (fig) keep sb/sth alive by providing food or other means of sustenance • *Dead organic matter enriches the soil and helps to ~ plants.* ➢ nourishment (n), nourishing (adj) ❖ (μετ) τρέφω, καλλιεργώ. See also **2.167** for literal meaning.

4.352 suppress (v) – stop sth from occurring • *~ a laugh or a cough, ~ the truth, ~ a rebellion* ➢ suppression (n), suppressed (adj) ❖ καταπνίγω, καταστέλλω

Paragraph 3

4.353 reverse (v) – go/make sth go in the opposite direction • *He carefully ~d the car out of the garage and backed out of the driveway. / The government is trying to ~ unemployment by creating new jobs.* ➢ reversal (n), reverse (n), in reverse (prep phr) ❖ αντιστρέφω

4.354 slacken (v) – decrease, become less intense; also, decrease or make sth less intense • *After a two-hour downpour, the rain finally began to ~. / In view of the recent terrorist threats, the government cannot afford to ~ security measures.* ❖ υποχωρώ, εξασθενώ, ελαττώνομαι

4.355 spawn (v) – (fig) produce, give birth to • *The industrial revolution has ~ed countless inventions that have improved our lives.* ❖ (μετ) γεννοβολώ. See **2.177** for literal meaning.

4.356 fuel (v) – increase the intensity of • *His desire to attend Harvard Law School has ~ed his desire to master the English language.* ➢ fuel (n) ❖ (μετ) τροφοδοτώ

4.357 veer (v) – turn sharply and suddenly • *The driver ~ed to avoid the child who had run out into the street.* ❖ αλλάζω κατεύθυνση ξαφνικά και απότομα

4.358 surge (v) – see **4.240**

4.359 prolonged (adj) – see **4.139**

4.360 havoc (n) → **play ~ with (sth)** (v phr) – completely disrupt or disturb; compare **wreak havoc** (see **3.369**)
• *Transatlantic travel plays ~ with her body clock. It takes her at least a week to recover from jet lag.* ❖ προκαλώ μεγάλη ζημιά, καταστρέφω

Writing (2) The opinion essay (pages 128-129)

Model essay (page 129)
Paragraph 1

4.361 culprit (n) – (thing) the cause of sth bad; also, (C) (person) sb who has done sth wrong • *(thing) As far as the fire goes, the fire department has determined that the ~ was faulty wiring in the TV. / (person) When the police catch the ~, he'll be sent to prison.* ❖ (πράγμα) αιτία, (άνθρωπος) δράστης, φταίχτης

4.362 pesticide (n) – see **4.167**

Environmentalism 101

Paragraph 2

4.363 produce (n) – (U) food products that are grown or produced by farming (e.g. fruit and vegetables, milk products, wheat, etc., but not meat) • *Because of the drought, the price of strawberries, mushrooms, and other ~ has gone through the roof!* ➢ production (n), producer (n), produce (v), productive (adj) ❖ γεωργικά προϊόντα

4.364 unsuspecting (adj) – having no idea or suspicion that sth bad is about to happen • *The lion crept forward in the long grass, slowly moving closer to the ~ zebra.* ❖ ανυποψίαστος

4.365 tissue (n) – (C) (anatomy) group of similar cells that perform the same function • *If the cancer cells spread, they will affect healthy ~ elsewhere in the body.* ❖ ιστός.
📖 : e.g., ~ paper, a box of ~s

4.366 absorb (v) – take/draw in, soak up (e.g., what roots do to water) • *The soil was dry and quickly ~ed the falling rain.* ➢ absorption (n), absorbent (adj), absorbed (adj), absorbing (adj) ❖ απορροφώ

4.367 concentration (of sth) (n) – (C) (chemistry) the relative amount of one substance that is dissolved or contained in another substance • *Ozone accumulates in dangerous ~s in the smog of big cities.* ➢ concentrate (n, v), concentrated (adj) ❖ συγκέντρωση. 📖 (U) powers of ~ , (C) ~s of foreigners in a big city

Paragraphs 3 and 4

4.368 alternative (n) – (C) choice, option • *When she discovered a bag with money under her son's bed, she had no ~ but to call the police.* ❖ εναλλακτική λύση, επιλογή

4.369 discontinue (v) – stop using, doing, or making • *The company has ~d the computer I bought last year. No wonder it was so cheap.* ➢ discontinuation (n), discontinued (adj) ❖ σταματώ, διακόπτω (τη χρήση, την παραγωγή κλπ.)

4 Exam practice (pages 130-133)

Cloze (page 131)

4.370 millennia (pl n) → **millennium** (n) – (C) period of one thousand years • *The year 2000 marked the end of the second ~ after the death of Christ, and the beginning of the third ~.* ➢ millennial (adj) ❖ χιλιετία

4.371 glory (n) – (C) (in context) sth that brings fame, honor, or greatness to sb/sth; also, (U) fame, honor or greatness that belongs to sb who has done sth great • *(C) To many people, the Parthenon is one of the ~ies of ancient Greece. / (U) For many Olympic gold medalists, ~ is often short-lived.* ❖ δόξα, μεγαλείο

4.372 sediment (n) – see **4.30**

4.373 inundate (v) – see **4.124**

4.374 superlative (n) – (C) exaggerated expression of praise • *If the ~s in the critics' reviews can be believed, the new production of Shakespeare's famous play is brilliant! We must see it!* ➢ superlative (adj) ❖ υπερβολή

4.375 fertilizer (n) – see **4.171**

4.376 ★ **salinity** (n) – (U) ➢ saline (adj) ❖ αλμύρα, περιεκτικότητα σε αλάτι

4.377 commercial (adj) – related to **commerce** (i.e., business, trade; the practice of buying and selling goods) • *The city's port, factories, banks, and other businesses make it an important ~ center.* ➢ commerce (n), commercial (n, adj), commercialize (v), commercially (adv) ❖ εμπορικός

4.378 residential (adj) – having **residences** (i.e., places where people reside/live), rather than offices or factories • *a ~ street/area* ➢ residence (n), resident (n, adj), reside (v) ❖ κατοικημένος, (αποτελούμενος) από κατοικίες, οικιστικός

4.379 sprawl (n) – (U) (of urban or industrial areas) disorganized and unattractive expansion into the surrounding countryside • *As a result of fifty years of urban ~ , the metropolitan area has tripled in size.* ❖ απλωσιά, άτακτα χτισμένη περιοχή. See also **4.318** for adjective.

4.380 concrete (n) – (U) grayish-white building material made of sand, cement, and small stones • *How many tons of ~ do you think went into the building of the new skyscraper?* ❖ μπετόν. 📖 : e.g., (adj) a ~ object, ~ proof, a ~ path

4.381 discharge (n) – (U) the process of **discharging** sth (i.e., sending out or emitting sth; see **4.104**) • *The court ruled that the ~ of chemicals into the lake is a violation of clean-air laws. / As the cut heals, expect to see a bloody ~ on the bandage.* ➢ discharge (v) ❖ εκροή

4.382 erode (v) – see **4.36**

4.383 coastal (adj) – on, near, or related to a **coast** (i.e., the edge of the land that touches the sea) • *If global warming continues, low-lying ~ areas are in danger of flooding.* ➢ coast (n) ❖ παραλιακός

4.384 province (n) – (C) political or geographical area (similar to a county within a state, or a state within a country) • *Canada is broken up into ten ~s and three territories.* ➢ provincial (adj) ❖ επαρχία

Vocabulary (page 132)

All of the answer choices in questions 21-30 appear in previous entries in this unit. Consult the Alphabetical Word List at the back of the book to locate any words you wish to review.

Reading (page 133)

Paragraph 1

4.385 inflict (sth) (on sb/sth) (v) – cause sb/sth to suffer/experience sth unpleasant or unwanted • *a disaster ~s pain and suffering on an area, a government ~s taxes on its citizens, the law ~s punishment on criminals* ➢ infliction (n) ❖ επιβάλλω

4.386 ★ **brush fire** (n phr) – (C) ❖ πυρκαγιά θάμνων / χαμόκλαδων

4.387 ravage (v) – see **4.97**

4.388 devastating (adj) – see **4.143**

4.389 drought (n) – see **4.125**

4.390 ★ **monsoon** (n) – (C) ❖ μουσώνας

4.391 conversely (adv) – (used to introduce an idea that reverses or is opposite to what has previously been said) alternatively, on the other hand • *You can get there by train or, ~, you can take a bus. It really doesn't matter.* ➢ converse (n) ❖ αντίστροφα

4.392 flurry (of) (n) – (C) (fig) wave, outbreak or rash of things in quick succession • *Police believe that the ~ of burglaries in the area are related.* ❖ (μετ) ξαφνικό ξέσπασμα. 📖 , a snow ~, a ~ of applause

4.393 demolish (v) – see **4.262**

Environmentalism 101

4.394 occurrence (n) – (C) event, incident, happening • *The crash was a tragic ~. / Burglary has become a daily ~ in the neighborhood.* ➢ occur (v) ❖ συμβάν, γεγονός. 📖 : e.g., the ~ of a disease

Paragraph 2

4.395 decline (n) – *see* **4.99**

4.396 alter (v) – change, make sth/sb become different • *Her new hairstyle is beautiful; it totally ~s her appearance.* ➢ alteration (n), altered (adj) ❖ μετατρέπω, αλλάζω, τροποποιώ

4.397 ★ prevailing winds (pl n) – (C) ❖ επικρατούντες άνεμοι

4.398 nutrient (n) – *see* **4.172**

4.399 fare (v) – get on, make progress • *How are you ~ing?* ❖ τα πάω, περνώ

4.400 predator (n) – *see* **4.92**

4.401 dine (v) – (formal, rarely used for animals) eat • *We thought we would ~ at the new French restaurant this evening. Would you care to join us?* ➢ dinner (n), dining (n, adj) ❖ γευματίζω

4.402 ★ salmon (n) – (C) ❖ σολομός

Paragraph 3

4.403 shear off (phr v) – cut off, usually with a quick, sharp motion (as if using a pair of sharp scissors known as **shears** • *It must have been frightening to see that bolt of lightning ~ the limb of that tree. It's a miracle no one was hurt.* ➢ shears (pl n) ❖ (μετ) κόβω, ψαλιδίζω

4.404 abort (v) – end sth (e.g., a planned activity) before the expected time, due to problems or difficulties • *The soldiers had to ~ their mission when the enemy suddenly changed position.* ➢ abortion (n), aborted (adj), abortive (adj) ❖ ματαιώνω. 📖 : e.g., ~ a pregnancy/fetus

4.405 precious (adj) – rare, valuable, and often hard to obtain • *In the desert, water is a ~ resource because there is so little of it.* ➢ preciousness (n), preciously (adj) ❖ πολύτιμος. 📖 : e.g., a ~ child/outfit

4.406 moisture (n) – *see* **4.145**

4.407 parched (adj) – dry, completely without water • *After a year without rain, the ~ soil was hardened and cracked. / The shipwreck survivors were ~ with thirst after a week at sea with no fresh water.* ➢ parch (v) ❖ ξεραμένος, καψαλισμένος (λόγω ζέστης ή ανομβρίας), άνυδρος, (μετ) διψασμένος

Technological transitions

As in units 2, 3, and 4, this unit contains a number of scientific, technical, and other non-essential terms, most of which are explained in the course book. For the sake of brevity, the entries for these words are marked with a star symbol (★) and include only derivatives (where they exist) and Greek equivalents.

Title

5.1 **transition** (n) – (C/U) change from one form or state to another • (C) *the ~ from winter to spring, the ~ from childhood to adulthood,* (U) *a company in ~* ➤ transition (v), transitional (adj), transitionally (adv) ❖ μεταβολή, αλλαγή, μετάβαση

Introduction Technology and innovation (pages 134-136)

5.2 **innovation** (n) – (U) the process of developing and introducing sth new (e.g., an invention, method, or idea); also, (C) a new invention, method, or idea • (U) *I~ is the key to progress.* / (C) *Many people find it hard to keep up with the constant ~s in computer technology.* ➤ innovator (n), innovate (v), innovative (adj), innovatively (adv) ❖ καινοτομία

A What is technology? (page 134)
Paragraph 1

5.3 **purposeful** (adj) – determined, focused, with a specific purpose or goal in mind • *Johnny rarely plays computer games when he's online. Most of the time he's engaged in ~ activities, like doing research for his latest science project.* ➤ purpose (n), purposefully (adv) ❖ σκόπιμος

5.4 **household appliance** (n phr) – (C) device or piece of equipment used in the home for a specific purpose (e.g., cooking or cleaning) • *Irons, washing machines, dishwashers, and toasters are examples of typical ~s.* ❖ οικιακή συσκευή

5.5 **aspiration** (n) – (C) strong desire or ambition to achieve sth • *The young senator has ~s of becoming president someday.* ➤ aspire (v), aspiring (adj) ❖ φιλοδοξία, βλέψη για το μέλλον

5.6 **impact** (n) – (C) strong effect or influence • *Renewed terrorism in the area is bound to have a negative ~ on tourism.* ➤ impact (v) ❖ επίδραση, αντίκτυπος. See also **4.3(1)**.

5.7 **aspect** (n) – (C) part, feature, characteristic • *The best ~ of the job is that it is well paid.* ❖ πλευρά, χαρακτηριστικό γνώρισμα

5.8 **profound** (adj) – deeply felt • *Ten years has passed since his wife died, but he still feels a ~ sense of loss whenever he thinks of her.* ➤ profundity (n), profoundly (adv) ❖ βαθύς, έντονος, σοβαρός

Paragraph 2

5.9 **context** (n) – (C) the general situation or set of circumstances that relates to an idea, event, etc. • *His poor grades are understandable when seen in the ~ of his parents' recent divorce.* ➤ contextual (adj) ❖ γενικό πλαίσιο

5.10 **hostile** (adj) – threatening, harsh, unfavorable to life, health, or development • *The desert is a ~ environment in which only the sturdiest of life forms can survive.* ❖ hostility (n), hostilely (adv) ❖ εχθρικός. 📖 : e.g., a ~ look, a ~ co-worker

5.11 **advent** (n) – (U) arrival of sth important, the act of coming into existence for the first time • *the ~ of spring, the ~ of a cure for cancer, the ~ of the computer* ❖ έλευση, ερχομός

5.12 **subsequent** (adj) – later, following • *S~ experiments confirmed the scientists' original findings.* ➤ subsequently (adv) ❖ επόμενος, μεταγενέστερος, επακόλουθος

5.13 ★ **hunter-gatherer** (n) – (C) ❖ κυνηγός-συλλέκτης

5.14 **crude** (adj) – simple, primitive, lacking refinement • *It's amazing how much the ancient Egyptians accomplished using ~ tools.* / *The experienced novelist looked back on his early work and found it strangely ~ compared to his most recent works.* ➤ crudity (n), crudely (adv) ❖ πρωτόγονος, πρόχειρος, φτιαγμένος χωρίς τέχνη. 📖 : e.g., ~ oil, a ~ person

5.15 **implement** (n) – (C) tool, instrument, or other piece of equipment • *farming ~s, prehistoric ~s carved from stone or bone* ➤ implement (v) ❖ εργαλείο

5.16 **manipulate** (v) – control or handle with skill • *She had trouble with the new software at first, but with a bit of practice she was able to ~ it like a pro.* ➤ manipulation (n), manipulated (adj), manipulative (adj) ❖ χειρίζομαι

B What drives technology forward? (page 134)
Word bank

5.17 **discover** (v) – learn or find out; also, find by chance • *Have the police ~ed the identity of the murderer yet?* / *Most students learn that Columbus ~ed America in 1492, but in fact the Viking Leif Ericson got there first, in the year 1000.* ➤ discovery (n) ❖ ανακαλύπτω

5.18 **experiment (with)** (v) – conduct a test (or experiment) in order to study what happens • *In the early 1750s the American inventor and diplomat Ben Franklin ~ed with kites to study electricity in the atmosphere.* ➤ experiment (n), experimental (adj), experimentally (adv) ❖ πειραματίζομαι

5.19 **inquire (into)** (v) – ask questions • *Scientists ~ into the nature of things.* ➤ inquiry (n), inquiring (adj) ❖ ερωτώ, προσπαθώ να μάθω, ζητώ πληροφορίες, ερευνώ

5.20 **invent** (v) – come up with; create or design sth that has not existed before • *Did you know that Samuel Morse ~ed the telegraph in 1844?* ➤ invention (n), inventor n), inventive (adj), inventively (adj) ❖ εφευρίσκω. 📖 : e.g., ~ an excuse

5.21 **observe** (v) – watch carefully • *After the accident, he was kept in the hospital overnight so the doctor could ~ him and make sure nothing was wrong.* ➤ observation (n), observant (adj), observed (adj), observably (adj), observantly (adv) ❖ παρατηρώ

5.22 **ponder** (v) – think deeply • *The more he ~s the situation, the more confused he gets.* ➤ imponderable (n, adj) ❖ συλλογίζομαι, ζυγιάζω (με το νου)

5.23 **refine** (v) – improve on • *She has an idea for the new ad campaign, but she wants to ~ it a little before presenting it to the boss.* ➤ refinement (n), refined (adj) ❖ βελτιώνω, ραφινάρω

5.24 **tinker** (v) – make small adjustments here and there to repair or improve sth • *The car mechanic spends his weekends ~ing with his motorcycle.* ➤ tinker (n), tinkerer (n) ❖ μαστορεύω, επιδιορθώνω. See note in **5.31**.

Technological transitions 5

Text

5.25 innate (adj) – natural, inborn • *Animals have an ~ ability to care for their young.* ➣ innately (adv) ❖ έμφυτος

5.26 curiosity (n) – (U) strong desire to learn or know • *She had an air of mystery that aroused his ~.* ➣ curious (adj), curiously (adv) ❖ περιέργεια

5.27 motivate (v) – (used passively in text) stimulate sb's interest in doing sth • *They promised their daughter a new guitar to ~ her to study harder.* ➣ motive (n), motivation (n), motivated (adj), motivating (adj) ❖ παρακινώ

5.28 procedure (n) – (C/U) set way of doing sth, established method • *If you need surgery, you must call your health insurance provider and find out what ~s they require you to follow. / A liver transplant is a difficult surgical ~.* ➣ proceed (v), procedural (adj) ❖ διαδικασία

5.29 trial and error (n phr) → **through/by ~** (prep phr) – by experimenting and learning from your mistakes • *Teaching is a skill that one gradually improves on year after year through ~.* ❖ με τη μέθοδος της δοκιμής και πλάνης (δηλ. μαθαίνω ή βελτιώνω κτ ψάχνοντας εμπειρικά)

5.30 millennia (pl n) → **millennium** (n) – (C) period of one thousand years • *The year 2000 marked the end of the second ~ after the death of Christ and the beginning of the third ~.* ➣ millennial (adj) ❖ χιλιετία

5.31 tinkerer (n) – a mechanically-minded person who likes to make constant adjustments and small repairs • *Most ~s are perfectionists who enjoy working on a project till it's as good as they can get it.* ❖ μαστορευτής. **Note:** Don't confuse with **tinker** (n) – (C) (old fashioned) a person who travels around mending pots and pans ❖ γανωτζής

5.32 insatiable (adj) – that cannot be satisfied • *The greedy businessman has an ~ appetite for power and wealth.* ➣ satiate (v) ❖ ακόρεστος, αχόρταγος, ανικανοποίητος

C Ingenious 19th-century innovations (A brief sampling) (page 135)

STEP 1: Word bank (page 135)

5.33 ★ oil well (n phr) – (C) ❖ πετρελαιοπηγή

5.34 ★ reaping machine (n phr) – (C) ❖ θεριστική μηχανή

STEP 2 (page 135)

Invention 1

5.35 grain (n) – (U/C) crop used for cereal • (U) *Wheat, rye, barley, corn, and oats are common types of ~.* / (C) *Wheat, rye, barley, corn, and oats are common ~s.* ❖ δημητριακά, σιτηρά. *See also* **2.360** and 📖: e.g., *wood ~, a ~ of intelligence*

5.36 ★ scythe (n) – (C) ❖ δρεπάνι

5.37 catch on (phr v) – become popular • *Cell phones have really become popular since the year 2000. I wonder what device will ~ next!* ❖ πιάνω, σημειώνω επιτυχία. **Note:** *catch* is irregular: **catch – caught – caught**.

5.38 prospect (n) – (C) (often plural) chance for success • *Your ~s for future employment will be better if you have a university education.* ➣ prospective (adj), prospectively (adv) ❖ προοπτική

5.39 pick up (phr v) – gain strength, improve • *If business doesn't ~ soon, the restaurant will have to close. / If the wind doesn't ~, we'll have to sail back to shore using the motor (and not the sails).* ❖ βελτιώνομαι, καλυτερεύω. 📖: e.g., *~ a language, ~ sth off the floor, ~ sth at the supermarket, ~ a friend at his/her home*

5.40 prosper (v) – become successful or wealthy • *All parents want their children to ~ and be happy.* ➣ prosperity (n), prosperous (adj) ❖ ευημερώ, επιτυγχάνω

Invention 2

5.41 demonstrate (v) – show how sth works or is done • *The salesman ~d the new kitchen appliance to us.* ❖ επιδείχνω, δείχνω

5.42 apparatus (n) – (C) piece of machinery or equipment • *The seismograph is an ~ that detects and measures the strength of earthquakes.* ❖ μηχανισμός, συσκευή

5.43 transmit (v) – send out sth (e.g., a TV, radio, or other electronic signal) • *The Hubble Space Telescope has ~ted brilliant images of space phenomena back to earth.* ➣ transmission (n) ❖ μεταδίδω. *See also* **3.317**.

5.44 impulse (n) → **electrical ~** (n phr) – wave or short pulse of electricity • *Telegraphic messages are transmitted as a string of electrical ~s.* ❖ ηλεκτρική ώθηση. *See also* **5.44** and 📖: e.g., *do sth on ~*.

Invention 3

5.45 drill (v) – make a hole with a special tool called a **drill** • *Oilmen ~ deep holes in the ground hoping to find oil. / Dentists use a drill to ~ away tooth decay. / Homeowners ~ holes in their walls to hang bookshelves.* ➣ drilling (n), drilled (adj) ❖ (για πετρέλαιο) κάνω γεώτρηση, (γενικά) ανοίγω τρύπα με τρυπάνι

5.46 strike – struck – struck/stricken (irreg v) – find sth (e.g., gold, silver, oil) by drilling or mining • *Miners are hoping to ~ gold in the area.* ❖ ανακαλύπτω (φλέβα πετρελαίου, χρυσού κλπ). 📖: e.g., *lightning ~s, workers ~, an idea / a disease ~s you.*

5.47 ★ lubricant (n) – (C) ➣ lubrication (n), lubricate (v), lubricated (adj) ❖ λιπαντικό

5.48 seep (v) – (of liquids) flow or come out slowly • *Oil ~s out of the ground. / Blood ~s out of a wound and through a bandage.* ➣ seepage (n), seeping (adj) ❖ διαρρέω, διαποτίζω

5.49 witness (v) – be present and see (sth significant happen) • *It's now fairly common for fathers to be present in the delivery room so they can ~ the birth of their children.* ❖ είμαι μάρτυρας/θεατής (ενός γεγονότος)

5.50 boom (n) – (C) (fig) period of sudden and increased activity (e.g., in economic activity, in the birth rate, etc.) • *It's usual for stores to experience a ~ in sales at Christmastime. / She was born during the so-called "Baby B~" after World War II.* ➣ boom (v), booming (adj) ❖ ξαφνική και μεγάλη αύξηση, έξαρση

Invention 4

5.51 inspire (v) – fill sb with a desire to do sth • *Her teacher loved poetry and ~d her to begin writing her own verses.* ➣ inspiration (n), inspired (adj), inspiring (adj) ❖ εμπνέω

5.52 prototype (n) – (C) first or early working model • *The finished product is a great improvement over the early ~s that we began working on.* ➣ prototypical (adj) ❖ πρωτότυπο, αρχέτυπο

5 Technological transitions

5.53 manufacture (v) – produce goods in large quantity
• *The Ford Motor Company began to ~ cars in the early 1900s.* ➣ manufacture (n), manufacturing (n), manufacturer (n), manufactured (adj) ❖ παράγω, κατασκευάζω (βιομηχανικά προϊόντα)

Invention 5

5.54 back (v) – support financially • *If you need a loan to start your business, the bank will probably ~ you.* ➣ backer (n), backing (n) ❖ ενισχύω, (υπο)στηρίζω. 📖 : e.g., ~ a car out of the driveway, ~ a horse

5.55 shed light on (v phr) – (lit) light up, illuminate; often used figuratively to mean "help to explain" (by providing further information) • *Edison's light bulb ~ the entire world. / Police are hoping that the DNA test will ~ the identity of the murderer.* ❖ (κυρ/μετ) ρίχνω φως, φωτίζω. **Note:** *shed* is irregular: **shed–shed–shed**.

5.56 ★ inert (adj) – ➣ inertia (n) ❖ (αέριο) αδρανής

5.57 ★ incandesce (v) – ➣ incandescence (n), incandescent (adj) ❖ πυρακτώνω

D Techno adjectives for a brave new world (page 136)
STEP 1
Words with a positive connotation

5.58 innovative (adj) – (people, ideas) imaginative; (machines) based on imaginative new ideas • *(people, ideas) The ~ sales manager suggested a brilliant new way to market the product. / (machines) In 1982, the Jarvik-7 artificial heart was an ~ device that quickly caught on.* ➣ innovation (n), innovator (n), innovate (v), innovatively (adv) ❖ νεωτεριστικός, καινοτόμος

5.59 revolutionary (adj) – involving a dramatic change of methods or conditions • *Advances in technology have had a ~ effect on society. The world is dramatically different than it was in 1900.* ➣ revolution (n), revolt (v), revolutionize (v) ❖ επαναστατικός

5.60 pioneering (adj) – at an early, exciting stage of development; bold, daring, never been done before • *The Wright brothers' ~ experiments in fixed-wing flight resulted in the first successful human flight on December 17, 1903.* ➣ pioneer (n, v) ❖ πρωτοποριακός

5.61 cutting-edge (adj) – at the forefront of research and development; likely to be among the first to make important and exciting new discoveries; also **at the cutting edge (of sth)** (prep phr) • *Microsoft has been a ~ software company since the mid-1970s.* ❖ αιχμής, προηγμένος, ο πιο σύγχρονος

5.62 state-of-the-art (adj) – the best available, using the most advanced technology or methods • *My computer needs are basic. I don't need a ~ machine; just a simple, functional laptop is sufficient.* ❖ τελευταίας τεχνολογίας

5.63 ingenious (adj) – (people, ideas) clever, original; (things) original in design, well-suited to its purpose • *Edison was an ~ and productive inventor with 1,093 patents to his name. / The robbers came up with an ~ plan to get past the museum's tight security.* ➣ ingenuity (n), ingeniously (adv) ❖ (για ανθρώπους, ιδέες) πολυμήχανος, εφευρετικός · (για πράγματα) έξυπνος, δεξιοτεχνικός

Words with a more neutral connotation

5.64 high-tech (adj) – sophisticated; having a high level of technological development • *Each year airport security systems are becoming more and more ~ in response to the increasing threat of terrorism.* ➣ Opp: low-tech (adj) ❖ υψηλής τεχνολογίας

5.65 low-tech (adj) – simple, unsophisticated, but not necessarily useless or impractical • *Paperclips and pencils are ~, but it's hard to imagine life without them.* ➣ Opp: high-tech (adj) ❖ χαμηλής τεχνολογίας

5.66 controversial (adj) – causing intense public discussion, disagreement, or disapproval • *Abortion and stem cell research are highly ~ issues that people will never agree on.* ➣ controversy (n), controversially (adv) ❖ επίμαχος, αμφιλεγόμενος

5.67 efficient (adj) – (people/machines) able to work or perform well with a minimum of waste • *The ~ secretary is not only fast but accurate as well. / An ~ car is one that burns a minimum of fuel.* ➣ efficiency (n), efficiently (adv). Opp: inefficient (adj) ❖ αποτελεσματικός, αποδοτικός

5.68 feasible (adj) – (ideas, methods) practical, possible, that can be put into practice • *Everyone agreed that the plan was ~ as it was logical and could be implemented with very little money.* ➣ feasibility (n), feasibly (adv). Opp: infeasible (adj) ❖ εφικτός, δυνατός

5.69 viable (adj) – capable of surviving or continuing to perform one's original function; also, workable, practical • *The company must close because it continues to lose money and is no longer ~. / The plan is ~ if we can raise the money.* ➣ viablility (n), viably (adv). Opp: unviable (adj) ❖ βιώσιμος

Words with a negative connotation

5.70 newfangled (adj) – (also **new-fangled**) modern or fashionable in an unattractive or unacceptable way • *Her grandmother says she has no need for ~ inventions like computers, microwaves, and cell phones.* ❖ καινοφανής

5.71 obsolete (adj) – no longer needed or used because something better has come along to take its place • *With the advent of the personal computer, both manual and electric typewriters have become virtually ~.* ➣ obsolescence (n) ❖ ξεπερασμένος, αχρηστευμένος

5.72 outmoded (adj) – (similar to **obsolete**) old-fashioned, no longer useful or relevant to modern life • *If you're still running Windows 95 on your computer, your system is seriously ~.* ➣ outmodedness (n) ❖ ξεπερασμένος, ντεμοντέ

5.73 antiquated (adj) – extremely old or old-fashioned (i.e., even more than **outmoded**) • *Isn't it time you got rid of that ~ manual typewriter and bought yourself a computer?* ➣ antique (n, adj), antiquity (n), antiquate (v) ❖ απαρχαιωμένος, παλαιάς μόδας

5.74 archaic (adj) – (similar to **antiquated**) extremely old or old-fashioned (i.e., even more than **outmoded**) • *The manual typewriter I used back in 1970 seems virtually ~ when I compare it to my new laptop.* ❖ αρχαϊκός, απαρχαιωμένος

Writing (1) Paragraph development (page 137)
Practice (page 137)
Text 1 (page 137)

5.75 efficiently (adv) – quickly and accurately, with a minimum of waste • *She did her work so ~ that her boss gave her a sizable Christmas bonus.* ➣ see **5.67**. Opp: inefficiently (adj) ❖ αποτελεσματικά, αποδοτικά

Technological transitions 5

5.76 **finite** (adj) – definite and limited in size or extent, not infinite • *Our supply of fossil fuel is ~ and is quickly being used up. / The distance from here to the sun is ~ and measurable.* ➣ finiteness (n), finitely (adv). Opp: infinite (adj) ❖ πεπερασμένος, περιορισμένος

5.77 **urgent** (adj) – requiring immediate action • *I have an ~ message for the boss; please ask him to call me as soon as he arrives.* ➣ urgency (n), urgently (adv) ❖ επείγον

5.78 ★ **renewable energy sources** (n phr) – ❖ ανανεώσιμη πηγή ενέργειας

Text 2 (page 137)

5.79 **breakthrough** (n) – (C) important development • *Scientists have made continual ~s in cancer research over the last few decades.* ❖ αποφασιστικό βήμα, εντυπωσιακή ανακάλυψη

5.80 ★ **retrofit** (v) – ❖ εξοπλίζω με πρόσθετα εξαρτήματα (π.χ., εργοστάσιο, μηχανή)

5.81 **commercial** (adj) – related to **commerce** (i.e., business, trade; the practice of buying and selling goods) • *The city's port, factories, banks, retail shops, and other businesses make it an important ~ center.* ➣ commerce (n), commercial (n, adj), commercialize (v), commercially (adv) ❖ εμπορικός

5.82 **yield** (v) – produce or generate sth (e.g., a certain result, higher profits, a certain quantity or amount) • *The innovative method of production has ~ed unexpected profits. / Each tree ~s more than a hundred kilos of fruit.* ➣ yield (n) ❖ δίνω, αποδίδω. 📖 : e.g., ~ to sb/sth

5.83 **install** (v) – (things, appliances) put sth in place and connect it to a power supply • *I have no idea how to ~ an air-conditioner, but I can certainly help you ~ that new software program.* ➣ installation (n), installed (adj) ❖ εγκαθιστώ, συνδέω

5.84 **cost-effective** (adj) – that will save money over a period of time • *Using public transportation is a more ~ way to get to work than driving a car.* ➣ cost-effectiveness (n), cost-effectively (adv) ❖ επικερδής, επωφελής, που αξίζει τα λεφτά του μακροπρόθεσμα

5.85 **tinted** (adj) – colored or dyed a certain color • *She wears ~ glasses to reduce the glare of the sun.* ➣ tint (n, v) ❖ χρωματισμένος

Vocabulary (1) — 20th-century milestones (pages 138-140)

1. Mass production (page 138)

5.86 **standardize** (v) – make uniform or the same • *The government has decided to ~ education throughout the country; from now on students will use the same books and learn the same material at each level.* ➣ standard (n, adj), standardization (n), standardized (adj) ❖ τυποποιώ, καθιερώνω (μεθόδους εργασίας κλπ.)

5.87 **streamline** (v) – (in context) make faster or more efficient (often by employing less time-consuming or simpler methods of working) • *Computers have made it possible for businesses to ~ office procedures.* ➣ streamlined (adj) ❖ τροποποιώ κτ (π.χ., παραγωγή εργοστασίου) για να είναι πιο αποδοτικό

5.88 **churn out** (phr v) – produce fast and steadily • *The factory ~s out thousands of plastic containers every single day. / Journalists are expected to ~ a steady stream of articles. / Students ~ homework assignments.* ❖ παράγω με ταχύ ρυθμό

5.89 **repository** (n) – (C) (lit) place for storing things; also, (fig) a rich source of sth (e.g., knowledge, stories, hopes) • *(lit) The government is said to have built a secret underground ~ for nuclear waste in the area. / (fig) Tim's grandfather was a ~ of fascinating World War II stories.* ❖ αποθήκη (π.χ., εμπορευμάτων, επίπλων) · (μετ) θησαυρός (γνώσεων, ελπίδων κλπ)

5.90 **convenience** (n) – (C) useful or helpful device • *Her dishwasher and washing machine are her two favorite ~s.* ➣ convenient (adj), conveniently (adv) ❖ ευκολία, άνεση, οικιακή συσκευή. 📖 : e.g., the ~ of having a car

5.91 **gadget** (n) – (C) clever or strange device • *Her kitchen is equipped with an egg-slicer, a corkscrew, and dozens of other labor-saving ~s that her children have no idea what to do with!* ❖ μηχανική επινόηση, μικροεφεύρεση, μαραφέτι

5.92 **in earnest** (prep phr) – seriously, with strong intent • *He needs a good grade on the final exam to pass the course, so he's been studying ~ for the past two weeks.* ❖ στα σοβαρά, για καλά

5.93 **come into its own** (idm) – show one's true worth or capabilities; receive the credit, recognition, or fame that one deserves • *Since the hospital began doing robotic surgery, it has really begun to ~. Last year it received several awards for medical excellence and innovation.* ❖ δείχνω τι αξίζω, τυχαίνω της οφειλόμενης αναγνώρισης

5.94 **ramification** (n) – (C) result, consequence • *Acid rain is just one of the disastrous ~s of industrialization.* ➣ ramify (v) ❖ επίπτωση, έμμεση συνέπεια

5.95 **stem (from)** (v) – originate, come from • *Hemophilia ~s from genetic causes. / Your composition problems ~ from the fact that you translate word for word from your own language.* ❖ κατάγομαι, προέρχομαι

5.96 **efficiency** (n) – (U) ability to perform well with a minimum of waste • *The extremely slow and inaccurate typist was fired for her lack of ~.* ➣ efficient (adj), efficiently (adv). Opp: inefficiency (n). ❖ αποτελεσματικότητα, αποδοτικότητα

5.97 **cost-effectiveness** (n) – (U) potential profitability, the quality of being **cost-effective** (see 5.84) • *In corporate America, ~ is a high priority.* ➣ see 5.84 ❖ που αξίζει τα λεφτά του μακροπρόθεσμα

2. Radar (page 138)

Paragraph 1

5.98 **transmission** (n) – (U) the action or process of broadcasting or sending out signals by electronic means; (C) a program or message that is sent out in this way • (U) *The public TV station is dedicated to the ~ of quality programs.* / (C) *The show was so popular that the radio station has agreed to broadcast several more ~s of it.* ➣ transmitter (n), transmit (v) ❖ μετάδοση. 📖 : e.g., the ~ of a communicable disease

5.99 **calculate** (v) – determine exactly how much • *After our trip, we ~d that we had spent exactly $950.* ➣ calculation (n), calculator (n), calculating (adj), calculated (adj) ❖ υπολογίζω, λογαριάζω υπολογίζω, λογαριάζω

5.100 **pinpoint** (v) – determine exactly where sth is • *With the aid of new diagnostic technology, doctors can ~ a patient's problem much more quickly and accurately than ever before.* ❖ εντοπίζω ακριβώς

5 Technological transitions

Paragraph 2

5.101 pursuit (n) – (C) activity, occupation • *She's a sophisticated person who enjoys opera, theater, and other cultural ~s.* ➢ pursuer (n), pursue (v), pursuable (adj) ❖ ενασχόληση, επιδίωξη. 📖 : e.g., the ~ of happiness

5.102 spawn (v) – (fig) produce (usually in large quantity), give birth to • *The industrial revolution has ~ed countless inventions that have improved our lives.* ❖ (μετ) γεννοβολώ, προκαλώ, παράγω (σε μεγάλη ποσότητα). See **2.177** for literal meaning.

5.103 ★ nuclear magnetic resonance imaging (n phr) – (U) ❖ απεικόνισμα πυρηνικού μαγνητικού συντονισμού

5.104 employ (v) – (of things) make use of, apply • *Doctors are beginning to ~ the new surgical technique in hospitals throughout the country.* ➢ employment (of) (n) ❖ χρησιμοποιώ. 📖 : e.g., ~ workers

5.105 monitor (v) – check, observe (e.g., by watching, listening) • *In an intensive care unit, hospital staff ~ critically ill patients around the clock.* ❖ παρακολουθώ, ελέγχω

5.106 volume (n) – (C/U) amount or quantity of sth • *The sales department always hires temporary help to handle the increased ~ of orders during the Christmas season. / The store experiences a sudden increase in ~ during December.* ➢ voluminous (adj) ❖ όγκος, ποσότητα. 📖 : e.g. the ~ of a TV, radio, etc.

3. Laser (page 139)

5.107 generate (v) – produce • *Unemployment is so high that the government is hoping to ~ jobs by giving tax breaks to large companies.* ➢ generator (n), generation (n), generative (adj) ❖ γεννώ, παράγω

5.108 intense (adj) – strong, concentrated • *The furnace produces heat that is so ~ it can easily melt metal.* ➢ intensity (n), intensify (v), intensely (adv) ❖ έντονος

5.109 medium (n) – (C) (science) substance or surroundings in which a reaction occurs • *Transmitting radio waves requires no special ~; the signals pass easily through the ~ of air.* ➢ media (pl n) ❖ μέσο. 📖 : e.g., a ~ at a séance; small, ~, large

5.110 stimulate (v) – activate, arouse, excite, encourage sth to begin or to develop further • *The clothing store decided to run a sale hoping to ~ business during the usually slow summer months. / A good teacher knows how to ~ interesting discussions. / Coffee contains caffeine, which ~s the body.* ❖ stimulation (n), stimulating (adj), stimulated (adj) ❖ διεγείρω

5.111 particle (n) – (C) tiny bit or piece of matter • *~s of dust in the air, subatomic ~s (e.g., electrons, protons, neutrons)* ❖ μόριο

5.112 amplification (n) – (U) increase, strengthening • *High-quality surround-sound speakers allow listeners to achieve undistorted ~ of sound.* ❖ ενίσχυση

5.113 trigger (v) – start, cause • *The noisy students ~ed the teacher's anger.* ➢ trigger (n) ❖ προκαλώ

5.114 beam (n) – (C) single, strong ray of light • *the ~ of a flashlight / a sun ~* ➢ beam (v), beaming (adj) ❖ ακτίνα, ακτίδα φωτός. 📖 : e.g., a ~ of wood

5.115 precision (n) – (U) accuracy, exactness, the quality of being **precise** (i.e., exact, accurate) • *The delicate surgery requires absolute ~ ; one wrong move and the patient could be paralyzed for life.* ➢ precise (adj), precisely (adv) ❖ ακρίβεια

4. Integrated circuits (page 139)

5.116 ★ integrated circuit (n phr) – (C) ❖ ολοκληρωμένο κύκλωμα

5.117 component (n) – (C) part of sth (e.g., of a system, a chemical compound); same as **component part** • *Speakers and amplifiers are ~s of a music system. / Hydrogen and oxygen are the ~s of water.* ➢ composition (n), compose (v), component (adj) ❖ συστατικό μέρος

5.118 ★ semiconducting (adj) – ❖ ημιαγώγιμος

5.119 compact (adj) – small, tightly built or packed • *What she likes about laptop computers is that they are so ~ and portable; the one she has hardly takes up any space at all in her tiny apartment.* ➢ compact (n, v), compactness (n), compactly (adv) ❖ συμπαγής, συμπυκνωμένος

5.120 refinement (n) – (C) improvement • *After a few ~s are made to the current design, the product will finally be ready for manufacturing.* ➢ refine (v), refined (adj) ❖ τροποποίηση, βελτίωση. 📖 : e.g., the ~ of crude oil, a person of unquestionable ~

5.121 miniaturization (n) – (U) reduction to a small scale • *Integrated circuits have undergone constant ~ since the late 1960s; they just keep getting smaller and smaller.* ➢ miniature (n, adj), miniaturized (adj) ❖ σμίκρυνση

5.122 incorporate (v) – include, combine sth into a larger thing • *I felt flattered when my supervisor decided to ~ my idea into his report.* ➢ incorporation (n), incorporated (adj) ❖ ενσωματώνω. See also **2.341**.

5.123 function (n) – (C) role, job • *The heart's main ~ is to pump blood. / Word processing is just one of a computer's many ~s.* ➢ function (v), functional (adj) ❖ λειτουργία. See also **1.340** and 📖 : e.g., kidney/heart ~.

5.124 capability (n) – (U/C) ability or power (to do sth) • (U) *She has the ~ to do anything she wants.* / (C) *Compared to computers, typewriters had only limited ~s.* ➢ capable (adj), capably (adv) ❖ ικανότητα, δυνατότητα

5.125 revolutionary (adj) – see **5.59**

5.126 reliability (n) – (U) dependability • *The company's excellent reputation comes from its ~: its products are of the highest quality and its service is excellent.* ➢ reliance (n), rely (v), reliable (adj), reliably (adv). Opp: unreliability (n) ❖ αξιοπιστία, σταθερότητα

5.127 consumption (n) – (U) use/usage, expenditure; the act of **consuming** (from the verb **consume** – use, use up, expend) • *The global ~ of electrical power has increased greatly over the past hundred years.* ➢ consumer (n), consume (v), consumable (adj) ❖ κατανάλωση. 📖 : e.g., food ~

Vocabulary (2) Techno buzz words (pages 144-146)

Warm-up (page 144)

Word bank

5.128 alloy (n) – (C) mixture of metals • *Common ~s include steel (a mixture of iron and carbon) and bronze (a combination of copper and tin).* ❖ κράμα

5.129 automation (n) – (U) use of machines to do work previously done by people. • *One of the disadvantages of ~ is that it inevitably results in unemployment.* ➢ automaton (n), automate (v), automated (adj). ❖ αυτοματοποίηση (στην παραγωγή)

5.130 ★ digitization (n) – (U) ➢ digit (n), digitize (v), digital (adj), digitally (adv) ❖ ψηφιοποίηση

Technological transitions 5

5.131 **fiber optics** (n phr) – (treated as singular) (scientific field based on) the use of thin flexible fibers of glass or other transparent solids to transmit light signals • *F~ is widely used in the telecommunications industry today.*
❖ ινο-οπτική τεχνολογία

5.132 ★ **internal combustion** (n phr) – (U) ❖ εσωτερική καύση

5.133 **miniaturization** (n) – *see* **5.121**

5.134 ★ **petroleum distillation** (n) – (U) ❖ διύλιση πετρελαίου

5.135 ★ **synthetic material** (n phr) – (C) ❖ συνθετική ύλη, συνθετικό υλικό

Ⓐ Interlocking revolutions (page 108)
Text 1 (page 108)

5.136 **internal-combustion** (n/adj) – *see* **5.132**

5.137 **debut** (n) – (C) first appearance • *The telegraph made its ~ in 1844. / The famous actor made his ~ more than thirty years ago.* ➤ debut (v) ❖ πρώτη εμφάνιση, ντεμπούτο

5.138 ★ **space probe** (n phr) – (C) ❖ μη επανδρωμένο διαστημόπλοιο

5.139 **demand (for)** (n) – (U) strong desire or need for sth (e.g., a product or service) • *The ~ has been so great for the medicine that the manufacturer has had to schedule a second production run.* ➤ demand (v), demanding (adj) ❖ ζήτηση. 📖 : e.g., terrorist ~s

5.140 **spawn** (v) – *see* **5.102**

5.141 **distillation of petroleum** (n) – *see* **5.134**

5.142 ★ **metallurgical** (adj) – ➤ metallurgy (n), metallurgist (n) ❖ μεταλλουργικός

5.143 **adept (at)** (adj) – skillful, proficient • *The child was an ~ reader by the age of five. / Screenwriters must be ~ at writing dialogue.* ➤ adeptness (n), adeptly (adv) ❖ επιδέξιος, ειδικευμένος

5.144 **extract** (v) – take out, remove • *Miners ~ rock from the earth. / A dentist ~s a rotten tooth. / Metal is ~ed from its ore via industrial smelting processes.* ➤ extract (n), extraction (n), extracted (adj) ❖ βγάζω, εξάγω, εξορύσσω

5.145 ★ **ore** (n) – (C) ❖ μετάλλευμα, ορυκτό

5.146 **alloy** (n) – *see* **5.128**

5.147 **abundant** (adj) – plentiful, existing in large quantities, more than enough • *South Africa is a country with an ~ supply of diamonds and other natural resources.* ➤ abundance (n), abundantly (adv) ❖ άφθονος

5.148 **feasible** (adj) – *see* **5.68**

Text 2 (page 145)

5.149 **spur** (v) – stimulate the development of • *Foreign investment ~s economic growth in an underdeveloped country. / Praise ~s a child to try harder.* ❖ κεντρίζω, παρακινώ

5.150 **substitute** (n) – (C) replacement • *Money is no ~ for happiness.* ➤ substitution (n), substitute (v) ❖ αντικατάσταση, υποκατάστατο, αναπληρωτής

5.151 **skyrocket** (v) – suddenly rise or increase ❖ ανεβαίνω στα ύψη

5.152 **insulation** (n) – (U) protective covering (e.g., on a wire) • *We had the plumber put ~ on the pipes to prevent them from freezing in the winter.* ➤ insulate (n), insulated (adj) ❖ μόνωση, μονωτικό υλικό

5.153 **transparent** (adj) – clear, see-through • *Glass is a ~ material.* ➤ transparency (n), transparently (adj) ❖ διαφανής. 📖 : e.g., a ~ lie/excuse

5.154 **dub** (v) – name, call • *The other students were quick to ~ him "Einstein" as he was by far the smartest in the class.* ❖ επονομάζω, κολλάω παρατσούκλι

5.155 **ubiquitous** (adj) – seeming to be everywhere • *Cell phones were a rarity twenty years ago; now they're ~. You can't go anywhere without seeing people using them.* ❖ πανταχού παρών

Ⓑ High-tech computer spin-offs (page 145)

5.156 **spin-off** (n) – (C) sth that develops, grows, or derives from sth else; offshoot, by-product • *Microwave ovens are a ~ of technology that was originally developed as a tool of war.* ❖ προϊόν ή όφελος, κτ που προέρχεται από μια συγκεκριμένη εξέλιξη

Text 1 (page 145)

5.157 **obsolete** (adj) – *see* **5.71**

5.158 **enhance** (v) – improve, make better • *Many women feel that black clothing ~s their appearance by making them look slimmer.* ➤ enhancement (n), enhanced (adj) ❖ βελτιώνω, επαυξάνω

5.159 **miniaturization** (n) – *see* **5.121**

5.160 **portability** (n) – (U) ability to be carried/moved ❖ φορητότητα

5.161 **digitization** (n) – *see* **5.130**

5.162 **sequence** (n) – (C) series, things one after another • *Your phone number is a unique ~ of numbers. / The article documented the ~ of events that led up to the terrorist attack.* ❖ σειρά, διαδοχή

5.163 **reassemble** (v) – put back together again • *It's easy to take a computer apart, but do you really think you can ~ it?* ➤ reassembly (n), reassembled (adj) ❖ ξανασυναρμολογώ, ξαναμοντάρω (μηχανή)

5.164 **application** (n) – (C) use, function • *the ~s of a computer program, a theory and its ~s* ➤ apply (v), applied (adj) applicable (adj) ❖ εφαρμογή, χρήση. 📖 : e.g., a job ~, study with great ~, the ~ of glue to a surface

5.165 ★ **fiber-optic cable** (n phr) – (C) ❖ καλώδιο φτιαγμένο από οπτικές ίνες

5.166 **tightly-bunched** (adj) – packed together in a tight group • *A muscle is made up of ~ muscle fibers. / A cable is composed of ~ lengths of wire that are twisted together.* ❖ σφικτά δεματιασμένος

5.167 **strand** (n) – (C) long thin piece (e.g., of metal, of hair) • *If you cut through a piece of wire, you can see that it is composed of several ~s of metal. / Police were able to identify the murderer by analyzing the DNA in a ~ of hair found at the crime scene.* ❖ κλώνος (σχοινιού ή καλωδίου), νήμα

5.168 **pulse** (n) – (C) short burst or signal • *radio ~s, a ~ of light* ❖ (ηλεκτρονικ) παλμός 📖 : e.g., take sb's ~, the financial ~ of the country

Text 2 (page 145)

5.169 **dimension** (n) – (C) measurement, proportion • *The ~s of a room are its length, height, and width.* ➤ dimensional (adj). ❖ μέγεθος, διάσταση. 📖 : e.g., (fig) an exciting new ~

5.170 **modify** (v) – change slightly, often (but not always) to improve • *Most scientists now believe that global warming has ~ied worldwide weather patterns.* ➤ modification (n), modified (adj) ❖ τροποποιώ

5. Technological transitions

5.171 offshoot (n) – (C) spin-off (see **5.156**), by-product; sth that develops or grows from sth else • *The small, portable laptop computer was a natural ~ of the larger personal computer.* ❖ βλαστός, παρακλάδι

5.172 automation (n) – see **5.129**

5.173 simulate (v) – imitate, be similar to • *The pilot did part of his training on a special computer equipped with software designed to ~ a wide range of flying conditions.* ➢ simulation (n), simulator (n), simulated (adj) ❖ εξομοιώνω

5.174 ★ **articulation** (n) – (U) ❖ διάρθρωση

5.175 ★ **weld** (v) – ❖ συγκολλώ, οξυγονοκολλώ

5.176 drilling (n) → from **drill** (v) – see **5.45**

5.177 ★ **riveting** (n) → from **rivet** (v) – ❖ καρφώνω (με πλατυκέφαλα καρφιά λαμαρίνας)

5.178 sort (v) – separate into categories • *After grading the essays, the examiners ~ed the papers into two piles: "pass" and "fail."* ➢ sorted (adj) ❖ ξεδιαλέγω

Cloze Parallel structure (pages 147-149)
Further practice (page 148)
Parallel verbs (page 148)

5.179 additive (n) – (C) substance, especially a chemical, that is added to sth else • *The company guarantees that the product is free of preservatives, artificial coloring, and other food ~s.* ➢ addition (n), add (v), additional (adj), additionally (adv) ❖ προσθετικό, πρόσθετο

5.180 stability (n) – (U) the quality or condition of being stable, constant, unchanging • *If a food has ~, it means it will not spoil quickly. / The lawyer presented evidence which caused the judge to question the mental ~ of the accused.* ➢ stabilization (n), stabilize (v), stable (adj), stabilizing (adj), stabilized (adj). Opp: instability (n) ❖ σταθερότητα, ευστάθεια

5.181 cathedral (n) – (C) large important church • *Notre Dame is the most famous ~ in Paris, France.* ❖ καθεδρικός ναός

5.182 soar (v) – (buildings) rise high into the sky • *The city's only skyscraper ~s high above the other buildings in the area.* ➢ soaring (adj) ❖ υψώνομαι. See also **2.289**.

5.183 ravages (pl n) → **the ~ of time** (n phr) – the destructive, ruinous effects of time • *The ~ of time showed clearly on the old woman's wrinkled face.* ➢ ravage (v), ravaged (adj) ❖ οι φθορές του χρόνου

5.184 clutter (v) – crowd untidily (e.g., with unnecessary objects or detail) • *Garbage ~ed the streets. / Stacks of paper and dirty coffee cups ~ her desk.* ❖ φορτώνω με άχρηστα αντικείμενα ή άχρηστες λεπτομέρειες

Parallel prepositions (page 148)

5.185 ★ **satellite** (n) – (C) ❖ δορυφόρος

5.186 data (pl n) – (plural of **datum**) facts, information • *The results of the experiment will be published after the scientists complete their analysis of the ~.* ❖ δεδομένα, στοιχεία

5.187 ★ **solar cell** (n phr) – (C) ❖ ηλιακό κύτταρο

5.188 ★ **nuclear generator** (n phr) – (C) ❖ πυρηνική γεννήτρια

Parallel structures for emphasis (page 148)

5.189 screw (n) – (C) metal object like a nail with a spiral edge running from the head down to the tip (see photo in course book, p. 148) • *The carpenter used ~s to hold the two pieces of wood together.* ➢ screwdriver (n), screw (v) ❖ βίδα

5.190 molecule (n) – (C) smallest unit of a chemical substance • *A ~ of water is made up of two parts hydrogen and one part oxygen.* ➢ molecular (adj) ❖ μόριο

5.191 manipulate (v) – see **5.16**

5.192 abundantly (adv) – in large quantity • *It rains ~ in the tropics.* ➢ abundance (n), abound (v), abundant ❖ άφθονα

Parallel structure with comparisons (page 148)

5.193 rapidity (n) – (formal) speed, quickness • *The ~ of technological advancement in the last hundred years has been nothing less than astounding.* ➢ rapid (adj), rapidly (adv) ❖ ταχύτητα

C CLOZE PRACTICE: Robo-revolution (page 149)
STEP 3:

For unknown vocabulary in this section, see analysis of the text in the next section.

STEP 4: Text

5.194 ingenuity (n) – (U) skill, cleverness, creativity, inventiveness • *The thieves showed surprising ~ in getting around the museum's tight security system* ➢ ingenious (adj), ingeniously (adv) ❖ ευφυΐα, εφευρετικότητα, πρωτοτυπία

5.195 devise (v) – create or invent as a result of careful thought • *The art thieves ~d a brilliant plan to enter the museum without being seen.* ➢ device (n) ❖ επινοώ, μηχανεύομαι, εφευρίσκω

5.196 cunning (adj) – clever, skillful (often in a way that is intended to deceive) • *Police would do anything to stop the ~ criminal, but so far their efforts have failed.* ➢ cunning (n), cunningly (adv) ❖ έξυπνος, καπάτσος, πονηρός

5.197 onerous (adj) – (of a task or responsibility) difficult, strenuous (i.e., involving effort that puts a great burden on sb) • *Grown children have the ~ responsibility of taking care of their elderly parents. / The president has the ~ task of preserving the welfare of the nation.* ➢ onus (n) ❖ επαχθής, βαρύς

5.198 compulsion (n) – (C/U) irresistible urge, force, or strong desire that often **compels** (i.e., forces) sb to behave in an unreasonable or illogical way • (C) *For some people gambling is a ~. / (U) Some say that ~ is what drives most inventors.* ➢ compel (v), compelling (adj), compellingly (adv) ❖ εξαναγκασμός, παρόρμηση

5.199 culminate (v) – reach a high point, conclusion, or result • *The 4th of July celebration ~d in a magnificent fireworks display.* ➢ culmination (n), culminating (adj) ❖ αποκορυφώνομαι

5.200 confer (sth on sb/sth) / confer (sb with sth) (v) – (formal) award, give, pass sth on to sb • *I would like to thank the Academy for ~ring this award on me. / Robotic engineers have ~red various human abilities on robots.* ❖ απονέμω. 📖 : e.g., ~ with sb (i.e., seek advice)

5.201 sidekick (n) – (informal) companion, pal, friend • *Robin was Batman's loyal ~, just as Dr. Watson was the trusted ~ of Sherlock Holmes.* ❖ δεξί χέρι, βοηθός ή σύντροφος, στενός φίλος (δηλ. κπ που είναι πάντα στο πλευρό σου)

5.202 quasi- (prefix) – (before adjectives or nouns) appearing to be sth that it is not • *If you want to lose weight, you should consult a doctor. Don't experiment with ~-medical products that you see on TV.* ❖ σαν, δήθεν, οιονεί, σχεδόν

Technological transitions 5

5.203 gizmo (n) – (C) (informal) gadget, contraption (i.e., small, clever, sometimes strange-looking device that does sth useful) • *The kitchens of gourmet cooks are full of odd-looking ~s such as corkscrews, wire whisks, and garlic presses.* ❖ μαραφέτι, μηχανική επινόηση

5.204 creeping (adj) – slow-spreading, gradual • *As the end of the school year draws near, teachers can always detect a ~ laziness in their students.* ➢ creep (v) ❖ που απλώνεται σιγά-σιγά

5.205 ubiquity (n) – (U) widespread existence or presence • *Eco-conscious Europeans are always amazed at the ~ of SUVs, mini-vans, and other big cars on American highways.* ➢ ubiquitous (adj) ❖ πανταχού παρουσία

5.206 drudgery (n) – (U/C) hard, boring work or task • *She finds most household tasks a ~, especially washing floors and ironing.* ❖ μόχθος, μονότονη και άχαρη εργασία, αγγαρεία

5.207 hum (v) – (fig) be busy (e.g. with activity or energy); (lit) make a low, continuous sound like a bee or a motor • *The busy office ~med with activity. / Bees ~ as they go from flower to flower collecting pollen and nectar.* ❖ (μετ/κυρ) βομβώ, βουίζω

5.208 ★ **automated teller terminal** (n phr) – (C) same as **automated teller machine** (ATM) ❖ αυτόματο ταμειακό μηχάνημα (ATM)

5.209 rote (adj) – memorized, mechanical • *The ~ learning of a new vocabulary word is a first step, but students must use a word again and again before it becomes an active part of their vocabulary.* ➢ by rote (prep phr) ❖ παπαγαλίστικος

5.210 transaction (n) – (C) (formal) an act of business (e.g., buying or selling sth) • *We knew exactly which TV we wanted to buy so the ~ was completed in a few minutes.* ➢ transact (v), transactional (adj) ❖ συναλλαγή, διεκπεραίωση

5.211 ★ **mine shaft** (n phr) – (C) ❖ αεραγωγός ορυχείου

5.212 ★ **mole** (n) – (C) ❖ τυφλοπόντικας

5.213 janitor (n) – (C) worker who is responsible for the cleanliness and maintenance of a building • *The ~ was tired after a hard day of washing floors and taking out the garbage.* ❖ επιστάτης κτιρίου (που σκουπίζει, φυλάει κλπ)

5.214 withstand – withstood – withstood (irreg v) – last under difficult conditions, stand up to, resist • *Spaceships are constructed to ~ extremes of heat and cold.* ❖ αντέχω σε, αντιστέκομαι σε

5.215 radiation (n) – (U) powerful and dangerous rays sent out from radioactive substances; similar to **radioactivity** ➢ radiate (v), radiant (adj), radiantly (adv) ❖ ραδιενέργεια. See also **4.151(1)**

Vocabulary (3) Other hot techno themes (pages 150-152)

A Food technology and the Green Revolution (page 150)
Text 1 (page 150)

5.216 strides (pl n) → **make ~ (in)** (idm) – (used passively in text) make great progress • *Medical researchers are making great ~s in understanding Alzheimer's syndrome.* ❖ σημειώνω μεγάλη πρόοδο

5.217 ★ **enzyme** (n) – (C) ❖ ένζυμο

5.218 ★ **spoilage agent** (n phr) – (C) ❖ παράγοντας που προκαλεί αλλοίωση τροφίμων

5.219 preservation (n/adj) – (U) protection, maintenance; (in context) the act of keeping food fresh and safe from spoilage • *Smoking meat is an age-old form of food ~.* ➢ preserve (n, v), preservative (n, adj), preserved (adj) ❖ συντήρηση, διατήρηση

5.220 texture (n) – (C) the characteristic way that sth feels when one touches it (e.g., rough or smooth, coarse or fine) • *Ice cream has a creamy, smooth ~. / The ~ of her hair was as smooth as fine silk.* ➢ textured (adj) ❖ υφή

5.221 intact (adj) – undamaged, complete • *The old house remained ~, despite the intensity of the earthquake.* ❖ ανέπαφος, άθικτος

5.222 sterilization (n) – (U) use of heat to kill germs and keep sth **sterile** • *Operating room procedure includes the careful ~ of all surgical instruments.* ➢ sterilize (v), sterile (adj) ❖ (απο)στείρωση

5.223 ★ **blanching** (n) → **blanch** (v) – ➢ blanched (adj) ❖ ζεματίζω

5.224 deterioration (n) – (U) (food) spoilage, worsening, loss of quality • *Refrigeration slows the ~ of foods.* ❖ (για τρόφιμα) αλλοίωση

5.225 ★ **ferment** (v) – ➢ fermentation (n), fermented (adj) ❖ προκαλώ ζύμωση. 📖 : e.g., ~ discontent or chaos

5.226 ★ **vacuum** (n) – (U) ❖ κενό (χωρίς αέρα ή ύλη)

5.227 ★ **irradiation** (n) – (U) ❖ βομβαρδισμός με ακτινοβολία

Text 2 (page 150)

5.228 mechanization (n) – (U) use of machines to do work once done by people; similar to **automation** (see **5.129**) ❖ μηχανοποίηση

5.229 ★ **pesticide** (n) – (C) ❖ φυτοφάρμακο (π.χ., εντομοκτόνο, ζιζανιοκτόνο)

5.230 ★ **herbicide** (n) – (C) ❖ ζιζανιοκτόνο

5.231 ★ **fertilizer** (n) – (C) ❖ λίπασμα

5.232 strain (n) – (C) kind, type, breed (e.g., of a germ, plant, or other life form) • *In recent years several new ~s of the virus have appeared that do not respond to antibiotics.* ❖ είδος, ράτσα. 📖 : e.g., the ~ of modern life, muscle ~

5.233 ★ **selective breeding** (n phr) – (U) ❖ επιλεκτική αναπαραγωγή

5.234 ★ **hybrid** (n) – (C) ❖ υβρίδιο

5.235 yield (n) – (C) total amount produced, esp. food (e.g., from crops or farm animals) or profit (e.g., from an investment) ➢ yield (v – see **5.82**) ❖ (γεωργικά προϊόντα) απόδοση, παραγωγή, σοδειά, (επένδυση) κέρδος

5.236 resistance (n) – (U) immunity, protection (i.e., the power to stand or endure sth without damage or harm) • *a plant's ~ to pests and disease, the body's ~ to infection or disease, the ~ of certain germs to antibiotics* ➢ resist (v), resistant (adj) ❖ αντίσταση. See also **3.254(2)**

5.237 trait (n) – (C) characteristic, attribute • *Genetically modified plants are bred to have ~s that make them more resistant to drought and disease. / Among his many admirable ~s are honesty, patience, and loyalty.* ❖ χαρακτηριστικό γνώρισμα

B Medicine and biotechnology (page 151)
Text 1
Paragraph 1

5.238 ★ **ultrasound** (adj) – ❖ υπερηχητικός

5.239 vaccine (n) – (C) a substance injected into the body or taken orally to protect against disease • *Scientists are hoping to discover a ~ against AIDS.* ➢ vaccination (n), vaccinate (adj), vaccinated (adj) ❖ εμβόλιο

63

5 Technological transitions

5.240 **immunize** (v) – protect against disease (e.g., by vaccinating or inoculating them) • *It is now common practice to ~ young children against diseases like polio and small pox.*
➢ immunity (n), immunization (n), immune (adj), immunized (adj)
❖ ανοσοποιώ, εμβολιάζω

5.241 **stamp out** (phr v) – destroy, put an end to • *It's unrealistic to think that we will ~ all disease in the near future.*
❖ εξαλείφω, καταπνίγω

5.242 **PET scan** (n phr) – (C) ❖ τεχνική εκτίμηση της λειτουργίας του εγκεφάλου κλπ

5.243 ★ **magnetic resonance imaging** (n phr) – (U) same as **nuclear magnetic resonance imaging** (NMRI or MRI)
❖ απεικόνισμα πυρηνικού μαγνητικού συντονισμού

5.244 **peer** (v) – look into hard-to-see places • *The sailor ~ed into the distance, looking for some sign of land.*
❖ κοιτάζω ερευνητικά

5.245 **battery (of sth)** (n) – (C) wide range or array (of sth) • *The doctor ordered a ~ tests to determine whether or not the patient's cancer had spread.* ❖ (μετ) σειρά, συστοιχία, σύνολο ομοειδών πραγμάτων. 📖: e.g., a ~ of soldiers, a rechargeable ~

Paragraph 2

5.246 **incision** (n) – (C) cut made by a sharp instrument, especially the cut made by a surgeon during an operation • *The surgeon made a five-inch ~ on the patient's abdomen.*
❖ τομή

5.247 ★ **saw** (n) – (C) ❖ πριόνι

5.248 **slender** (adj) – thin ❖ λεπτός, λυγερός

5.249 **probe** (n) – (C) any instrument used (e.g., by doctors or scientists) to examine places that otherwise cannot be reached • *a surgical ~, a space ~* ➢ probe (v), probing (adj)
❖ ανιχνευτήρας: π.χ., (χειρουργική) καθετήρας, διαστημικό σκάφος εξερεύνησης

5.250 **emerging** (adj) – gradually developing • *The increasing frequency of terrorist attacks in Great Britain indicate that the nation has an ~ crisis on its hands.* ➢ emergency (n), emerge (v), emergent (adj) ❖ αναδυόμενος, ανερχόμενος

5.251 ★ **scalpel** (n) – (C) ❖ χειρουργικό νυστέρι

Text 2 (page 151)
Paragraph 1

5.252 ★ **yeast** (n) – (U) ❖ μαγιά
5.253 ★ **sewage** (n) – (U) ❖ λύματα
5.254 ★ **genetic engineering** (n phr) – (U) ❖ γενετική μηχανική
5.255 ★ **recombinant DNA technology** (n phr) – (U)
❖ τεχνολογία ανασυνδυασμένου DNA
5.256 ★ **cloning** (n) – (U) ❖ κλωνοποίηση
5.257 **isolate** (v) – (chemistry) separate out a chemical or biological material from sth else in order to identify and/or study it • *Forensic scientists can ~ DNA from a blood or saliva sample.* ➢ isolation (n), isolated (adj) ❖ (χημεία) διαχωρίζω, απομονώνω. 📖: ~ sb with a contagious disease, ~ oneself from society

5.258 **splice** (v) – join together, recombine • *The surgeon ~d together the two ends of the severed nerve in the patient's hand. / Genetic engineers can splice DNA into the DNA of another species.* ❖ ενώνω, συγκολλώ

5.259 ★ **replicate** (v) – ❖ αναδιπλασιάζομαι

Paragraph 2

5.260 **application** (n) – *see* **5.164**
5.261 ★ **insulin** (n) – (U) ❖ ινσουλίνη
5.262 ★ **hepatitis** (n) – (U) ❖ ηπατίτιδα
5.263 **fault** (n) – imperfection, flaw, defect, weak point • *The condition is caused by a ~ on a specific chromosome. / No one is perfect; we all have our ~s.* ➢ fault (v), faulty (adj); flaw (v), flawed (adj) ❖ ελάττωμα, σφάλμα, ατέλεια. 📖: e.g., be sb's ~, find ~ with sb/sth

5.264 ★ **cystic fibrosis** (n phr) – (U) ❖ κυστική ίνωση
5.265 ★ **hemophilia** (n) – (U) – (Brit: **haemophilia**)
➢ hemophiliac (n) ❖ αιμοφιλία
5.266 **virus** (n) – (C) kind of tiny, disease-causing life form; also, a disease caused by such a life form • *Antibiotics can fight diseases that are caused by bacteria, but they are no help against ailments like the flu and common cold, both of which are caused by ~es.* ➢ viral (adj) ❖ ιός

5.267 ★ **bioremediation** (n) – (U) ❖ βιοχημική επανόρθωση του περιβάλλοντος

Reading Coping with ... techno passages (pages 153-155)

READING PRACTICE: Seeing is believing (pages 154-155)

Note: In the following sections (i.e., Extracts A-E), the wealth of cross-references is intended to show you that you have already met a great many of the words you need to handle ECPE technology passages in the course of this book. Chemical terms have not been included, as these are not crucial to your overall understanding of the passages.

Extract A (page 154)

5.268 **bioremediation** (n) – *see* **5.267**
5.269 **strewn (with)** (pp) → **be ~ with** (v phr) – be spread or scattered with sth • *After the wind storm, the roads were ~ with leaves and broken branches.* ❖ διασπείρομαι, σκορπίζομαι

5.270 **waste** (n) – *see* **4.160**

Extract B (page 154)

5.271 **consumption** (n) – *see* **5.127**
5.272 **harvest** (v) – *see* **2.82**
5.273 **innovation** (n) – *see* **5.2**
5.274 ★ **grape vine** (n) – ❖ αμπελόκλημα
5.275 **prune** (v) – (used passively in text) *see* **2.88**
5.276 **accommodate** (v) – (in context) provide sufficient space for, meet the needs or requirements of • *The hotel is specially fitted with ramps and other equipment to ~ guests in wheelchairs.* ➢ accommodation (n) ❖ εξυπηρετώ, διευκολύνω. 📖: e.g., ~ guests for the weekend, ~ sb's demands

5.277 **automation** (n) – *see* **5.129**
5.278 **yeast** (n) – *see* **5.252**
5.279 **strain** (n) – *see* **5.232**
5.280 **ferment** (v) – *see* **5.225**
5.281 ★ **oak cask** (n) – (C) ❖ δρύινο βαρέλι

Technological transitions 5

Extract C (page 155)

5.282 ★ **pick** (n) – (C) ❖ σκαπάνη, κασμάς

5.283 ★ **shovel** (n) – (C) ❖ φτυάρι

5.284 ★ **trench** (n) – (C) ❖ χαντάκι, χαράκωμα

5.285 ★ **tundra** (n) – (U) ❖ τούνδρα

5.286 **germinating** (adj) → from **germinate** (v) – *see* **2.76**

5.287 **simulate** (v) – *see* **5.173**

5.288 **efficient** (adj) – *see* **5.67**

5.289 **sprout** (v) – same as **germinate** – *see* **2.76**

5.290 **carbon-dating** (n phr) → **radiocarbon dating** (n phr) – (U) ❖ ραδιοχρονολόγηση με άνθρακα

5.291 **radioactive** (adj) – containing **radiation/radioactivity** – *see* **4.151(2)**

5.292 **fossil** (n) – *see* **2.53**

Extract D (page 155)

5.293 **eliminate** (v) – *see* **4.86**

5.294 **distortion** (n) – (C/U) 1. (U) the quality of being changed in a way that makes sth appear or sound strange and unnatural • *Playing music too loudly results in audio ~. / Looking in a mirror whose surface is curved or not smooth results in visual ~.* 2. (C) sth that is changed in this way • *a ~ of the truth* ➢ distort (v), distorted (adj), distorting (adj) ❖ (évs. 1-2) παραμόρφωση, παραποίηση

5.295 **beam** (n) – *see* **5.114**

5.296 ★ **lens** (n) – (C) ❖ φακός

5.297 **magnified** (adj) → from **magnify** (v) – *see* **4.120**

5.298 **spectacles** (pl n) – (slightly old-fashioned) same as **glasses/eyeglasses** • *He has excellent eyesight, so he has never needed to wear ~.* ❖ γυαλιά, ματογυάλια

5.299 **defect** (n) – (C) fault, imperfection • *a disease caused by genetic ~, ~s in a car's electrical system* ➢ defective (adj), defectively (adv) ❖ ελάττωμα, ατέλεια

Extract E (page 155)

5.300 **preserve** (v) – *see* **5.129**

5.301 **speculate** (v) – make guesses, form an opinion without having all the facts • *It's impossible to ~ about the future of the stock market when the economy is so bad.* ➢ speculation (n), speculative (adj), speculatively (adv) ❖ διαλογίζομαι, εικάζω, κάνω υποθέσεις

5.302 **preservative** (adj) – (of food) having the ability to act as a **preservative** (i.e., a substance that protects sth from decay or spoilage) • *Our Neolithic ancestors discovered that smoke has ~ qualities.* ➢ preserve (n, v), preservative (n), preserved (adj) ❖ (για τρόφιμα) συντηρητικός

5.303 ★ **rack** (n) – (C) ❖ σχάρα, ράφι

5.304 **cure** (v) – (food) preserve sth by one of several methods • *Smoking, salting, and drying are some of the common ways in which we ~ food to keep it fresh.* ❖ (για τρόφιμα) συντηρώ κτ με διάφορες μεθόδους (π.χ., καπνίζω, αλατίζω, παστώνω). *See also* **3.37** 📖 : e.g., ~ leather.

5.305 **retard** (v) – delay or slow down the development of sth • *Cold weather ~s plant growth. / An economic crisis ~s industrialization.* ❖ επιβραδύνω, καθυστερώ

5.306 ★ **oxidation** (n) – (U) ❖ οξείδωση

5.307 **spoilage** (n) – *see* **5.218**

5.308 **compound** (n) – *see* **3.412**

5.309 **inhibit** (v) – slow down, limit • *Certain food preservatives are used to ~ the growth of mold.* ➢ inhibition (n), inhibited (adj), inhibiting (adv) ❖ παρεμποδίζω, περιορίζω

5.310 **fungi** (pl n) – *see* **2.354**

5 Exam practice (pages 158-161)

Cloze (page 159)

Paragraph 1

5.311 **spawn** (v) – *see* **5.102**

5.312 **decipher** (v) – figure out the meaning of sth that is difficult to understand • *~ a code, ~ sb's illegible handwriting* ❖ αποκρυπτογραφώ, (μετ) βγάζω νόημα

5.313 **inquiry** (n) – (U/C) – (in context) (U) the process of **inquiring** or looking into the nature of sth to find out more about it (*see* **5.19**); also, (C) a request for help or information about sb/sth or a formal investigation into sth • *The researcher enjoys the process of scientific ~. / Police have been making ~ies about the victim's husband. / The government has called for an ~ into the scandal.* ➢ inquisition (n), inquire (v), inquisitive (adj), inquisitively (adv) ❖ έρευνα, εξέταση

Paragraph 2

5.314 **virus** (n) – *see* **5.266**

5.315 **rational** (adj) – logical, reasonable, sensible • *Calm down. You're so upset that you're not being ~.* ➢ rationality (n), rationalization (n), rationale (n), rationalize (v), rationally (adv). Opp: irrational (adj) ❖ λογικός

Reading (page 161)

Paragraph 1

5.316 ★ **bucket** (n) – (C) ❖ κουβάς

5.317 ★ **malaria** (n) – (U) ❖ ελονοσία

5.318 ★ **yellow fever** (n phr) – (U) ❖ κίτρινος πυρετός

5.319 **contrive** (v) – create, design, invent or bring about sth (e.g., an object or a situation) • *She ~d an interesting bedside table by placing a glass top over the opening of a large ceramic vase.* ➢ contrivance (n), contrived (adj) ❖ εφευρίσκω, επινοώ. 📖 : e.g., ~ to do sth

5.320 **saturate** (v) – make sth very wet, soak, drench • *The pouring rain ~d our clothing.* ➢ saturation (n), saturated (adj) ❖ διαποτίζω, μουσκεύω

5.321 **comfort** (v) – bring sb relief from distress or anxiety, soothe sb's pain or sorrow • *The widow's friends did their best to ~ her at her husband's funeral.* ➢ comfort (n), comfortable (adj), comforting (adj), comfortably (adv), comfortingly (adv) ❖ παρηγορώ, συμπαραστέκομαι

5.322 **consume** (v) – *see* **5.127**

Paragraph 2

5.323 ★ **dehumidify** (v) – ❖ αφαιρώ την υγρασία

5.324 **apparatus** (n) – (C) *see* **5.42**

5.325 **humidity** (n) – (U) amount of water in the air • *I can tell it's going to rain. There's so much ~ in the air you can feel it on your skin.* ➢ humidify (v) humid (adj) ❖ υγρασία (στην ατμόσφαιρα)

5 Technological transitions

5.326 foil (v) – see **4.339**

5.327 coil (n) – (C) continuous, tight spiral shape made by winding sth (e.g., a rope, wire, or garden hose) around and around • *After he finished watering the grass, he wound the hose into a neat ~.* ➢ coil (v), coiled (adj) ❖ πηνίο · κουλούρα, σπείρα

5.328 wondrous (adj) – (literary) beautiful and impressive • *The sky at sunset was a ~ combination of purple, pink, and orange.* ➢ wonder (n, v) wondrously (adv) ❖ θαυμαστός

5.329 ★ template (n) – (C) ❖ περίγραμμα, φόρμα

Paragraph 3

5.330 ★ printing plant (n phr) – (C) ❖ τυπογραφείο

5.331 ★ textile mill (n phr) – (C) ❖ κλωστοϋφαντουργείο

5.332 manufacturer (n) – (C) from **manufacture** – see **5.53**

5.333 ★ coolant (n) – (C) ❖ ψυκτικό υγρό

5.334 breakthrough (n) – see **5.79**

5.335 benign (adj) – (of a substance) not harmful to the environment • *Nowadays you can buy ~ aerosol products which do not harm the ozone layer.* ➢ benignly (adv) ❖ αβλαβής, ήπιο. See also **3.312**.

5.336 ★ compressor (n) – (C) ❖ συμπιεστής

5.337 compact (adj) – see **5.119**

5.338 spurt (n) – (C) (fig) short intense burst of sth (e.g., energy interest, action, or speed); also, (lit) sudden stream of liquid or gas, forced out under pressure • *Teenagers often undergo a growth ~ as their bodies begin to mature. / If you shake that bottle of champagne, you'll get a ~ in the face when you open it.* ➢ spurt (v), spurting (adj) ❖ (μετ.) κύμα ανάπτυξης, (κυρ) εκτόξευση

5.339 dripping (adj) → from **drip** (v) – come out slowly and fall (or allow to fall) in drops, one at a time • *Careful! Your ice cream is melting, and it's ~ onto your new jeans.* ➢ drip (n) ❖ στάζω

5.340 jut (v) → **~ out** (phr v) extend out, over, or beyond sth (or the main line of sth) • *The top of the cliff ~s out over a sandy beach.* ➢ jutting (adj) ❖ προεξέχω

5.341 ★ aerial (n) – (C) ❖ κεραία

5.342 ubiquitous (adj) – see **5.155**

5.343 suburban (adj) – characteristic of or related to a suburb/ the suburbs • *Many people feel that ~ life is a good compromise between the noise of the city and the quiet of the countryside.* ❖ των προαστίων

Alphabetical word list

Following is a list of all the words and phrases defined in the Glossary. The number to the right of each word or phrase refers to the entry in which the word or phrase is defined for the first time. Where more than one entry appears, each entry represents a unique meaning.

A
abdominal cavity (n phr) - 3.141
aberration (n) - 4.312
ablaze (adj) - 1.193
abnormal (adj) - 3.237
abort (v) - 4.404
absentminded (adj) - 1.73
absorb (v) - 2.72
abstracted (adj) - 1.332
abundant (adj) - 5.147
abundantly (adv) - 5.192
abuse (n) - 3.346
accelerate (v) - 2.31
accelerating (adj) - 4.98
access (n) - 4.189
accommodate (v) - 5.276
account (for) (v) - 4.286
acid rain (n phr) - 4.147
acquired disease (n phr) - 3.382
adamantly (adv) - 1.282
adapt (v) - 2.30
adaptation (n) - 2.349
addicted (adj) - 3.351
additive (n) - 5.179
adept (at) (adj) - 5.143
adrenal (n) - 3.169
advance (v) - 2.298, 4.34
advent (n) - 3.265, 5.11
aerial (n) - 5.341
aerosol spray (n phr) - 4.155
afflicted (pp), be afflicted with (v phr) - 3.223
affliction (n) - 3.20
afloat (adj) - 1.194
aftermath (n), in the aftermath (of sth) (prep phr) - 4.267
agent (n) - 2.359
aggravate (v) - 4.131
aggravating (adj) - 1.76
aggression (n) - 2.383
aggressive (adj) - 1.68
antagonistic (adj) - 1.69
aghast (adj) - 1.195
agitated (adj) - 1.67
aglow (adj) - 1.196
agonizing (adj) - 3.242
agricultural (adj) - 4.161
ailment (n) - 3.21
alarming (adj) - 3.411
algae (pl n)) - 2.8
alleviate (v) - 3.35
alloy (n) - 5.128
aloof (adj) - 1.72
alter (v) - 4.396
alternative (n) - 4.368
alveolus (n) - 3.126

amiable (adj) - 1.63
amniocentesis (n) - 3.334
amniotic sac (n phr) - 3.77
amok (adv), run amok (v phr) - 4.317
amphibian (n) - 2.152
amphibious (adj) - 2.151
amplification (n) - 5.112
ancestor (n) - 3.15
anesthetize (v) - 3.36
angiogram (n) - 3.307
angiosperm (n) - 2.99
animated (adj) - 1.64
anther (n) - 2.108
antibody (n) - 3.159
anticipation (n) - 4.248
antigen (n) - 3.154
antiquated (adj) - 5.73
antler (n) - 2.213
appalling (adj) - 1.71
apparatus (n) - 5.42
application (n) - 3.428
appointment (n) - 1.321
appropriate (adj) - 3.352
aquatic (adj) - 2.147
aquifer (n) - 4.185
arch (n) - 4.52
archaic (adj) - 5.74
ardent (adj) - 1.66
arrangement (n) - 2.236
array (n) - 2.141
arrogance (n) - 1.30
arrogant (adj) - 1.31
arteriosclerosis (n) - 3.217
artery (n) - 3.116
articulate (adj) - 1.65
articulation (n) - 5.174
artificial insemination (n phr) - 3.335
artificial limb (n phr) - 3.330
as stubborn as a mule (idm) - 2.309
aspect (n) - 5.7
aspiration (n) - 1.187
assassin (n) - 1.281
assessment (n) - 4.108
associated (adj) - 4.295
association (n) - 2.353
assume (v) - 2.350
asthma (n) - 4.330
attribute (n) - 1.19
attribute (to) (v) - 3.1
auditorium (n) - 1.270
austere (adj) - 1.74
authority (n) - 1.337
automated teller terminal (ATM) (n phr) - 5.208
automation (n) - 5.129
avalanche (n) - 4.192
avaricious (adj) - 1.75

averse (adj) - 1.197
aviator (n) - 1.173

B
back (v) - 5.54
backbone (n) - 2.145
bacteria (pl n) - 2.7
baffling (adj) - 1.77
ban (v) - 4.111
bare (v), bare one's teeth (v phr) - 2.286
barely (adv) - 1.61
barren (adj) - 2.51
barrier (n) - 1.174
bat (v) - 2.277
battery (of sth) (n) - 5.245
be in the doghouse (idm) - 2.313
beach (n) - 4.22
beak (n) - 2.214
beam (n) - 5.114
beat a dead horse (idm) - 2.316
bedrock (n) - 4.236
begging call (n phr) - 2.371
beleaguered (adj) - 2.20
belittling (adj) - 1.79
benevolent (adj) - 1.80
benign (adj) - 3.312, 5.335
beverage (n) - 2.362
bewildering (adj) - 2.10
biased (adj) - 1.78
bile (n) - 3.142
bill (n) - 2.215
billow (v) - 4.144
bind (irreg v) - 3.88
binoculars (pl n) - 2.241
biodiversity (n) - 2.12
biopsy (n) - 3.308
bioremediation (n) - 5.267
biosphere (n) - 4.1
bird of prey (n phr) - 2.194
birds of a feather flock together (idm) - 2.307
bladder (n) - 3.162
blanching (n) - 5.223
blastula (n) - 3.72
blessed (adj) - 4.261
blizzard (n) - 4.193
blood corpuscle (n phr) - 3.94
blood vessel (n phr) - 3.114
bloodless (adj) - 3.320
blossom (v) - 2.74
blueprint (n) - 3.67
bluff (n) - 4.50
blunder (v) - 2.304
bog (n) - 2.58
bogged down (adj), get bogged down (in sth) (idm) - 2.129

boisterous (adj) - 1.82
boldly (adv) - 2.252
bone marrow (n phr) - 3.93
boom (n) - 5.50
brain stem (n phr) - 3.107
branch (n) - 1.13, 2.93
branch (v), branch out (into sth) (phr v) - 2.122
breakthrough (n) - 3.17
breast (n) - 2.216
breed (irreg v) - 2.79
breeding (n/adj) - 2.380
breeding ground (n phr) - 3.418
breezy (adj) - 1.176
broad-minded (adj) - 1.81
bronchiole (n) - 3.125
bronchus (n) - 3.122
browser (n) - 2.195
bruising (n) - 3.262
brunt (n), the brunt of sth (idm) - 4.266
brush fire (n phr) - 4.386
bubonic plague (n phr) - 3.293
bucket (n) - 5.316
buckle (v) - 4.217
buck-toothed (adj) - 2.283
bud (n) - 2.105
bud (v) - 3.81
budding (adj) - 2.128
bulk (of) (n) - 4.294
burrow (v) - 3.419
burst (v) - 1.272
bursting (n/ger), fill (sth) to bursting (v phr/idm) - 4.244
bush (n) - 2.94
bustle (with) (v) - 4.272
bypass (n) - 3.321
bystander (n) - 1.277

C
calamity (n) - 4.221
calculate (v) - 5.99
campaign (v) - 1.269
cancer (n) - 3.303
canopy (n) - 2.89
canyon (n) - 4.28
capability (n) - 5.124
capillary (n) - 3.119
carbon dioxide (n phr) - 2.45
carbon-dating (n phr), radiocarbon dating (n phr) - 5.290
cargo (n) - 4.340
carnivore (n) - 2.182
carve (v) - 4.24
cataract (n) - 3.322
catch on (phr v) - 5.37

cathedral (n) - 5.181
cauldron (n) - 4.229
cavity (n) - 3.250
cell (n) - 3.57
cellulose (n) - 2.59
central nervous system (n phr) - 3.102
cerebellum (n) - 3.108
cerebral cortex (n phr) - 3.106
cerebrum (n) - 3.105
charismatic (adj) - 1.287
charm (n) - 3.3
charred (adj) - 4.219
chasm (n) - 4.225
check (v) - 3.357
chest (n), get it off (sb's) chest (idm) - 3.277
chilling (adj) - 4.310
chlorophyll (n) - 2.60
chorus (n) - 2.247
chromosome (n) - 3.64
chronic (adj) - 3.54
chubby (adj) - 1.109
churn out (phr v) - 5.88
circulatory (adj) - 3.82
circumstances (pl n) - 1.289
clash (v) - 4.233
claw (n) - 2.217
cliff (n) - 4.21
climate (n) - 2.26
clog (v) - 4.345
cloning (n) - 3.342
clot (v) - 3.258
clutter (v) - 5.184
coastal (adj) - 4.383
coercive (adj) - 1.86
coexist (v) - 4.57
coil (n) - 5.327
coincide (v) - 4.302
coincidence (n) - 2.266
cold-blooded (adj) - 2.156
collapse (v) - 4.237
collide (v) - 4.16
collision (n) - 2.29
combat (v) - 3.301
come down with (phr v) - 3.275
come into its (one's) own (idm) - 3.344
comfort (v) - 5.321
commandeer (v) - 3.368
commando (n) - 3.366
commendable (adj) - 1.83
commercial (adj) - 4.377
commercial exploitation (n phr) - 2.40
communicable (adj) - 3.47
compact (adj) - 5.119

Alphabetical word list

compassion (n) - 1.300
compassionate (adj) - 1.261
complex (adj) - 2.143
component (n) - 2.61
compose (oneself) (v) - 1.284
composed (adj) - 1.88
conceive (v) - 1.315
compound (n) - 3.412
compressor (n) - 5.336
compromise (sth/sb) (v) - 4.157
compulsion (n) - 5.198
Computerized Axial Tomography (CAT/CT scan) (n phr) - 3.318
conceiving (n) - 3.336
concentration (of sth) (n) - 4.367
concept (n) - 2.11
conception (n) - 3.70
conceptual (adj) - 3.353
concerned (adj) - 1.262
concrete (n) - 4.380
condense (v) - 4.2
conduct (n) - 1.12
confer (v) - 5.200
congenial (adj) - 1.84
congenital (adj) - 3.337
congestion (n) - 3.249
conscientious (adj) - 1.87
consciously (adv) - 1.313
consciousness (n) - 3.234
consequence (n) - 3.358
considerate (adj) - 1.299
consistent (adj) - 1.302, 3.199
conspicuous (adj) - 2.264
constant (adj) - 1.186
consume (v) - 2.334
consumption (n) - 4.280
contagious (adj) - 3.48
contain (v) - 4.334
contaminate (v) - 4.148
contamination (n) - 4.315
content (to do sth) (adj) - 3.415
context (n) - 5.9
continent (n) - 4.14
contract (v) - 2.137, 3.172
contraction (n) - 3.91
contrive (v) - 5.319
controversial (adj) - 5.66
convenience (n) - 5.90
convention (n) - 1.344
conversely (adv) - 4.391
convert (v) - 2.67
coolant (n) - 5.333
cooperative (adj) - 1.85
coordination (n) - 3.230
core (n) - 4.8
corpse (n) - 4.276
cost-effective (adj) - 5.84

cost-effectiveness (n) - 5.97
count on (phr v) - 1.60
countless (adj) - 4.59
court (v) - 2.374
cove (n) - 2.240
cower (v) - 2.269
cranium (n) - 3.251
crater (n) - 4.242
crawl (v) - 2.164
creep (irreg v) - 2.163
creeping (adj) - 5.204
crest (n) - 2.218
croaking (adj) - 2.248
crude (adj) - 5.14
crumble (v) - 4.214
crust (n) - 4.6
culminate (v) - 5.199
culprit (n) - 4.361
cultivate (v) - 2.80
cultivated (adj) - 2.130
cunning (adj) - 5.196
curb (v) - 4.122
cure (v) - 3.37
curiosity (n) - 5.26
cutting-edge (adj) - 5.61
cystic fibrosis (n phr) - 3.374

D

dappled (adj) - 4.53
daring (n) - 1.172
dart (v) - 2.257
dashing (adj) - 1.178
data (pl n) - 5.186
dawn (of) (n) - 1.8
deadly (adj) 3.178
deathly (adj) - 3.177
debris (n) - 4.259
debut (n) - 5.137
decay (v) - 2.75
decimate (v) - 3.294
decipher (v) - 5.312
decline (n) - 3.289
decompose (v) - 2.55
decomposer (n) - 2.183
decorum (n) - 1.339
defect (n) - 5.299
defiant (adj) - 3.198
deforestation (n) - 2.33
defy (v) - 1.338
degrade (v) - 4.82
dehumidify (v) - 5.323
dejected (adj) - 1.89
deluge (n) - 4.194
demand (for) (n) - 5.139
demolish (v) - 4.262
demonstrate (v) - 5.41
denizen (n) - 2.181
denude (v) - 4.89
deplete (v) - 4.88

deploy (v) - 3.378
deposit (n) - 3.266
detached (adj) - 1.90
deter (v) - 2.339
detergent (n) - 4.338
deteriorate (v) - 4.149
deterioration (n) - 5.224
determined (adj) - 1.91
detrimental (adj) - 4.152
detritus (n) - 2.193
devastating (adj) - 4.143
devise (v) - 5.195
devour (v) - 2.192
diagnose (v) - 3.27
diaphragm (n) - 3.130
digest (v) - 2.135
digestive (adj) - 3.83
digitization (n) - 5.130
diligence (n) - 1.53
diligent (adj) - 1.54
dimension (n) - 5.169
dimness (n) - 3.228
dine (v) - 4.401
dire (adj) - 4.290
disability (n) - 3.22
discharge (n) - 3.239, 4.381
discharge (v) - 4.104
discontinue (v) - 4.369
discover (v) - 5.17
disease (n) - 3.23
disillusioned (adj) - 1.94
disorder (n) - 3.24
displace (v) - 4.209
disruptive (adj) - 4.348
dissolve (v) - 4.70
distillation of petroleum (n) - 5.141
distortion (n) - 5.294
distracted (adj) - 1.93
distributed (pp) - 4.283
ditch (n) - 2.260
diverse (adj) - 2.52
diverse (adj) - 4.300
dizziness (n) - 3.229
dome (n) - 4.47
domestication (n) - 4.83
draw (irreg v) - 4.346
drift (v) - 4.15
drill (v) - 3.13
drilling (n), - 5.176
dripping (adj) - 5.339
drive (irreg v) - 2.268
drive out (phr v) - 3.14
drop out (of sth) (phr v) - 1.318
drought (n) - 4.125
drove (n) - 3.170
drudgery (n) - 5.206
dual (adj) - 3.109
dub (v) - 5.154
dump (v) - 3.424
dwell (v) - 3.414

E

ear (n), be all ears (idm) - 3.278
earthquake (n) - 4.196
eccentric (adj) - 1.323
ecosystem (n) - 2.14
efficiency (n) - 5.96
efficient (adj) - 1.100
efficiently (adv) - 5.75
eke out a living (v phr) - 4.326
elaborate (adj) - 3.379
elbow (v), elbow (sb's) way through/to (a place) (idm) - 3.279
electrocardiogram (n) - 3.309
electroencephalogram (n) - 3.310
elemental (adj) - 4.232
elevated (adj) - 4.215
eliminate (v) - 4.86
eloquent (adj) - 1.97
embody (v) - 1.175
embryo (n) - 2.175
emerge (v) - 3.375
emerging (adj) - 5.250
emission (n) - 4.136
emit (v) - 4.123
employ (v) - 2.343
enchanting (adj) - 1.96
encounter (n) - 2.239
encounter (v) - 3.417
endangered (adj) - 2.23
endocrine system (n phr) - 3.150
endure (v) - 2.325
enhance (v) - 5.158
enlightened (adj) - 1.188
enlist (v), enlist the help of (sb/sth) (v phr) - 4.74
enlisted (pp) - 3.376
ensue (v) - 4.254
enterprising (adj) - 1.98
envious (adj) - 1.35
envy (n) - 1.34
enzyme (n) - 3.139
eons (pl n) - 4.63
epilepsy (n) - 3.218
epitome (n) - 1.24
epitomize (v) - 1.57
eradicate (v) - 3.174
erect (v) - 1.192
erode (v) - 2.125
erosion (n) - 2.46
erratic (adj) - 1.99
esophagus (n) - 3.135
ethical/moral (adj) - 1.15
ethics (n) - 1.14
evacuate (v) - 4.253
eventually (adv) - 4.29
evolution (n) - 2.24
evolving (adj) - 1.179
exacerbate (v) - 4.117

exasperating (adj) - 1.244
exceptional (adj) - 1.249
excessive (adj) - 1.246
exhalation (n) - 3.129
exhaust fumes (pl n phr) - 4.323
expel (v) - 3.9
experiment (with) (v) - 5.18
exploit (v) - 2.39
exposure (n) - 3.52
exquisite (adj) - 2.244
extend (v) - 2.356
extensible (adj) - 2.297
extent (n) - 1.258
external (adj) - 2.358
extinction (n) - 2.22
extract (v) - 5.144
extraordinary (adj) - 1.294
exuberant (adj) - 1.95

F

facilitate (v) - 2.378
factor (n) - 4.296
famine (n) - 4.197
fare (v) - 4.399
farsighted (adj) - 1.104
fatal (adj) - 1.183
fatalistic (adj) - 3.176
fatality (n) - 3.175
fatigue (n) - 3.28
fault (n) - 4.17
fault/flaw (n) - 1.20
faulty (adj) - 3.341
fauna (pl n) - 2.5
feasible (adj) - 5.68
feat (n) - 3.343
ferment (v) - 5.225
ferocious (adj) - 4.204
fertile (adj) - 2.131, 4.32
fertility (n) - 3.338
fertilization (n) - 2.174
fertilize (v) - 2.81
fertilizer (n) - 4.171
fetus (n) - 3.75
fever (n) - 3.29
fiber optics (n phr) - 5.131
fiber-optic cable (n phr) - 5.165
fickle (adj) - 1.105
fierce (adj) - 1.296, 2.249
fiery (adj) - 4.226
figure out (phr v) - 1.247
fin (n) - 2.159 flank (n) - 2.203
finger (n), have (sb) wrapped/twisted around (sb's) little finger (idm) - 3.280
finite (adj) - 5.76
flap (v) - 2.291
flash flooding (n phr) - 4.126
flit (v) - 2.293

Alphabetical word list

flood (n) - 4.198
flop (v) - 2.300
flora (pl n) - 2.4
floral (adj) - 2.365
flow (v) - 3.115
flowered (adj) - 2.366
flowering (adj) - 2.364
flowery (adj) - 2.363
fluid (n) - 3.145
flurry (of) (n) - 4.392
foe (n) - 3.243
foil (v) - 4.339
follow suit (idm) - 3.404
food web (n phr) - 2.189
foolhardy (adj) - 1.103
forecast (v) - 4.287
foreleg (n phr) - 2.204
forest (n), can't see the forest for the trees (idm) - 2.115
fossil (n) - 5.292
fossil fuel (n phr) - 2.48
fossilize (v) - 4.64
fossilized (adj) - 2.53
four-chambered (adj) - 3.111
fraction (of sth) (n) - 2.234
fracture (n) - 3.30
fractured (adj) - 3.16
framework (n) - 3.354
frank (adj) - 1.102
frenzy (n) - 3.423
freshwater (n/adj) - 2.149
frizzy (adj) - 1.328
frolic - (irreg v) - 2.242
frugal (adj) - 1.101
fruitful (adj) - 2.172
frustrated (adj) - 1.106
fuel (v) - 2.186
fulfillment (n) - 1.181
fumes (pl n) - 4.133
function (n) - 1.340
funeral (n) - 4.207
fungi (pl n) - 2.354
furiously (adv) - 3.421

G

gadget (n) - 5.91
gall bladder (n phr) - 3.143
gasp (v) - 1.292
gastric acid (n phr) - 3.137
gastroenteritis (n) - 4.332
gene (n) - 3.65
generate (v) - 5.107
generous (adj) - 1.112
genetic engineering (n phr) - 5.254
genial (adj) - 1.114
geothermal (adj) - 4.241
germ (n) - 3.46
germinate (v) - 2.76
germinating (adj) - 5.286
get it straight from the horse's mouth (idm) - 2.319

gill (n) - 2.157
give way (phr v) - 4.213
gizmo (n) - 5.203
glacial (adj) - 4.228
glacier (n) - 4.23
gland (n) - 3.165
glare (n) - 2.250
glide (v) - 2.290
glint (v) - 4.271
glisten (v) - 4.275
global warming (n phr) - 4.121
gloomy (adj) - 1.113
glory (n) 4.371-
gluttonous (adj) - 1.37
gluttony (n) - 1.36
go away (phr v) - 3.194
go back (phr v) - 3.193
go down (phr v) - 3.195
go off (phr v) - 3.196
go to the dogs (idm) - 2.315
gobble (v) - 2.288
gorge (n) - 4.27
gorge (on sth) (v) - 2.262
gracious (adj) - 1.111
grain (n) - 2.360, 5.35
grandeur (n) - 4.56
grape vine (n) - 5.274
grasp (v) - 2.275
grazing (n) - 2.190
grease (n) - 4.166
greed (n) - 1.32
greedy (adj) - 1.33
greenhouse effect (n phr) - 4.114
gregarious (adj) - 1.110
grim (adj) - 3.224
groundwater (n) - 4.182
grow (v), grow on sb (idm) - 2.126
gullible (adj) - 1.115
gully (n) - 4.71

H

hopeless (adj) - 1.116
habitable (adj) - 4.115
habitat (n) - 2.16
habitat loss (n phr) - 2.34
hallmark (n) - 3.256
hapless (adj) - 3.420
harsh (adj) - 4.62
harvest (v) - 2.82
haunting (adj) - 4.68
have a frog in (sb's) throat (idm) - 2.318
have/get butterflies in (sb's) stomach (idm) - 2.312
havoc (n), play havoc with (sth) (v phr) - 4.360
hazard (n) - 1.184
haze (n) - 4.158

head (n), two heads are better than one (idm) - 3.281
headway (n), make
headway (v phr) - 3.381
heat stroke (n phr) - 4.129
heedless (of) (adj) - 1.117
helpless (adj) - 1.119
hemophilia (n) - 3.219
hemorrhage (v) - 4.341
hemorrhaging (n) - 3.264
hepatitis (n) - 5.262
herb (n) - 2.101
herbicide (n) - 5.230
herbivore (n) - 2.184
herd (n) - 2.255
herding (n) - 4.84
hereditary (adj) - 3.63
hesitant (adj) - 1.118
hibernator (n) - 2.196
high-tech (adj) - 5.64
hind leg (n phr) - 2.206
hint (at sth) (v) - 1.311
hollow (adj) - 3.71
honest (adj) - 1.42
honesty (n) - 1.41
hoof (n) - 2.207
hoof it (idm) - 2.227
horn (n) - 2.208
horny (adj) - 2.165
host (n) - 2.238
hostile (adj) - 5.10
household appliance (n phr) - 5.4
hover (v) - 2.294
howling (adj) - 4.55
hum (v) - 5.207
human nature (n phr) - 1.11
humble (adj) - 1.120
humble (v) - 4.222
humid (adj) - 4.141
humidity (n) - 5.325
humiliated (adj) - 1.121
hunter-gatherer (n) - 5.13
hurricane (n) - 4.199
hybrid (n) - 5.234

I

icon (n) - 1.326
ignorant (adj) - 1.122
illness (n) - 3.25
imaginative (adj) - 4.106
imminent (adj) - 4.246
immune system (n phr) - 3.151
immunity (to sth) (n) - 3.188
immunize (v) - 5.240
immunology (n) - 3.298
impact (n) - 4.3
impairment (n) - 3.26
impertinent (adj) - 1.124

impetuous (adj) - 1.126
implement (n) - 5.15
impulse (n), electrical impulse (n phr) - 3.317
in earnest (prep phr) - 4.93
inattentive (adj) - 1.334
incandesce (v) - 5.57
incision (n) - 3.323
incongruous (adj) - 4.218
incorporate (v) - 2.341, 3.66
indignant (adj) - 1.125
indispensable (adj) - 1.317
indolence (n) - 1.38
indolent (adj) - 1.39
induce (v) - 3.11
indulge (in) (v) - 1.189
industrialized (adj) - 3.51
inert (adj) - 5.56
infant (n) - 3.76
infant mortality (n phr) - 3.290
infection (adj) - 3.203
infestation (of sth) (n) - 3.201
infiltrate (v) - 3.367
inflame (v) - 3.245
inflammation (n) - 3.202
inflict (sth) (on sb/sth) (v) - 4.385
inflict mayhem (v phr) - 3.365
influential (adj) - 2.323
influenza (n) - 3.45
infraction (n) - 3.204
ingenious (adj) - 5.63
ingenuity (n) - 5.194
ingest (v) - 2.134
inhalation (n) - 3.128
inhibit (v) - 5.309
inject (v) - 3.38
innate (adj) - 5.25
innately (adv) - 2.370
innovation (n) - 5.2
innovative (adj) - 5.58
inoculated (adj) - 3.216
inquire (into) (v) - 5.19
inquiry (n) - 5.313
insatiable (adj) - 5.32
insectivore (n) - 2.197
insectivorous (adj) - 2.64
insidious (adj) - 4.308
inspire (v) - 5.51
install (v) - 5.83
insufficiency (of sth) (n) - 3.260
insulation (n) - 5.152
insulin (n) - 5.261
intact (adj) - 5.221
integrated circuit (n phr) - 5.116
integrity (n) - 1.312

intense (adj) - 5.108
interact (v) - 2.15
internal combustion (n phr) - 5.132
intolerant (adj) - 1.123
intrigue (v) - 3.422
introverted (adj) - 1.324
intruder (n) - 2.301
inundate (v) - 4.124
invade (v) - 4.58
invasion (n) - 1.171
invent (v) - 5.20
invertebrate (n) - 2.144
involuntary (adj) - 3.99
irksome (adj) - 1.127
irradiation (n) - 5.227
irreparable (adj) - 3.316
irresistible (adj) - 3.214
irrigate (v) - 2.83
irrigation (n) - 4.184
irritate (v) - 4.138
isolate (v) - 3.426
isolate (v) - 5.257

J

jagged (adj) - 4.43
janitor (n) - 5.213
jealous (adj) - 1.131
jerking (n) - 3.235
joint (adj) - 2.329
joint (n) - 3.90
jovial (adj) - 1.128
jubilant (adj) - 1.130
judicious (adj) - 1.133
jumbled (adj) - 2.42
just (adj) - 1.132
jut (v), jut out (phr v) - 5.340
juvenile (adj) - 1.129

K

keen (adj) - 1.136
keep up with (phr v) - 3.409
keyed-up (adj) - 1.137
kidney (n) - 3.161
kindhearted (adj) - 1.134
kneel (v) - 4.40
knowing (adj) - 1.138
knowledgeable (adj) - 1.135

L

landscape (n) - 4.42
landslide (n) - 4.200
lapse (v) - 3.247
large intestine (n phr) - 3.147
latter (adj) - 2.389
laudable (adj) - 1.144
launch (v) - 2.282
leak (n) - 4.288
leakage (n) - 4.177

69

Alphabetical word list

leap (irreg v) - 2.261
legion (adj) - 1.329
lend (sb) a hand (idm) - 1.62
lenient (adj) - 1.143
lens (n) - 5.296
lesion (n) - 3.233
let sleeping dogs lie (idm) - 2.305
let the cat out of the bag (idm) - 2.314
lethal (adj) - 4.293
liberal (adj) - 1.139
lick (v) - 2.272
life expectancy (n phr) - 3.288
ligament (n) - 3.89
limb (n) - 2.90
limb (n), go out on a limb for sb (idm) - 2.116
limestone (n) - 4.60
linger (v) - 4.128
lingering (adj) - 3.252
literate (adj) - 1.142
liver (n) - 2.233
lodge (v) - 1.285
log (n) - 2.95
log (n), sit around like a log on a log (idm) - 2.117
long-term (adj) - 4.314
low-grade fever (n phr) - 3.189
low-tech (adj) - 5.65
loyal (adj) - 1.52
loyalty (n) - 1.51
lubricant (n) - 5.47
lucid (adj) - 1.141
lumber (v) - 2.279
lung (n) - 3.113
lung (n), scream at the top of (sb's) lungs (idm) - 3.282
lure (v) - 2.302
lymphocyte (n) - 3.158

M

macrophage (n) - 3.156
magma (n) - 4.224
magnanimous (adj) - 1.149
magnetic resonance imaging (n phr) - 5.243
magnified (adj) - 5.297
magnify (v) - 4.120
make sense of (v phr) - 1.10
malaria (n) - 3.405
malevolent (adj) - 3.2
malicious (adj) - 1.147
malignant (adj) - 3.313
mammal (n) - 2.153
mane (n) - 2.209
manifestation (n) - 3.236
manipulate (v) - 5.16

mantle (n) - 4.7
manufacture (v) - 5.53
manufacturer (n) - 5.332
marine (adj) - 2.148
marsupial (n) - 2.170
mass immunization (n phr) - 3.299
massacre (n) - 4.279
massive (adj) - 3.259
mate (n) - 2.324
materialistic (adj) - 1.148
maternal (adj) - 1.150
mating (n) - 2.379
matter (n) - 3.68
mechanization (n) - 5.228
medieval (adj) - 4.227
mediocre (adj) - 1.146
medium (n) - 5.109
mere (adj) - 1.276
metallurgical (adj) - 5.142
metamorphosis (n) - 2.162
mettle (n), prove (sb's) mettle (idm) - 1.182
microbe (n) - 3.388
microsurgical (adj) - 3.324
migratory animal (n phr) - 2.198
millennia (pl n) - 4.370
mimic (v) - 2.346
mimicry (n) - 2.344
mine shaft (n phr) - 5.211
mineral (n) - 3.148
miniaturization (n) - 5.121
minor (adj) - 1.267
misgiving (n) - 2.278
misleading (adj) - 3.348
missing link (n phr) - 4.269
mobility (n) - 1.177
mobilization (n) - 3.356
moderate (adj) - 1.44
moderation (n) - 1.43
modest (adj) - 1.145
modify (v) - 2.56
moisten (v) - 2.274
moisture (n) - 4.145
mole (n) - 5.212
molecule (n) - 5.190
molten (adj) - 4.5
monitor (v) - 5.105
monsoon (n) - 4.390
mortality (n) - 3.50
mortally (adv) - 1.291
mosquito-borne (adj) - 3.406
motivate (v) - 5.27
mound (n) - 2.253
mountain chain (n phr) - 4.18
multicellular (adj) - 2.65
multiply (v) - 2.173
municipal (adj) - 4.327
muscular (adj) - 3.84
muted (adj) - 4.54

N

narrow-minded (adj) - 1.154
nasty (adj) - 1.153
natural disaster (n phr) - 2.27
natural selection (n) - 2.345
nectar (n) - 2.296
needle (v) - 1.342
needless to say (idm) - 1.58
negligent (adj) - 1.155
nervous (adj) - 3.85
nervous system (n phr) - 2.138
network (n) - 3.95
neuron (n) - 3.96
newfangled (adj) - 5.70
nibble (v) - 2.276
night owl (idm) - 2.308
nip (v) - 2.287
noble (adj) - 1.156
non-infectious (adj) - 3.49
nose (n), nose out (sth/sb) (idm) - 3.283
nosy (adj) - 1.152
notorious (adj) - 1.151
nourish (v) - 2.167
nourishment (v) - 2.237
noxious (adj) - 4.322
nuclear generator (n phr) - 5.188
Nuclear Magnetic Resonance Imaging (MRI or NM) (n phr) - 3.319
nucleus (n) - 3.59
numbness (n) - 3.227
nutrient (n) - 2.188
nutrient-laden (adj phr) - 3.110

O

oak cask (n) - 5.281
objection (to) (n) - 4.100
objectionable (adj) - 1.164
objective (adj) - 4.105
obligation (n) - 1.308
oblivious (adj) - 1.163
obnoxious (adj) - 1.157, 2.351
observe (v) - 5.21
obsolete (adj) - 5.71
obstinate (adj) - 1.161
obstruct (v) - 3.269
obstruction (n) - 3.270
occurrence (n) - 4.394
offensive (adj) - 1.159
offshoot (n) - 5.171
offshore oil rig (n phr) - 4.179
oil slick (n phr) - 4.335
oil spill (n phr) - 4.176
oil well (n phr) - 5.33

old hat (idm) - 3.340
omnivore (n) - 2.185
on the brink (of sth) (prep phr) - 2.32
on the move (prep phr) - 3.212
on the rise (prep phr) - 3.211
on the verge of (prep phr) - 2.21
on the wane (prep phr) - 3.209
onerous (adj) - 5.197
ooze (n) - 4.44
operate (v) - 3.39
oral contraceptive (n phr) - 3.339
orator (n) - 1.288
orbiting (adj) - 4.109
ore (n) - 5.145
organic matter (n phr) - 2.49
ornamental (adj) - 2.321
ostentatious (adj) - 1.162
outmoded (adj) - 5.72
outrageous (adj) - 1.160
outskirts (pl n), on the outskirts (of) (prep phr) - 2.44
outspoken (adj) - 1.158
ovary (n) - 2.110
overburden (v) - 4.163
overgrazing (n) - 4.85
overhunting (n) - 2.35
overpopulation (n) - 2.36
oversight (n) - 1.341
overwhelming (adj) - 3.349
ovule (n) - 2.111
ovum (n) - 2.176
ovum (n) - 3.61
oxidation (n) - 5.306
oxygen (n) - 2.50
oxygenation (n) - 3.118
ozone layer (n phr) - 4.153

P

pale (v) - 4.265
palette (n) - 4.48
pancreas (n) - 3.144
paradigm (n) - 1.23
paragon of virtue (n phr) - 1.25
parasite (n) - 2.62
parched (adj) - 4.407
particle (n) - 4.304
pattern (n) - 2.347
paw (n) - 2.220
peak (v) - 4.243
peer (v) - 5.244
penetrate (v) - 2.355
pensive (adj) - 1.166
pent-up (adj phr) - 4.250
perch (n) - 2.285
perch (v) - 4.278

peripheral nervous system (n phr) - 3.104
persistent (adj) - 1.167
personable (adj) - 1.169
personality (n) - 1.18
perspective (n) - 1.1
pertussis (n) - 3.185
pest (n) - 3.425
pesticide (n) - 4.167
PET scan (n phr) - 5.242
petal (n) - 2.106
petri dish (n phr) - 3.427
petroleum distillation (n) - 5.134
phagocyte (n) - 3.155
photosynthesize (v) - 2.68
physician (n) - 3.18
pick (n) - 5.282
pick (v) - 2.84
plant (v) - 2.85
pick up (phr v) - 5.39
pinpoint (v) - 5.100
pioneering (adj) - 5.60
pistil (n) - 2.109
pituitary (n) - 3.167
plague (n) - 3.393
plain (n) - 4.33
plant (n) - 4.344
plaque (n) - 3.267
plateau - 4.19
plow (v) - 2.86
plumage (n) - 2.320
plume (n) - 2.322
poaching (n) - 2.41
poised (adj) - 1.168
pollen (n) - 2.98
pollination (n) - 2.114
pollutant (n) - 4.103
pollution (n) - 2.37
ponder (v) - 5.22
portability (n) - 5.160
postdoctoral (adj) - 1.320
posture (n) - 2.384
potable (adj) - 4.183
potential (adj) - 2.352
potion (n) - 3.10
poverty (n) - 4.191
praise (n) - 4.37
precious (adj) - 4.405
precision (n) - 3.316
predation (n) - 2.191
predator (n) - 2.199
preening (n) - 2.327
pretension (n) - 1.343
prescribe (v) - 3.40
preservation (n/adj) - 5.219
preservative (adj) - 5.302
preserve (v) - 3.41
presumed (adj) - 3.173
pretentious (adj) - 1.170
prevailing winds (pl n) - 4.397

70

Alphabetical word list

prevalent (adj) - 4.142
prey (n) - 2.200
prey on (phr v) - 2.228
pride (n) - 1.28
primate (n) - 2.171
prime rib (n phr) - 2.263
primer (n) - 1.7
primitive (adj) - 2.6
printing plant (n phr) - 5.330
pristine (adj) - 4.342
proactive (adj) - 4.101
probe (n) - 5.249
probe (v) - 2.295
procedure (n) - 3.328
process (n) - 3.100
produce (v) - 4.363
profound (adj) - 5.8
prognosis (n) - 3.359
proliferate (v) - 4.127
prolonged (adj) - 4.139
prompt (v) - 4.245
proposition (n) - 3.355
prospect (n) - 5.38
prosper (v) - 5.40
prosthetic (adj), prosthetic device (n phr) - 3.325
prototype (n) - 5.52
proud (adj) - 1.29
province (n) - 4.384
provoke (v) - 2.246
proximity (n) - 2.235
prudence (n) - 1.45
prudent (adj) - 1.46
prune (v) - 5.275
puddle (n) - 4.337
pulse (n) - 5.168
pump (v) - 3.112
purposeful (adj) - 5.3
pursuit (n) - 5.101

Q

quackish (adj) - 1.203
quarrelsome (adj) - 1.200
quasi- (prefix) - 5.202
querulous (adj) - 1.199
quibbling (adj) - 1.201
quirky (adj) - 1.198
quiver (v) - 2.270
quixotic (adj) - 1.202

R

rack (n) - 5.303
radiate (v) - 4.9
radiation (n) - 4.151
radioactive (adj) - 5.291
radioactive decay (n phr) - 4.4
rage (v) - 4.206
ramification (n) - 5.94
rampant (adj) - 4.333
range (of) (n) - 2.13
range wide (v phr) - 1.314

rank (v) - 3.226
rapidity (n) - 5.193
rash (adj) - 1.209
rash (n) - 3.31
rational (adj) - 5.315
ravage (v) - 4.97
ravages (pl n), the ravages of time (n phr) - 5.183
ravine (n) - 4.26
raw sewage (n phr) - 4.165
reap (v), reap the rewards (idm) - 2.127
reaping machine - 5.34
rear (v) - 2.375
reassemble (v) - 5.163
recombinant DNA technology (n phr) - 3.384
recruit (v) - 3.372
rectum (n) - 3.149
recurrence (n) - 3.274
recurrent (adj) - 3.255
reef (n phr) - 2.18
refine (v) - 5.23
refined (adj) - 1.206
refinement (n) - 5.120
refinery (n) - 4.178
reflect (v) - 4.113
refrigerant (n) - 4.154
refugee (n) - 4.313
rehabilitation (n) - 3.273
reject (v) - 1.322
reliability (n) - 5.126
reliable (adj) - 1.205
remote (adj) - 1.210
render (v) - 3.5
renewable energy sources (n phr) - 5.78
replicate (v) - 3.385
repository (n) - 5.89
reproduce (v) - 2.77
reproductive (adj) - 3.69
reproductive system (n phr) - 3.152
reptile (n) - 2.154
reputable (adj) - 1.204
resent (v) - 1.335
reserve (n) - 4.95
reside (v) - 3.416
resident (n) - 4.252
residential (adj) - 4.378
resilient (adj) - 4.301
resist (v) - 1.336
resistance (n) - 3.254, 5.236
resistant (adj) - 3.197
resisting (adj) - 3.215
resolute (adj) - 1.56
resolve (v) - 1.55
resource (n) - 4.96
respiratory (adj) - 3.86
restrict (v) - 3.268

restrospect (n), in restrospect (prep phr) - 4.264
resurgence (n) - 3.180
resurgent (adj) - 3.181
retard (v) - 5.305
retreat (n) - 4.79
retreat (v) - 4.35
retrofit (v) - 5.80
reverse (v) - 4.353
revolutionary (adj) - 5.59
ridge (n) - 4.46
righteous (adj) - 1.207
rigid (adj) - 1.211, 2.66
rival (v) - 4.49
riveting (n), - 5.177
robust (adj) - 4.299
rodent (n) - 2.169
rogue (n/adj) - 3.386
root (n) - 2.92
root (n), put down new roots (idm) - 2.118
root (n/adj), root cause (of sth) (n phr) - 2.132
rote (adj) - 5.209
rousing (adj) - 1.286
rubble (n) - 4.78
rumble (v) - 4.230
runny nose (n phr) - 3.190
runoff (n) - 4.168
rural (adj) - 4.187
rush (n) - 2.243
ruthless (adj) - 1.208

S

salinity (n) - 4.376
saliva (n) - 3.132
salivary gland (n phr) - 3.133
salmon (n) - 4.402
sampler (n) - 1.27
sand dune (n phr) - 4.61
sanitary (adj) - 4.291
sanitation (n) - 3.296
sap (n) - 2.338
saprophyte (n) - 2.63
sarcastic (adj) - 1.212
satellite (n) - 5.185
saturate (v) - 5.320
saw (n) - 5.247
scalding (adj) - 4.223
scale (n) - 2.166
scalpel (n) - 5.251
scamper (v) - 2.299
scarcity (n) - 4.190
scatter (v) - 4.336
scavenger (n) - 2.201
scoop (v) - 4.45
scourge (n) - 3.240
scrambled (adj) - 1.107
scratch the surface (idm) - 2.9
screen (v) - 3.171

screw (n) - 5.189
sculptor (n) - 4.73
scythe (n) - 5.36
seagull (n) - 4.277
secrete (v) - 2.328
sediment (n) - 4.30
seed (n), go to seed (idm) - 2.119
seep (v) - 1.275
segment (n) - 3.295
seizure (n) - 3.231
selective breeding (n phr) - 5.233
semiconducting (adj) - 5.118
sense organ (n phr) - 2.139
sensitive (adj) - 1.217
sensory (adj) - 3.98
sepal (n) - 2.104
sequence (n) - 5.162
set (irreg v) - 3.42
sever (v) - 4.212
severed (adj) - 3.326
sewage (n) - 5.253
sewage system (n phr) - 3.297
sewer (n) - 4.164
shaggy (adj) - 2.258
shallow (adj) - 1.190
shanty (n) - 4.319
shatter (v) - 4.238
shear off (phr v) - 4.403
shed light on (v phr) - 5.55
sheer (adj) - 4.208
shellfish (n) - 4.170
shelter (v) - 2.57
shift (sth) (v) - 3.402
shift (v) - 4.349
shortcoming (n) - 1.21
shoulder (n), cry on (sb's) shoulder (idm) - 3.285
shove (v) - 4.65
shovel (n) - 5.283
shred (n) - 4.255
shrewd (adj) - 1.214
shrink (irreg v) - 2.232
sidekick (n) - 5.201
simulate (v) - 5.173
sinusitis (n) - 3.220
skeletal (adj) - 3.87
sketchy (adj) - 1.26
skyrocket (v) - 5.151
slacken (v) - 4.354
slaughter (v) - 4.90
sleeping sickness (n phr) - 3.221
slender (adj) - 1.108
slink (v) - 2.256
slip (v) - 3.377
slum (n) - 3.390
small intestine (n phr) - 3.138

smallpox (n) - 3.292
smash (v) - 1.273
smog (n) - 4.137
smoldering (adj) - 4.220
snarled (adj) - 4.321
soar (v) - 2.289, 5.182
solar cell (n phr) - 5.187
solitary (adj) - 2.373
sophisticated (adj) - 1.213
sort (v) - 5.178
sought (pp) - 1.180
sow (irreg v) - 2.87
space probe (n phr) - 5.138
spatter (v) - 1.274
spawn (v) - 2.229
spawning (n) - 2.177
special forces (n phr) - 3.373
species (n/pl n) - 2.3
spectacles (pl n) - 5.298
speculate (v) - 5.301
sperm (n/pl n) - 2.178
spew (v), spew forth (v phr) - 4.251
spinal cord (n phr) - 3.103
spine (n) - 2.337
spin-off (n) - 5.156
spire (n) - 4.51
splice (v) - 5.258
spoilage (n) - 5.307
spoilage agent (n phr) - 5.218
spontaneous (adj) - 1.303
sprawl (v) - 4.379
sprawling (adj) - 4.318
sprint (v) - 2.267
sprout (v) - 5.289
spur (v) - 5.149
spurt (n) - 5.338
squalid (adj) - 4.324
squat (v) - 2.271
squint (v) - 2.280
stumble (v) - 2.281
stability (n) - 5.180
stagnant (adj) - 4.140
stamen (n) - 2.107
stamp out (phr v) - 5.241
stampede (v) - 2.265
standardize (v) - 5.86
starch (n) - 3.146
starve (v) - 3.8
state-of-the-art (adj) - 5.62
stem (from) (v) - 3.383
stem (n) - 2.102
stench (n) - 4.320
sterilization (n) - 5.222
stigma (n) - 2.113
stimulate (v) - 5.110
stimulated (adj) - 3.182
stimulation (n) - 3.183

71

Alphabetical word list

stimuli (pl n) 2.140
stitch (v) - 3.43
stomach (n) - 3.136
stomach (v), can't stomach (sb/sth) (idm) - 3.284
strain (n) - 3.253
strand (n) - 5.167
streak (v) - 2.284
streamline (v) - 5.87
strewn (with) (pp), be strewn with (v phr) - 5.269
stride (n), make great strides (v phr) - 3.332
strike (irreg v) - 5.46
strode (v) - 1.271
stroke (n) - 3.222
struggle (to do sth) (v) - 1.9
strut (v) - 2.251
stubborn (adj) - 1.216
stump (n) - 2.96
stunning (adj) - 3.287
style (n) - 2.112
subdue (v) - 1.278
subjectivity (n) - 1.345
subsequent (adj) - 5.12
substitute (n) - 5.150
suburban (adj) - 5.343
succinct (adj) - 1.330
suck (v) - 3.120
sufficient (adj) - 4.281
sum (n) - 3.56
superficial (adj) - 1.215
superlative (n) - 4.374
supplement (v) - 2.69
suppress (v) - 4.352
surge (v) - 4.240
surreal (adj) - 4.75
surround (v) - 3.157
susceptible (to) (adj) - 3.53
sustain (v) - 2.292
sustained (adj) - 3.347
swath (n) - 4.305
sway (v) - 4.216
sweep (irreg v) - 4.41
swelling (n) - 3.32
swollen (adj) - 2.385
swoop (v) - 2.303
symptom (n) - 3.33
synthetic material (n phr) - 5.135

T
tactile (adj) -2.372
tadpole (n) - 2.161
take exception (to sth) (v phr) - 1.245
take the bull by the horns (idm) - 2.306

take to sth like a duck takes to water (idm) - 2.310
talon (n) - 2.221
tap (n) - 4.289
technique (n) - 3.329
tectonic plate (n phr) - 4.13
teeming (adj) - 2.2
temper tantrum (n phr) - 4.347
temperament (n) - 1.22
temperate (adj) - 1.218, 2.326
template (n) - 5.329
tenacious (adj) - 1.219
tend (v) - 1.290
tendency (n) - 1.310
tenderness (n) - 3.34
tendon (n) - 3.92
tentacle (n) - 2.211
terrestrial (adj) - 2.150
textile mill (n phr) - 5.331
texture (n) - 5.220
the black sheep of the family (idm) - 2.311
theory of relativity (n phr) - 1.316
there are plenty more fish in the sea (idm) - 2.317
thermal (adj) - 4.234
thorn (n) - 2.103
thorn (n), be a thorn in (sb's) side (idm) - 2.121
thorny (adj) - 2.133
thrifty (adj) - 1.221
thrive (v) - 3.408
thumb (n), be all thumbs (idm) - 3.286
thunder (v) - 1.283, 2.259
thyroid (n) - 3.168
tightly-bunched (adj) - 5.166
tinker (v) - 5.24
tinkerer (n) - 5.31
tinted (adj) - 5.85
tissue (n) - 2.136
tolerance (n) - 1.49
tolerant (adj) - 1.50
toll (n) - 3.225, 4.309
tongue (n) - 3.134
topple (v) - 4.210
topsoil (n) - 4.31
tornado/cyclone/twister (n) - 4.201
torrent (n) - 4.239
torture (v) - 3.7
toxic (adj) - 4.134
trachea (n) - 3.121
train of thought (n phr) - 4.270
trait (n) - 1.6

transaction (n) - 5.210
transfer (v) - 3.97
transform (v) - 1.191
transition (n) - 3.401
transmission (n) - 5.98
transmit (v) - 3.241, 5.43
transparent (adj) - 5.153
transplant (n/adj) - 3.327
trap (v) - 4.112
treat (v) - 3.44
tree (n), bark up the wrong tree (idm) - 2.120
tremor (n) - 4.205
trench (n) - 5.284
trial and error (n phr), - 5.29
trigger (v) - 2.382
trim (v) - 2.88
trouble-plagued (adj) - 1.185
trunk (n) - 2.91
trusting (adj) - 1.222
trustworthy (adj) - 1.223
tube (n) - 3.124
tuberculosis (n) - 3.399
tumor (n) - 3.311
tundra (n) - 5.285
twig (n) - 2.97
twist (n) - 3.371
twist (v) - 4.211
typhoon (n) - 4.202

U
ubiquitous (adj) - 5.155
ubiquity (n) - 5.205
udder (n) - 2.212
ultimately (adv) - 1.307
ultrasound (adj) - 3.315
ultraviolet (adj) - 4.150
umbilical cord (n phr) - 3.79
unambiguous (adj) - 2.377
unbearable - 1.226
uncanny (adj) - 1.227
uncouth (adj) - 1.229
unethical/immoral (adj) - 1.16
undergo (irreg v) - 3.272
underlying (adj) - 3.232
unevenly (adv) - 4.282
uninhabitable (adj) - 2.54
unique (adj) - 1.225
unmotivated (adj) - 1.59
unpalatable (adj) - 2.348
unsanitary (adj) - 3.19
unsuspecting (adj) - 4.364
untreated (adj) - 4.292
unvaccinated (adj) - 3.213
unwitting (adj) - 3.394
unwittingly (adv) - 2.361

upgrade (v) - 4.102
uproarious (adj) - 1.224
uproot (v) - 4.258
urban (adj) - 4.188
urbane (adj) - 1.228
urbanization (n) - 2.38
urgent (adj) - 5.77
urinary system (n phr) - 3.153
urine (n) - 3.160
uterus (n) - 2.179

V
vaccinate (v) - 3.300
vaccination (n) - 3.187
vaccine (n) - 5.239
vacuum (n) - 5.226
vague (adj) - 1.232
vain (adj) - 1.237
valiant (adj) - 1.48
valley (n) - 4.25
valor (n) - 1.47
vanquish (v) - 3.398
vapor (n) - 4.11
vast (adj) - 2.1
veer (v) - 4.357
vegetate (v) - 2.71
vegetation (n) - 2.70
vein (n) - 3.117
versatile (adj) - 1.234
versus (prep) - 1.3
vertebrate (n) - 2.146
viable (adj) - 5.69
vibration (n) - 2.387
vice (n) - 1.2
vice versa (adv) - 1.5
vicious (adj) - 1.231
vicious cycle (n phr) - 2.43
vigorous (adj) - 1.235
villainous (adj) - 1.230
vindictive (adj) - 1.233
viral (adj) - 3.387
virtue (n) - 1.4
virus (adj) - 3.363
void (n) - 4.72
volatile (adj) - 4.10
volcanic eruption (n phr) - 2.28
volcano (n) - 4.203
volume (n) - 5.106
vomiting (n) - 3.12
voracious (adj) - 1.236

W
wage war (v phr) - 3.350
wager (v) - 2.245
wake (n), in the wake of (sth) (prep phr) - 3.410, 4.107
wane (v) - 4.249

ward off (v) - 3.4
warm-blooded (adj) - 2.160
wart (n) - 3.370
wary (adj) - 1.240
waste (n) - 4.160
waste disposal (n phr) - 4.162
wasteland (n) - 2.17
wax (v), wax eloquent (v phr) - 4.38
wear off (phr v) - 3.206
wear away (phr v) - 3.207
wear down (phr v) - 3.208
wear out (phr v) - 3.205
webbed (adj) - 2.222
weird (adj) - 3.246
weld (v) - 5.175
welfare (n) - 1.306
well up (phr v) - 4.235
whimsical (adj) - 1.238
whiny (adj) - 1.241
whip (v) - 4.298
wickedness (n) - 1.17
widespread (adj) - 2.100
wildebeest (n/pl n) - 2.254
wilderness (n) - 2.19
will (n) - 3.362
wilt (v) - 2.78
wily (adj) - 1.243
wing (n) - 2.223
wing it (idm) - 2.231
wipe out (phr v) - 2.25
wishy-washy (adj) - 1.239
withdraw (irreg v) - 3.184
withstand (irreg v) - 5.214
witness (v) - 5.49
witty (adj) - 1.242
wondrous (adj) - 5.328
would-be (adj) - 1.280
wreak havoc (on sth) (v phr) - 3.369
wrestle (v) - 1.279

X
xenophobic (adj) - 1.248

Y
yeast (n) - 5.252
yellow (adj) - 1.250
yellow fever (n phr) - 5.318
yield (v) - 5.82
yielding (adj) - 1.251
young (adj) - 1.252
youthful (adj) - 1.253

Z
zany (adj) - 1.254
zealous (adj) - 1.257
zestful (adj) - 1.255
zippy (adj) - 1.256
zygote (n) - 3.62

www.ingramcontent.com/pod-product-compliance
Ingram Content Group UK Ltd.
Pitfield, Milton Keynes, MK11 3LW, UK
UKHW060050240426
12048UKWH00019B/1416